EDUCATION FOR PRESERVATION?

EDUCATION FOR PRESERVATION?

EXAMINING NATIVE AMERICAN EDUCATION POLICY IN THE NEW DEAL, 1933–1945

GABRIELLA A. TREGLIA

UNIVERSITY PRESS OF KANSAS

© 2025 by the University Press of Kansas
All rights reserved

Published by the University Press of Kansas (Lawrence, Kansas 66045), which was organized by the Kansas Board of Regents and is operated and funded by Emporia State University, Fort Hays State University, Kansas State University, Pittsburg State University, the University of Kansas, and Wichita State University.

This book will be made open access within three years of publication thanks to Path to Open, a program developed in partnership between JSTOR, the American Council of Learned Societies (ACLS), University of Michigan Press, and the University of North Carolina Press to bring about equitable access and impact for the entire scholarly community, including authors, researchers, libraries, and university presses around the world. Learn more at https://about.jstor.org/path-to-open/.

Library of Congress Cataloging-in-Publication Data
Names: Treglia, Gabriella A. author
Title: Education for preservation?: examining Native American education policy in the New Deal, 1933–1945 / Gabriella A. Treglia.
Description: Lawrence: University Press of Kansas, 2025. | Includes bibliographical references and index.
Identifiers: LCCN 2025008537 (print) | LCCN 2025008538 (ebook) | ISBN 9780700640713 cloth | ISBN 9780700640720 paperback | ISBN 9780700640737 epub
Subjects: LCSH: Indians of North America—Education—Government policy—United States—History—20th century | Off-reservation boarding schools—United States—History—20th century | New Deal, 1933–1939 | Biculturalism—United States
Classification: LCC E97.5 .T74 2025 (print) | LCC E97.5 (ebook)
LC record available at https://lccn.loc.gov/2025008537.
LC ebook record available at https://lccn.loc.gov/2025008538.

British Library Cataloguing-in-Publication Data is available.

EU Authorised Representative Details:
Easy Access System Europe
Mustamäe tee 50, 10621 Tallinn, Estonia | gpsr.requests@easproject.com

For my family

CONTENTS

Acknowledgments   ix

Introduction   1

1. Federal Government Attitudes to Native American Cultures, c. 1880–1945   13

2. Presenting Native "Pasts" in the Classroom   39

3. Soil Conservation, Science, and Health on the Curriculum   73

4. Indigenous Religions and the Indian Service School Program   115

5. Bilingual Education and Dual-Language Primers   141

6. Evaluating the New Deal Education Reforms   173

Epilogue: Monocultural Resurgence and Bicultural Education in Practice   191

Notes   201

Selected Bibliography   253

Illustrations Sources   269

Index   271

A photo gallery follows page 110.

ACKNOWLEDGMENTS

I would like to thank the excellent archivists and staff at the NARA Federal Record Centers at Denver (Rocky Mountain region) and Laguna Niguel (Pacific region), who were so helpful and welcoming. Many thanks also to the staff at the Center for Southwest Research (University of New Mexico), the Hayden Library (Arizona State University), the Roosevelt Study Center (now the Roosevelt Institute for the Study of the Americas) at Middelburg, and the Sterling Memorial Library (Yale). The guidance and assistance offered was invaluable.

My research at NARA Denver and Laguna Niguel was supported by a British Academy Small Research Grant and a Durham University Faculty research grant. I would like to thank both the Academy and Durham University for their generosity.

I would also like to thank David Congdon and the University Press of Kansas for their support and advice. John Gram and the anonymous reviewer for UPK both offered insightful and constructive feedback, which helped me to think about wider implications and contextualization of some research findings and new directions to consider—I am so grateful for your suggestions. This book includes adapted material from my previously published essay "Cultural Pluralism or Cultural Imposition? Examining the Bureau of Indian Affairs' Education Reforms during the Indian New Deal (1933–1945)," *Journal of the Southwest* 61, no. 4 (Winter 2019): 821–862. Many thanks to *Journal of the Southwest* for their kind permission to include this material in this book.

My thanks are due to colleagues who have offered feedback and advice on this project over the years—I have learned so much from you. And also to my students, undergraduate and postgraduate, whose enthusiasm for history and whose questions concerning the "Indian New Deal" have both inspired and challenged my own views and interpretations.

And finally, a huge thank you to my family, whose support and encouragement throughout this project have meant so much. To my mother and to my sisters Sara and Gemma, all greatly missed, whose resilience and strength remain so inspirational. To my father for his optimism and belief that this book would one day be completed. And my deepest gratitude to my husband, James—your support has made all the difference.

INTRODUCTION

In 2000 the Powhatan-Renapé and Lenape historian and educator Jack D. Forbes issued the following warning concerning public school education in the United States: "This past decade [1990s] has witnessed a growing interest, on the part of Anglo-Americans especially, in promoting English-language and Anglo-European perspectives, in spite of strong pressures in the direction of multiculturalism, globalism, and interethnic understanding and reconciliation."[1] Forbes feared that a growing drive towards standardized curricula marked "an attempt to destroy multiculturalism, pluralism, and non-Anglo-ethnic-specific curriculum by forcing all public schools to adhere to a curriculum approved by centralized agencies controlled by white people."[2] Standardization invariably implies adherence to the culture, mindset, and values of the dominant society or ethnic grouping—in effect a monocultural curriculum that advances a Eurocentric perspective and worldview.

Native Americans have historically experienced the full brunt of state-directed monoculturalism, epitomized most overtly by the attempted cultural genocide advanced by the federal Indian boarding schools of the late nineteenth and early twentieth centuries. The destructive legacy of the boarding schools is undisputed—while Indigenous resistance and resilience ensured policymakers failed in their goal of erasing Indigenous cultures and identities, the schools strove to disrupt community and familial systems of cultural transmission and thus caused significant cultural damage in addition to the physical menaces of disease, overcrowding, and corporal punishment.[3] Yet even without the violent abuse, deliberate cultural destruction, and unhealthy environments characteristic of the historic boarding schools, monocultural education at public schools and some government schools serving Native children *continues* to cause harm. The psychologist Keith James has drawn attention to the deleterious impact of ethnocentric teaching, particularly the prioritization of "Euroscience," on student self-esteem and cultural identity.[4] An education based on "ethnocentric cultural chauvinism" has been linked to high levels of depression and anxiety for those students who face conflict between the values of home and school.[5] Indeed, cultural conflict generated by a Eurocentric education system is cited as a factor in a large percentage of Native

American school dropout cases.⁶ And imposed monocultural education, involving replacement of Indigenous narratives and knowledge systems, has grave implications for the cultural sovereignty of Native nations. As law scholar Rebecca Tsosie notes, "For Native people, culture is an inseparable aspect of their daily existence, and the survival of Native nations depends upon cultural maintenance."⁷

Yet in the early 1930s, the Lakota author and educator Luther Standing Bear, himself a survivor of Carlisle Indian Boarding School, issued a powerful challenge to the federal government to forsake monocultural schooling for Native Americans and instead adopt a bicultural education model. The author of a series of impassioned defenses of Lakota culture and Indigenous cultural sovereignty, Standing Bear firmly rejected the either/or rationale underpinning the government schools, which assumed the individual had to reject their Indigenous identity while receiving an "American" education in English, math, and vocational training. Instead, he proposed a culturally inclusive and integrated curriculum: "To the end that young Indians will be able to appreciate both their traditional life and modern life they should be doubly educated. Without forsaking reverence for their ancestral teachings, they can be trained to take up modern duties that relate to tribal and reservation life."⁸ Standing Bear emphasized the vital importance of Indigenous cultures, histories, and traditional values, urging the federal government to "give back to Indian youth all, everything in their heritage that belongs to them and augment it with the best in the modern schools." And he reiterated that Indigenous cultures and histories could and should be a part of school-based learning, preferably taught by Native American educators. This "double education" clearly anticipated what we now term bicultural learning.⁹ Significantly, Standing Bear's call for educational reform coincided with a short-lived change in the direction of federal government policy that professed "cultural tolerance"—the so-called Indian New Deal (1933–45).

The Indian New Deal remains a controversial and divisive policy, subject to interpretations ranging from praise to condemnation. The term applies to a series of reforms implemented by the Bureau of Indian Affairs (BIA) under the commissionership of John Collier, aptly described by one historian as a "wild-eyed idealist."¹⁰ A reaction against the previous policy of coercive assimilation to US social, cultural, and economic norms, the Indian New Deal marked a shift to a pro-reservation, ostensibly pro-tribal approach to "Indian Affairs." Collier professed cultural pluralism, expressed admiration for Indigenous cultures and social structures, and claimed to seek self-determination for Indigenous communities. He was also highly paternalistic, at times dictatorial, and has been criticized both for holding romanticized, inaccurate views of Native cultures and for continuing assimilation efforts with certain policies.[11] The 1930s did witness some major reforms, notably the reorganization of many tribal governments, the ending of land allotment, the lifting of bans on ceremonial dances, and the prioritization of day schools for younger children.[12] However, boarding school education continued into the postwar era; many New Deal day schools suffered significant water supply and transportation problems, not to mention staff shortages; and tribal government reorganization fueled damaging factionalism in some cases. Whatever its achievements, the Indian New Deal was no savior of Indigenous sovereignty, nor was it a panacea for the economic and social damage wrought by the dispossession and attempted ethnocide that preceded it.

This book examines the extent to which the New Deal reflected Standing Bear's call for a bicultural approach to teaching. This is a study of school-based education only—as Matthew Sakiestewa Gilbert reminds us, "Education for indigenous people did not originate at US government schools" but was carried out by elders, families and communities outside the confines of the schoolroom.[13] Through an examination of teaching materials, reports, correspondence, memoirs, and petitions, this book explores what was taught at the schools, what reactions the curricula generated, and whether the reforms matched Standing Bear's vision of a "double education."

Evolving and Conflicting Interpretations of New Deal Education Policy

Government education policy towards Native Americans has attracted considerable academic attention since the 1980s, with a focus on the ethnocidal residential program of the period 1880–1930. Scholarship on the BIA-controlled boarding schools has flourished, ranging from David Wallace Adams's seminal overview study *Education for Extinction* to case studies of individual institutions, such as Jacqueline Fear-Segal's analysis of Carlisle Indian School and Matthew Sakiestewa Gilbert's study of the experiences of Hopi pupils at Sherman Institute.[14] The case studies offer valuable insights into how the boarding schools were run and, more recently, have examined student experiences and the relationship between the schools and the communities they served. However, with a few exceptions, the boarding school scholarship has tended to end in 1928 or 1930, with scant attention paid to the 1930s and 1940s.[15] The day schools have also been underrepresented, with Thomas Andrews's insightful article on Lakota day schools in the early twentieth century and Adrea Lawrence's *Lessons from an Indian Day School: Negotiating Colonization in Northern New Mexico, 1902–1907* the stand-alone analyses.[16] Given the day schools' innate status as spaces of contested influence (espousing a BIA-controlled curriculum, while located in or close to Native communities and by extension the influence of parents, elders, and political and religious leaders), this neglect is surprising.

The New Deal education program has received contrasting appraisals in two key works which offer overviews of twentieth-century government education policy. The first, Margaret Connell Szasz's pioneering 1974 study *Education and the American Indian: The Road to Self-Determination since 1928*, is a policy history which examines the ideological underpinnings of New Deal reforms—notably the progressive education sympathies of Directors of Indian Education Carson Ryan and Willard Beatty—and the main areas of reform, such as the prioritization of day schools, and the attempt to develop cross-cultural curricula.[17] Szasz offers a cautiously sympathetic appraisal of New Deal education policy: she acknowledges the limitations of the curricular developments, the impact of evaporating funding, and the practical failings of the day schools but concludes that policymakers were sincere in their attempts to improve education and to move away from the relentless monoculturalism of previous administrations. Szasz argues that Beatty and Ryan, with the aid of anthropologists, embarked on a "prodigious effort" to develop a "cross-cultural education program" consisting largely of bilingual learning and traditional arts and crafts.[18] With the exception of bilingual primers, however, Szasz argues that cross-cultural education was informal and undeveloped.[19] This lack of curricular cohesion, stemming from underfunding, haste, and inadequate resources, effectively torpedoed the attempt to transform government schools into meaningful bicultural centers. Interestingly, Szasz suggests that the cross-cultural program enjoyed greater success at day schools "simply because of daily cultural reinforcement in the home and community"—this, however, implies that Native cultures were being taught not at the schools but in the home environment, which contradicts the notion of school-based cross-cultural teaching.[20]

K. Tsianina Lomawaima and Teresa McCarty agree that the day schools did not offer much in the way of bicultural instruction. However, they suggest this was *deliberate* based on BIA fears that "as a result of close community ties" the day schools were "less controlled and thus less safe environments than the large off-reservation schools to introduce Native-focused curriculum."[21] This supports the "safety-zone thesis"—their groundbreaking conceptual framework published in 2006 that challenges long-held notions of divergent "swings" in federal government policy towards Native Americans. Rather than an abrupt and total shift from cultural destruction to cultural tolerance, Lomawaima and McCarty argue that assimilation to Eurocentric tenets remained the BIA's overriding goal throughout both the Assimilation and New Deal eras. They conclude that policymakers permitted a narrow, tightly controlled "safety zone" of "harmless" Indigenous cultural expression, restricted to practices which posed no threat to assimilationist aims—notably children's songs and traditionally female-associated (and potentially marketable) crafts. "Safe" in this context means "safe for the agendas and interests of dominant power structures," with a goal to negate "dangerous" cultural difference and thus eliminate Indigenous sovereignty.[22] Lomawaima and McCarty argue the safety zone was expanded slightly in the 1930s to include bilingual primers and an isolated "Indian history and lore" course; however, these served respectively to transmit assimilationist ideals of thrift and "good housekeeping" and to confine Native cultures to the distant past.[23] In essence, the safety zone thesis argues that Native cultural contexts were employed to sugar the pill of cultural change by presenting assimilationist values in a familiar milieu. The New Deal curricular reforms were therefore cosmetic, and rather than a genuine attempt at bicultural or even pluralist education, they represented assimilation by stealth. This renders the New Deal education policy akin to the Settlement House Movement which adopted a softly-softly approach to the full cultural assimilation of "new immigrants" in northern US cities in the late nineteenth century.[24]

In contrast, some scholars have identified a significant cultural shift in the New Deal education policy. Education scholar Jon Reyhner suggests that Collier, together with "culturally sensitive teachers ... and the recent policy of Indian self-determination," heralded a "forward-looking" (in other words, positive) approach to American Indian education policy.[25] Reyhner argues that this *attempted* cultural tolerance distinguishes the New Deal education program from earlier BIA approaches. Paul Boyer, in his 1989 report on tribal colleges, briefly cited the New Deal as heralding a tangible change in education policy, marking a recognition of Indigenous "values" and "heritage" on the government school curriculum.[26] Peter Iverson, in his long-range study of Diné history, noted that the BIA had a "greater commitment to cultural pluralism during the Collier era" and claimed the 1940 *Little Herder* bilingual primer series "represented a real breakthrough in bilingual, bicultural education."[27] He concluded, however, that "although some progress was achieved," the disastrous program of livestock reduction prevented the realization of a culturally pluralistic policy.[28] For the Lakota anthropologist Beatrice Medicine, the New Deal "rejected the traditional policy of assimilation and 'Americanization' of the Indians in favor of a policy of cultural pluralism"—although she acknowledges that a sometimes glaring "dissonance" between policy intent and implementation meant that biculturalism "was initiated but not completely incorporated into the education of the indigenous people of the U.S."[29] Both Medicine and Iverson suggest that the New Deal's educational intent was pluralist, but the implementation was, to put it mildly, disappointing. Kevin Whalen has described the New Deal as marking "a significant philosophical shift," claiming that "Native cultures abruptly received respect and admiration from Collier and his administration." According to Whalen, this government "about-face with regard to Indian culture" produced some short-lived curricular changes—again suggesting that something more than cosmetic tweaking was occurring.[30] In contrast, Farina King, in her groundbreaking analysis of Diné educational experiences in the twentieth century, argues that while the Crownpoint Boarding School curriculum did include some elements of Diné history and culture, they were taught entirely out of context, so pupils missed the essential traditional knowledge and moral guidance.[31] These interpretations and insights indicate the debate over the New Deal education program's relationship to both assimilation and pluralism is far from closed.

Deconstructing the New Deal Education Program

This book deconstructs and challenges the cultural dimensions of the New Deal education program to try to make sense of its intentions, flaws, and the divergent assessments it continues to attract. It explores the extent to which New Deal education policy was culturally tolerant in both intention and practice by examining what was taught at the BIA boarding and day schools to determine if and how Indigenous cultures were included on the curricula, along with whose voices and knowledge were prioritized. Community responses to the schools are also considered and reveal both the limitations of policymakers' attempts to "Indianize" the curriculum and the disconnect between parents' and teachers' expectations of what the schools should teach. Reflecting the New Dealers' keen interest in day school education, community organization, and range management, this book focuses primarily on the schools of the Navajo Reservation and United Pueblos Agency (UPA), which bore the brunt of many of the education reforms.[32] However, reflecting wider education policy and students' passage between schools, it also includes examples of lessons and teaching from off-reservation boarding schools, as well as teaching materials produced for use in schools across the Indian Service.

Throughout this study I consider questions of power and control over education and culture, and I explore the reasons behind the often confused and contradictory cultural messages sent out by policymakers and education personnel. It is possible to reassess the nature of government policy in the 1930s and 1940s and to partly reconcile its contradictory components and conflicting interpretations, primarily through a focus on the treatment and incorporation/exclusion of Native cultures and knowledge systems in the government school curriculum. I argue that, rather than just continuing assimilation, New Deal education policy represented a *new* set of dangerous flaws—a distorted interpretation of cultural pluralism that often ignored the realities of Native American cultures, societies, and lives. New Dealers did champion what they understood to be "religious" and "cultural" freedom. Yet they simultaneously prioritized Western science over Indigenous worldviews and never wavered from a Eurocentric understanding and framing of cultural, historical, and natural phenomena. What constrained New Deal cultural pluralism wasn't so much a "safety zone" that deliberately divided Native cultures into "safe" and "dangerous" aspects but rather an intrinsic Euro-American worldview that simultaneously failed to recognize the clash between religious freedom and Western scientific "truth" and valued academic and invariably non-Native "expertise" over Indigenous knowledge systems.

This book thus highlights debates over power relations between Indigenous communities and policymakers in the first half of the twentieth century and demonstrates the dangers of top-down education approaches that can, both intentionally and inadvertently, perpetuate colonialist attitudes and generate cultural conflict. It is helpful to consider the New Deal in relation to wider colonial education paradigms. These include Paulo Freire's concept of "cultural invasion," which more closely resembles coercive assimilation while also complicating the necessity of destructive intent in colonization, and Francis Nyamnjoh's theory of "epistemicide," by which colonizers consciously seek to destroy the epistemologies of the colonized.[33] As I will show in later chapters, both of these paradigms have some applicability to the Indian New Deal, but they do not explain all of its contradictions. Another mode of domination, settler colonialism, has also had strong influence in the relationship between the federal government and Native nations. Characterized initially as a power process geared towards erasing Indigenous peoples from the land, settler colonialism runs into difficulties vis-à-vis the New Deal, given its reversal of allotment policy and stated emphasis on conserving tribal lands.[34] However, settler colonialism also extends to the transfer and attempted erasure of Indigenous *narratives*—and this aspect arguably has some resonance for New Deal education initiatives.[35] Ultimately, the Indian New Deal as a policy is an example of "messy" history; it contains contradictions and inconsistencies which defy the neat application of set academic models. The Indian New Deal reflects both policymakers' own unreconcilable misconceptions and confusions and Indigenous communities' concerted efforts to interpret and utilize a program they had little voice in creating.

By unpacking the nature, implementation, and reception of 1930s school policy, rather than grouping it together with earlier federal government initiatives, this study offers an opportunity to understand and therefore learn from the specific mistakes of the Indian New Deal. The 1930s show us that colonialism can wear different, at times obfuscatory guises (even to its perpetrators) and that assimilationist intent is not the only threat to Indigenous cultural sovereignty; the imposition of knowledge hierarchies and of subjective regimes of "truth" are incompatible with bicultural education and represent an insidious form of cultural invasion, irrespective of policymakers' intent. Rather than a straightforward continuation of assimilationist ideals with a smattering of cosmetic cultural additions, the New Deal demonstrated a new threat to Native American cultural sovereignty, while simultaneously removing overt obstacles to religious performance and cultural expression.

This study explores the New Deal education program from the policymaker stage through to its implementation at the reservation schools. To do so, it draws upon the records of individual schools and school districts, including lesson plans, attendance records, and correspondence between school personnel and regional directors of education; the teaching materials commissioned for use in the government schools; the guidance issued by nongovernment sources (notably anthropologists); as well as policymakers' correspondence and reports. Student writings and published memoirs by both teachers and students are also used, in addition to reports by nongovernment organizations—notably the Phelps-Stokes Fund and the New Mexico Association on Indian Affairs (NMAIA).[36] By moving beyond a focus on the official statements of the commissioner of Indian Affairs and his directors of education, it is possible to follow the path of policies as they were understood, and at times refashioned, by teachers and school personnel, council delegates, BIA field workers, students, and parents. This study therefore challenges the depiction of policy as a monolithic entity and instead views it as a dynamic process of reinterpretation and adaptation.

Such sources also pose challenges in terms of the voices they represent—school records, like higher policy documents, were invariably written by BIA employees in positions of relative authority and thus risk telling a one-sided history. Yet, as Lomawaima and McCarty have shown, the government archive should not be viewed as devoid of Indigenous voices, input, and agency.[37] Native voices and actions speak through the government and school records: sometimes directly, in letters and student compositions, and sometimes indirectly, as reported by BIA employees, by BIA-commissioned anthropologists, and by organizations investigating Native concerns about government policy. The latter may have undergone distortion, or at best an unconscious editing process by the reporter, yet taken together what these sources reveal is Native peoples' concerted interest in, and engagement with, school policy. Indeed, the NMAIA's highly critical 1940 report was commissioned specifically in response to Diné concerns about New Deal policy, including education reforms. The report was based upon interviews with 150 Diné households and the researcher's attendance at eight community meetings, as well as consultation with government field workers and missionary groups. In a similar vein, the Phelps-Stokes Fund sent four researchers, including the Dakota anthropologist Ella Deloria, to the Navajo Reservation in 1939 to investigate tensions between the Diné and government personnel. Deloria proved an invaluable member of the research team: according to the director, her efforts "guaranteed that the interpretations and views of the Indians themselves are sincerely recognized in the conclusions drawn."[38] While the authors of these published reports were not Diné, and the tone is at times paternalistic and undeniably Eurocentric, the concerns and opinions of Navajo Nation members form significant parts of their content.

Structure

The structure of this study reflects the government school curricula in the New Deal era. Vocational education remained a priority at the government schools in the 1930s and has been the focus of earlier research, as has the implementation of controversial progressive education techniques.[39] In contrast, this book examines the teaching of (and schools' attitudes towards) history and the past; science, healthcare, and the environment; traditional religions; and Native languages. These topics reflect the rigid Eurocentric subject categorization inherent in the New Deal curriculum that failed to acknowledge Indigenous perspectives. However, these categories also speak to key elements of cultural sovereignty: how a nation views and interprets its past; the relationship between a nation and its surrounding environment; religious freedom; and the power of language and its relationship to identity and culture. These elements were subject to concerted attack through the Assimilation Era boarding schools and land policy; therefore, a study of how they were treated at the schools in the 1930s will reveal the extent to which the New Deal marked a change from attempted government-mandated ethnocide.

This book begins with an overview of federal government attitudes and policy towards Indigenous cultures from the assimilation policy of the late nineteenth and early twentieth centuries through the Meriam Report

(1928) and Indian New Deal (1933–45), which will show the contextualization and evolution of policymakers' cultural views and their impact on education policy. The first chapter demonstrates the Meriam Report's cultural conservatism and introduces the wider ideology and aims of New Deal architects.

The second chapter explores the ways in which Native histories and "the Native American past" were taught at the schools. It takes a broad view of "the past" to include formal history units and textbooks, school-based arts and crafts lessons, the government's bid to "preserve" traditional songs and plant knowledge, and the Pageant of Navajo History (1940). This interpretation reflects policymakers' tendency both to prioritize historic artistic patterns and techniques and to depict many Native traditions as teetering on the brink of extinction—thus blurring the boundaries of "history" and "culture." The chapter contrasts individual teachers' incorporation of Native historical knowledge in the classroom with policymakers' prioritization of academic expertise and explores the BIA preoccupation with historical "authenticity" as presented by non-Native anthropologists and historians. It concludes with an analysis of Native teachers' contribution to curriculum design in the 1930s and reveals tensions over the control of historical narratives and the differing perceptions of what constitutes "history."

From history, the analysis shifts to science lessons at the Navajo schools. Chapter 3 examines policymakers' decision to use schools to propagandize the government's unpopular stock reduction program through the teaching of soil conservation based on Western scientific principles. The health and sanitation program, both at the schools and across the reservation, is also analyzed. The emphasis on Western concepts of weather formation, drought and growth patterns, and contagion theory contradicted traditional Diné metaphysical beliefs, religious values, and medical practices. This chapter explores policymaker and community reactions to these tensions, fleeting attempts at cultural tolerance, and the implications the science program held for a supposedly pluralist curriculum.

The fourth chapter considers the treatment of religion at the government schools. Indigenous religions were not formally included on BIA school curricula in this period. However, proselytization by Christian missionaries was actively curtailed—from early 1934 onward, missionaries could only teach those children at government schools who had written parental permission for Bible study and Christian services. This chapter examines the extent to which school-based proselytization was regulated. It also considers the newly formalized policy by which pupils on the Navajo Reservation and United Pueblos Agency were permitted to leave school to attend religious ceremonies and festivals in their home communities.

Chapter 5 focuses on bilingual education, notably the attempt to develop a written form of Diné bizaad in the late 1930s. The dispute between the academic experts hired by the Indian Service and the Diné translators and educators who would use the written language reveals tensions over who held the power and the authority to determine the Diné orthography. In the 1940s the BIA produced bilingual primers, written by non-Native authors, for use at the Diné, Pueblo, and Lakota schools. This chapter examines the stated aims, themes, and content of some of these primers to demonstrate their treatment of Native cultures. Despite the Eurocentric framing and composition of the stories, some of the themes and messages complicate interpretations of the primers as assimilationist texts.

The last chapter offers an evaluation of the New Deal education program as fledgling pluralist experiment, exploring the issues of power, authority, and colonization revealed by the curriculum and by both its critics and supporters. It evaluates the education program in the context of established colonial education models (safety zone; cultural invasion; epistemicide; and settler colonialism) and considers the reasons behind the New Deal's inherent confusion and "messiness," notably the persistence of colonizer notions of "truth" and objectivity, and the compartmentalization of cultures and knowledge spheres.

The epilogue explores the resurgence of monoculturalism in Indian Service schools in the later decades of the twentieth century and the challenges facing supporters of bicultural education for Indigenous communities. The book concludes with an examination of the Diné History and Culture program devised by Navajo Community College in 1970, which offers a powerful insight into how bicultural education can be realized. Indigenous cultural survivance is a testament to the resistance and resilience demonstrated by Indigenous communities, educators, parents, and children who have persistently defended their identity and cultural sovereignty against the aggressions and impositions of colonization.

FEDERAL GOVERNMENT ATTITUDES TO NATIVE AMERICAN CULTURES, C. 1880–1945

1

For Indigenous nations, the struggle to retain sovereignty in the face of hostile government interference, land loss, and the dislocation of traditional economic systems has characterized the period of Euro-American colonization and remains ongoing. From the late nineteenth century onward, the federal government viewed Native Americans as its wards, supposedly guiding them through the processes of adjustment to "modern" American life and US citizenship. In practice, this pronounced congressional guardianship translated into paternalistic dominance, treating Native nations as errant children who needed to be protected from themselves, even if not from unscrupulous outsiders. From the 1880s through the 1950s, paternalism, often accompanied by coercion, continued to characterize the federal-tribal relationship, albeit in varying degrees of intensity. One aspect of attempted government control that has evolved over time concerns traditional Indigenous cultures and the extent to which the federal government has sought their oppression in favor of assimilation to Euro-American sociocultural values. This chapter explores and contextualizes federal government attitudes towards Indigenous cultures from the Assimilation Era (c. 1880–1930) to the Indian New Deal (1933–45), tracing the evolution from a coercive assimilation policy to the limited tolerance shown in the Meriam Report and the confused synthesis of preservation and assimilation promoted in the 1930s. While paternalistic guidance remained entrenched throughout this period, contextual factors such as changes in American anthropological thought, the failure of flagship assimilationist programs, and concerted Indigenous resistance to cultural oppression combined to steer policy away from unabashed monoculturalism and towards professed cultural tolerance.

Assimilation Policy (c. 1879–1930): Attempted Ethnocide in Action

The coercive assimilation strategy that constituted federal government "Indian" policy for the five decades before the New Deal has garnered deserved notoriety both for its inhumanity towards Indigenous families and its abject failure to improve the economic situation of most Native Americans. Presented as a bid to ensure Native American survival in "modern" US society, the policy rested firmly upon the federal government's belief in the inferiority of non–Anglo-Saxon cultures. A climate of cultural intolerance strengthened in the United States in the late nineteenth century against a backdrop of rising immigration from supposedly "backward" nations and concerns that the new arrivals were clinging tenaciously to their "old world" cultures and languages, thereby threatening national cohesion.[1] Civilization hierarchies conceived by anthropologists depicted a world in which alleged "savage" and "barbaric" societies either evolved into the perceived apex of progress—Anglo-American culture—or expired through inability to compete with their culturally and technologically "superior" rivals.[2] This hierarchical presentation of human "progress" that emphasized necessary assimilation to American mores permeated the public sphere in the late nineteenth and early twentieth centuries—shaping museum exhibitions, world fairs, and public school education. Geography textbooks used "cartographies of climate" to justify imperial and continental expansion, presenting European and Euro-American settlers as masters of the environment, exempt from the geographic determinism that governed Indigenous and so-called barbarous races in tropical climes.[3] History lessons taught narratives of manifest destiny, Anglo-American "civilization," and benevolent colonization, depicting Native Hawaiians and Filipinos as fortunate beneficiaries of American uplift and Native Americans as historic (and transient) obstacles in the path of national security and natural progress.[4] Such de facto imperialist narratives arguably strove to bolster national cohesion and confidence while projecting a monocultural, uniform concept of citizenship based on Anglo-American values of individualism and capitalist production. Anything regarded as alien to this national identity had to be neutralized, either through exclusion (immigration restriction) or a rigorous assimilation process that eliminated perceived undesirable qualities.

To the federal government in the late nineteenth century, Native American cultures were outmoded relics of a bygone era, which should be jettisoned before Native peoples could contribute to the American nation as productive, obedient citizens. This citizenship preparation involved three key "civilized" values: individualist capitalism, Christianity, and the English language.[5] Capitalism was imposed via the General Land Allotment Act (Dawes Act) of 1887, which divided selected reservations into individual plots of land leased by the federal government to a (usually) male head of household who would then pass the farm on to immediate heirs. Through allotment the government strove to kill three birds with one stone: to make Native Americans economically self-sufficient; to free up so-called surplus land for non-Native usage (in practice the most successful goal); and to break extended Indigenous kinship ties and communitarian values and replace them with individualist capitalism.[6]

The bid to sever cultural and social ties continued with the restricting of traditional Indigenous ceremonies and dances, some of which were formally banned under the Court of Indian Offences (1883). Policymakers and some Christian missionaries justified the bans by luridly smearing ceremonies as smokescreens for ritualized violence, debauchery, and inebriation—and downplaying any links to religious significance.[7] As late as 1923 one commissioner of Indian Affairs referred to dances as "*so-called* religious ceremonies."[8] Reservation superintendents and commissioners fretted over the crop-tending time they feared was lost to dances and the property they viewed as squandered during giveaways.[9] Not only did the BIA seek to reduce the frequency of ceremonial gatherings, but it strove to divorce younger generations from their cultural heritage: as Commissioner Charles Burke directed, "None [should] take part in the dances or be present who are under 50 years of age." As additional insurance against cultural continuation, Burke urged that "a careful propaganda be undertaken to educate public opinion against the dance and to provide a healthy substitute."[10] Native communities employed creative strategies to subvert the bans and to maintain religious and cultural knowledge, frustrating BIA officials with their resilience and ingenuity.[11] However, the price of defiance—including imprisonment, physical violence, and the withholding of vital rations—should not be underestimated; this was a state-driven effort to euthanize Indigenous cultural expression by actively discouraging its performance. Excepting some arts and crafts (those valued by policymakers for their potential pecuniary value), Indigenous cultures were viewed by policymakers as at worst, actively harmful, and at best, "a waste of time."[12]

This deliberate attempt at cultural extinction was aided by the BIA's education policy. As Commissioner Thomas Morgan stated in 1889, the government sought to raise the next generation of Native Americans "not as Indians, but as Americans."[13] Under the aggressive slogan "Kill the Indian and save the man," policymakers championed residential schools for young children and ignored cultural and regional diversity through a rigidly applied "Uniform Curriculum." At least half of each day was devoted to vocational training—linked to the government's equation of economic self-sufficiency with good citizenship. In this they mirrored the agricultural training schools for African Americans that in reality offered very basic vocational training and which arguably, under the guise of industrial education, sought to solidify the existing labor hierarchy in the South rather than enable equal economic opportunity.[14] Yet economic self-sufficiency constituted just one part of citizenship preparation for Native Americans—the schools simultaneously strove to eradicate tribal identity, and by extension, sovereignty. It was not enough for children to learn Euro-American values; they had also to reject those of their home nation—a process described recently as "curricular genocide."[15] Pupils faced brutal punishments for speaking their own languages and for holding traditional ceremonies.[16] The curriculum consciously left little room for Native identities: religion was taught, but it was strictly Christian; history lessons revolved around Washington and Jefferson, not Sequoyah or Barboncito. True, there were sporadic, short-lived attempts to include "Indian art" at some schools, and Commissioner Francis Leupp conceded that "little children's songs" and women's crafts might be sufficiently harmless as to escape prohibition.[17] However, Leupp's commissionership lasted just four years, witnessed scant actual hiring of Native art teachers, and the overriding message conveyed by the schools remained one of total cultural assimilation. Writing for the Indian Service newsletter *Indians at Work*, Miguel Trujillo of Isleta Pueblo, who graduated from Albuquerque and Haskell Boarding Schools and went on to a long career as a day-school teacher, painted a grim picture of cultural oppression:

> The youngsters were forbidden to speak their native language in order that they might better learn the white man's language. If the little Indians forgot and spoke Indian they were subjected to corporal punishment that was reminiscent of the feudal times in the white man's history. Jails were part of the educational institutions and were used to retract those who persisted to cling to their primitive ways and also those that managed to run away from the "school" and were later re-captured. Throughout this "recreation" the Indian youth was made to understand that everything his parents had taught him was wrong. If his parents objected and interfered they were given jail sentences also.

As Trujillo poignantly concluded, "One is not apt to forget soon one's own subjection to such an 'educative process.'"[18]

Some pupils and teachers did, however, successfully subvert the monocultural ethos. Esther Burnett Horne, a Shoshone teacher, recalled her own schooldays at Haskell: "We students nurtured a sense of community among ourselves, and we learned so much from each other. Traditional values such as sharing and cooperation helped us to survive culturally at Haskell, even though the schools were designed to erase our Indian culture, values, and identities."[19] Indeed, the deliberate bid to extinguish tribal identity by mixing up different nations at the schools backfired: rather than adopting an Anglo-American identity, many children created a pan-tribal one. According to Horne, the bonding of children from different nations transformed the boarding school experience for some into a "historical and cultural feast"—a far cry from policymakers' assimilationist intentions.[20] Native teachers, such as Ruth Muskrat Bronson, Polingaysi Qoyawayma, and later Horne—themselves boarding school graduates—clandestinely incorporated elements of Native cultures into their lessons, while some sympathetic non-Native teachers turned a blind eye to student expressions of traditional culture or language.[21] However, despite this concerted resistance and resilience, the *objective* of the schools remained ethnocidal: to detach children from their cultures and communities and to ignore Indigenous knowledge and learning systems. Indigenous philosophies, customs, and knowledge systems were presumed to be wrong, and their Euro-American equivalents right—mirroring the epistemicide which Francis Nyamnjoh has identified in European colonial education policies in early twentieth-century African nations.[22]

The Meriam Report (1928): Cultural Choice?

The 1920s witnessed both the extension of US citizenship to all Native Americans (1924) and the attempted intensification of the dance bans (1921–25).[23] While Congress continued to exercise extraordinary guardianship powers over Native Americans, changes in government attitudes did occur toward the decade's end. Much has been made of the 1928 publication *The Problem of Indian Administration*, a detailed 847-page report produced by the Brookings Institution at the behest of Secretary of the Interior Hubert Work. Dubbed the "Meriam Report" after its lead researcher, Lewis Meriam, the investigation was based on fieldwork conducted in 1926 on reservations across the United States. The final report consisted of fourteen chapters examining the state of Native American education, health, economics, family life, and more. The Ho Chunk educator and missionary Dr. Henry Roe Cloud was a member of the survey team and played a vital role in the fieldwork—according to Meriam his presence, and his "wide acquaintanceship among the Indians," ensured that "conferences with Indians and Indian councils became a regular part of the work of the survey."[24] The Meriam Report therefore marked a watershed moment in US research on Native American living conditions—while the opinions of superintendents, BIA personnel, and missionaries featured most prominently in the narrative, Indigenous voices did also appear, and researchers conducted home visits on reservations with a view to gaining grassroots opinions of government policy.

The Meriam Report is widely regarded as a progressive investigation that sounded the death knell of the coercive assimilation policy. It presented a scathing criticism of land allotment and boarding school management, arguing that neither had achieved the assimilation objective. In the opening chapter, Meriam offered a stark indictment of government policy: "An overwhelming majority of the Indians are poor, even extremely poor, and they are not adjusted to the economic and social system of the dominant white civilization."[25] This was, Meriam detailed, the result of grave Indian Service incompetence: "It almost seems as if the government assumed that some magic in the individual ownership of property would in itself prove an educational civilizing factor, but unfortunately this policy has for the most part operated in the opposite direction."[26] A caustic denunciation, substantiated with grim statistics charting bad harvests, unchecked manipulation by unscrupulous grifters, and eventual land loss and poverty—indeed, with few exceptions, allotment had not created a generation of self-sufficient agriculturalists.[27] Meriam also publicly revealed that the boarding schools of the 1920s bore closer resemblance to Victorian workhouses than educational establishments. Overcrowded and underfunded, the schools increasingly relied on students to perform arduous menial tasks including cleaning, cooking, and general plant maintenance—such as would "constitute a violation of child labor laws in most states."[28] In addition, the caliber of intellectual education was disappointing, consisting largely of a Uniform Curriculum that bore little relevance to the pupils' experience or identity.[29] Despite their lofty professed aims, the schools offered few lucrative career options.

The Meriam Report did not just expose the economic and moral failures of existing policies: it emphasized the necessity of *choice* in the assimilation process. In a chapter proposing "A General Policy for Indian Affairs," the authors issued a groundbreaking statement: "The work with and for the Indians must give consideration to the desires of the individual Indians. He who wishes to merge into the social and economic life of the prevailing civilization of this country should be given all practicable aid and advice in making the necessary adjustments. He who wants to remain an Indian and live according to his old culture should be aided in doing so."[30] The report thus undermined the keystone foundation of assimilation policy—the assumption that Native American cultures and identities could not endure and that total acceptance of Euro-American culture was the only viable future. Crucially, Meriam acknowledged the right of Native individuals to choose their identity and argued against a coercive assimilation strategy. This emphasis on choice has led scholars to hail the Meriam Report as a watershed moment in federal government policy that both criticized assimilation and offered Native Americans the "radical notion" of retaining their cultural identity.[31] Certainly, its suggestion that Native cultures *could* continue was a challenge to prevailing BIA ethnocentrism.

Yet the Meriam Report stopped far short of advocating either cultural pluralism or the ending of assimilation policy. While they decried allotment's botched implementation, the authors believed it should continue—albeit in a reformed manner. Rather than detailing the positive and dynamic aspects of Native cultures, Meriam devoted considerable word space to criticizing their *artificial* preservation—the so-called glass-case policy by which "liberal whites" sought to preserve Native Americans "as museum specimens for future generations to study and enjoy, because of the value of their culture and its picturesqueness in a world rapidly advancing in high organization and mass production."[32] Such a stance was, to Meriam, "impracticable" because the "advancing tide of white civilization has ... largely destroyed the economic foundation upon which the Indian culture rested." In short, "The hands of the clock cannot be turned backward."[33] The language and tone in these sentences are striking. By equating cultural preservation with the romanticized whims of non-Native antimodernists and sightseers, Meriam reduced the viability and resilience of Native traditional cultures in the eyes of his predominantly non-Native readers. Then, by referring to the "advance" of modern civilization and the futility of turning back time, he placed Indigenous cultures firmly in the past. This appears to reflect what Lorenzo Veracini has identified as part of the "narrative transfer" aspect of settler colonialism, whereby Indigenous peoples and their cultures are depicted "as hopelessly backward, as unchanging specimens of a primitive form of humanity inhabiting pockets of past surrounded by contemporaneity."[34] The report then listed the benefits of "white civilization" that some Native Americans "even in the most conservative pueblos" desired: "white industrial pursuit"; "modern sanitary conveniences"; "to have their wives in childbirth attended by skilled physicians in a hospital"; to consult trained doctors "as the white man does"; automobiles "and other things made possible by the white man's mass production." Meriam cautioned against forcing these individuals "back to the old"—once again implying that traditional cultures were outmoded and belonged to the past. What also emerges from these passages is an assumption of "good" and "bad" cultural elements: while Meriam saw no harm in Native "art, music, religion," he implicitly suggested traditional cultures were devoid of basic sanitation and medical knowledge and that these were somehow the preserve of "white civilization."[35]

Meriam did champion the *right* of Native Americans to choose their cultural identity. Yet the choice itself was framed as a binary model: a person could choose either an assimilated or an "Indian" identity, not any semblance of biculturalism or dual identity. This assumption ignored the multifaceted reality of Native identities and wrongly depicted Native cultures as static relics of a fading past. Furthermore, the choice was qualified by assimilationist sentiment. Those who had chosen to "remain an Indian" would still face major "adjustments" to their "economic, social and legal" systems. These adjustments, when outlined by the author, largely targeted health and sanitation, and they were necessitated by the apparent associated risks posed by close proximity of Native "villages" to "white settlements." Indeed,

> Both the Indians and their white neighbors are concerned in having those Indians who want to stay Indians and preserve their culture, live according to at least a minimum standard of health and decency. Less than that means not only that they may become a menace to the whites but also that they themselves will go through a long drawn out and painful process of vanishing. They must be aided for the preservation of themselves.[36]

In other words, the denigration of Native traditional cultures and communities by policymakers and commentators remained intact in 1928. Traditional culture was depicted as synonymous with disease, while Native communities were characterized as incapable of helping themselves. In Meriam's view, only the dynamic, advanced, and, in effect, superior Euro-American culture and technology could save Native communities. True, the report did acknowledge the historic role played by Euro-American aggression and incursion in destroying "the old economic basis" of Native cultures and so stopped short of the classic BIA trope of blaming Native communities for the difficulties they faced.[37] Yet the overall impression given by the authors is that, artistic elements aside, they saw little in Native traditional cultures that was worth saving or that could survive unaided by Euro-American guidance.

Meriam's uneasy blend of professed cultural tolerance and denigration of Indigenous health and hygiene had a precursor. Progressive Era reformers who sought to facilitate the assimilation of immigrants into American urban life had also promoted a gospel of combined "tolerance" and "improvement." At a 1913 conference on education for immigrant children, the associate superintendent of New York City Public Schools denounced "narrow-minded zealots [who] imagine that to become a good American citizen the immigrant must eradicate all the ideals and sentiments that have characterized the race from which he came."[38] Yet the very same conference proceedings contain condescending references to immigrant women's apparent ignorance of "proper" domestic and hygiene standards—and the need for a staff of "visiting housewives" to instruct them in basic American homemaking.[39] Indeed, the representative of the Association of Practical Home-Making Centers advocated an instructive model home in every immigrant neighborhood to impart American standards of cooking, cleaning, and infant care.[40] The parallel with the Meriam Report's dismissal of Native homemaking is striking.

Meriam's criticism of Indigenous traditional life didn't stop at health, sanitation, and homemaking. In addition to lamenting nomadic or "wandering" economic practices and arguing that Native Americans should be taught how to beautify their own homes, the report spoke of "objectionable features" in Native cultural and recreational expression. According to the authors,

> That some of their dances and other activities have objectionable features is of course true. The same thing is true of the recreation and the community activities of almost any people. The object should not be to stamp out all the native things because a few of them have undesirable accompaniments but to seek to modify them gradually so that the objectionable features will ultimately disappear. The native activities can be supplemented by those activities borrowed from the whites ... notably athletics, music, and sewing, and other close work demanding manual skill.[41]

In one brief passage, the report dismissed Native dances—some of which are religious in nature—as mere recreational pursuits and then advocated their gradual replacement with Euro-American leisure activities, those presumably deemed more wholesome. The authors did not elaborate on the "objectionable" features yet evidently felt qualified to position themselves as moral adjudicators of Indigenous cultural practice.

The closing chapter of the report went even further, demonstrating a condescending attitude toward traditional religious beliefs:

> Superstition gives way before scientific knowledge. Once the Hopi is reasonably supplied with water by the government engineers, as he

will be some day, the Hopi rain god, the Snake, will depart to return no more. Great advance in sanitation and hygiene and in the elimination of malnutrition by economic improvement and proper dietary habits will demonstrate to the Indians that the medicine man is a useless adjunct of Indian society.[42]

The authors' dismissal of Hopi religion as mere "superstition," followed by the simultaneous denigration of traditional medicine and the sacred role of "medicine men," demonstrates the underlying assimilationist impulse at the Meriam Report's heart. While the authors were horrified at the poverty and dislocation caused by botched allotment and boarding school policies, and while they lamented the practice of coercive assimilation, they could not bring themselves to view Native traditional cultures—including religions—as equal to their own.

The chapter on education authored by W. Carson Ryan Jr., a professor of education at Swarthmore College, came perhaps the closest to a culturally inclusive stance. Ryan was a member (and future president) of the Progressive Education Association (PEA), hence his promotion of Dewey-esque teaching techniques and his criticism of the Uniform Curriculum. Placed amongst the progressive education tenets, however, is a challenge to prevailing government attitudes towards Native families. Ryan championed day schools for young children, noting that it "leaves the child in the home environment, where he belongs."[43] And he seemed to accept that traditional cultures held elements of value and that parents had a role to play in their children's learning process:

> We have learned, in the case of children from foreign homes, that there are values in the customs of other peoples that ought to be preserved and not destroyed; so with Indians; there is a contribution from Indian life that likewise needs to be safeguarded and not sacrificed to unnecessary standardization.... The day school principal and teacher have the parents close at hand, and can, if they will, get the interest and point of view of the parents in a way that would be almost out of the question for the boarding school.[44]

Ryan appeared to indicate that not only were Native cultural values worth keeping but that parents should be consulted in the education of their children.

Again, however, the proposed progression was limited. The knowledge transfer between the day schools and homes was conceived as a largely one-sided channel. The close proximity of day school to home would, Ryan believed, ensure that "whatever worthwhile changes the school undertakes to make are soon reflected in the home." In this way, "Ideas of cleanliness, better homekeeping, better standards of living, have their influence almost immediately in the home and community."[45] Once again, Native communities and homes were portrayed as benighted centers of dirt and poverty—hardly a culturally pluralist stance. Indeed, while the Meriam Report did criticize the policy of destroying all that was "Indian" in Native cultures, it devoted remarkably little word space across its many chapters to outlining positive aspects of traditional customs, social networks, and cultural practices.

The "Indian New Deal" (1933–45): A Future for Community?

In 1933 President Franklin Roosevelt appointed a new commissioner of Indian Affairs who had different views on Indigenous cultures, communities, and lands. A newcomer to government office, John Collier had spent much of the 1920s aggressively lobbying against government policies, notably the 1922 Bursum Bill, which attacked Pueblo land titles; the 1924–25 joint BIA-missionary bid to outlaw Pueblo dances; and the 1926 Leavitt Bill which sought to ban traditional marriages. As executive secretary of the newly established pressure group the American Indian Defense Association (AIDA), Collier campaigned against bids to curtail Native land rights and cultural freedom, forming formidable coalitions with the All-Pueblo Council and the General Federation of Women's Clubs. By shrewdly asserting the integral role of dances in religious worship, the All-Pueblo Council played a vital role in the quiet demise of Commissioner Burke's smear campaign against so-called secret dances.[46] For his part, Collier bombarded national newspapers and liberal journals with alarm calls of federally sponsored religious persecution on US soil—effectively inviting public condemnation of an Indian Office that appeared hell-bent on trampling the First Amendment.[47] Given the collapse of the Bursum Bill, "secret dance file," and the Leavitt Bill, it is fair to say that the All-Pueblo Council and AIDA successfully raised public and congressional awareness of Native American land and religious freedom rights in the 1920s.

Before 1920, Collier had had no experience of Indian Affairs, having previously worked with immigrant communities in New York. In 1920 he was invited by the art patron and socialite Mabel Dodge Luhan to visit Taos Pueblo, and his enchantment at the community's social, religious, and cultural existence has been widely discussed.[48] His writings and memoirs suggest this marked the beginning of a lifelong admiration for Native Americans, or rather of *his* particular perception of Indigenous cultures.[49] However, it was hardly a watershed moment in his wider views on culture and community—as a social worker he had voiced concern at ongoing aggressive attempts to assimilate immigrants into American culture at the cost of their "old world" identities. He feared that individualism and the dislocating effect of modern, urbanized existence—"its sick spirit, its atomizing intellectual and moral aims and purposes"—would harm people of all races, nationalities, and cultures, both collectively and psychologically.[50] For Collier, and fellow devotees of Tonnies's "brotherhood of man" social theory, a community motivated by shared purposes was integral to human wellbeing: "The individual fares best when he is a member of a group faring best."[51] As the Onondaga artist and council member Oren Lyons has commented: "What was it that Collier saw of value in Indian life? What was he trying to preserve? You know what he was trying to preserve: it was a peaceful community. The United States as it stands today has very little community. Indian nations still have community."[52] This emphasis on community formed a major part of Collier's 1934 speech to the American Federation of Arts, in which he defended Pueblo and Diné cultures and social organization: "Here, then, are ancient social orders, organisms of communal life from thousands of years ago—institutionalized common life, all-embracing in the experience of its members, and striving at this hour to make profound adaptations to the demands of necessity while still keeping alive the ancient values and ancient sources of joy, of belief, of courage and of power."[53]

In contrast to some of the cohesive immigrant communities he had worked with and the Pueblo nations of Taos, Zia, and Tesuque, Collier viewed urban, industrialized US society as "a shattered race—psychically, religiously, socially and esthetically shattered, dismembered, directionless."[54] Indeed, when describing Tesuque society, he wrote, "I have not personally encountered anything else equally powerful in social life. Measured by that spirit and that world-view of the Tesuques, most of our white life seemed very weakly self-centered, undisciplined and unbeautiful."[55] Contrast this depiction of an "ancient," harmonious culture with his description of contemporary white society: "Let us do our best and let us be full sure that ours is a quickly passing day."[56] In this view, the enduring Native communities, far from being moribund and dying, were in some ways superior to "modern" American society—and rather than being the potential contaminants suggested by Meriam, they had something valuable to teach Euro-Americans.

Collier's veneration of community and communitarianism played a large role in his policies as commissioner of Indian Affairs. One of his first steps was to end the process of land allotment. As he informed BIA personnel in 1936: "The basic policy of this Indian Administration is to halt the process by which the Indians have been deprived of two-thirds of their lands and to begin a reverse process of restoring and building up and developing the entire Indian estate as a basis of Indian culture, independence, and self-support."[57] Land loomed large in the Indian Reorganization Act (IRA), the flagship legislation of the Indian New Deal, reflecting New Dealers' belief that land was essential to both economic success and spiritual and community wellbeing. The BIA also promised to restore parts of the tribal land base to tribal councils, notably the land lost under the Dawes Act's surplus land clause. More controversially, the IRA encouraged the reorganization of tribal governments along a Euro-American model of democratic governance—simultaneously suggesting BIA recognition that tribes had a future as political institutions, while also encouraging the structural assimilation of tribal councils. The reorganized governments were given increased self-governance powers in some areas, notably the right to employ legal counsel and to negotiate with federal, state, and local governments. In contrast to allotment policy, tribal government reorganization was meant to be voluntary: the secretary of the interior was directed to organize tribal referenda, decided by a majority vote of a tribe's adult population. Under such referenda, 181 Native nations accepted reorganization, while seventy-seven rejected it. The latter included the Diné, the largest nation.

The IRA marked an aggrandizement in tribal self-determination compared to earlier policy—yet the powers granted to reorganized governments were sadly limited. Indeed, as Laurence Hauptman has noted, "In the manner of a 'liberal imperialist,' Collier improved upon the situation, but did not create complete self-rule."[58] The act witnessed an expansion of the powers of the secretary of the interior, who had final approval of proposed constitutions, bylaws, business charters, and even of a nation's legal counsel appointment. Collier—by his own admission—was a fan of indirect administration, the system favored by contemporary British colonial authorities in Kenya and Uganda in which administration was executed through existing political and social organizations.[59] The IRA did not mark an end to the colonization of Native peoples by the federal government. It did, however, differ from previous policy in its promotion of a reservation-centric and community-orientated future for Native nations. To this end, the IRA sought to boost tribal economies via promotion of cooperative businesses and through the marketing of traditional arts and crafts. The latter was facilitated by the Indian Arts and Crafts Board Act (1935), which seed-funded crafts cooperatives and sought to reduce non-Native competition by establishing authenticity ("Indian-made") hallmarks and strict production regulations for "traditional" products.[60] Agriculture and ranching were also seen as key to economic success: "Unless the Indian land situation can be met, there is no future for the Indians."[61]

While the move to a community and land-centric policy marked a significant change for the BIA, it wasn't dramatically out of step with wider New Deal government attitudes towards rural America. Burgeoning concern at soil erosion and environmental despoliation spurred the rollout of conservation projects designed to protect the land as an economic resource.[62] Against a backdrop of Mississippi flood surges and denuded slopes, one Resettlement Administration documentary cautioned, "Poor land makes poor people, and poor people make poor land."[63] Government policy actively sought to keep people *on* the land, fearful of mass migration to crowded urban centers ravaged by unemployment.[64] But economic and employment concerns weren't the sole motivators of rural reform. Some of the academic experts and educators involved in rural policies, such as the Subsistence Homestead program and the Community Farms projects, sought to *reshape* rural communities—not just to revive them economically but to effect social change and promote community cooperation which could strengthen both society and the national economy.[65] Rural schools were reimagined as community centers that would offer more than just academic lessons; they would uplift the entire community by dispensing health care, distributing information, and housing women's clubs and community gatherings.[66] New communities were also created. The Farm Security Administration relocated landless farmers to purpose-built, centralized communities intended to be self-supporting through cooperative enterprises and small-scale agriculture.[67] And educators enthusiastically promoted what they viewed as positive rural character traits—independence and resourcefulness—as well as rural contributions to American culture including "certain cultural patterns in music, handicrafts, and other arts."[68] As one rural education reform advocate declared in 1936, rural community offered a potential solution to the dislocating effects of urban individualism, proven by "the recent collapse of our present industrial system with its tragic unemployment and general economic insecurity." Rather, "It should be possible under proper federal safeguards and vocational guidance to develop a cooperative type of life upon the land which would far surpass anything yet realized by the average citizen in either economic security or the enjoyment of living."[69] The Indian New Deal therefore unfurled against a backdrop of increased government and academic interest in promoting rural communities and experimental rural planning and amidst investment in the land as an economic resource. Rural community, the government believed, should be strengthened, revitalized, and preserved, and those living on the land should be encouraged, and helped, to stay there.

Circular 2970 (1934) and "Cultural Tolerance"

The Indian Reorganization Act focused on land, economics, and political restructuring, with little direct reference to Indigenous cultures or religions. However, in a 1934 article promoting the proposed legislation, Collier cited both land loss *and* religio-cultural suppression as policies he sought to overturn. In his view, the Wheeler-Howard bill "strikes a double blow at the two fatal weaknesses of Indian administration across a whole century: first, the dissipation of the Indian estate and the progressive pauperization of the Indians, and, second, the suppression of Indian tribal and social and religious institutions and the steadfast failure of the Government to organize any effective plan of collective action by which the Indians could advance in citizenship and protect their rights."[70] While land was listed as the primary area of concern for New Dealers, cultural oppression was a close second. Religious freedom for Native Americans was not enshrined in legislation until 1978, but it was the subject of an influential New Deal Indian

Service directive. In January 1934 Collier issued Circular 2970 on "Indian Religious Freedom and Indian Culture" to all BIA superintendents to affirm the BIA's new policy of cultural tolerance. The commissioner claimed to have discovered, through visits to jurisdictions and correspondence, that "some" bureau personnel, missionaries, and "many" Native Americans "are not clearly advised as to the policy of this office toward Indian religious expression and toward ceremonial and art expression of Indians and the use of Indian native language." He noted that in some areas Native Americans still believed they had to secure bureau permission to hold "dance ceremonies of native religious or folk significance"—indeed, the widespread perception was that the recently lifted dance bans were still active. He lamented the existence of government schools "into which no trace of Indian native symbolism or art or craft expression has been permitted to enter." In other words, many Indian Service personnel had not implemented the new approach. The remainder of the circular spelt out the policy: "No interference with Indian religious life or ceremonial expression will hereafter be tolerated. The cultural liberty of Indians is in all respects to be considered equal to that of any non-Indian group.... The fullest constitutional liberty, in all matters affecting religion, conscience, and culture, is insisted on for all Indians. In addition, an affirmative, appreciative attitude toward Indian cultural values is desired in the Indian Service."[71] The communiqué also championed bilingualism and Native American art.

Circular 2970 did two things. Firstly, it affirmed (on paper) the protection of Native American freedom of conscience under the First Amendment. It specifically warned superintendents against using punishments for statutory violations in ways that would "constitute an interference with, or to imply a censorship over, the religious or cultural life, Indian or other." The reference to "ceremonial expression" clearly protects worship, as well as belief.[72] Secondly, Circular 2970 went beyond mere removal of religio-cultural restrictions: it encouraged a change in BIA mindset—the need to *appreciate* Native cultures and religions and to view them as equal to Euro-American culture. This reflected the views of Collier and other leading New Dealers, who made public statements highlighting the merits of Indigenous religious beliefs and ceremonies. For example, the arts advisor Leslie Van Ness Denman, who was involved in New Deal art sponsorship, described the Zuni Shalako ceremony in awed tones to the readers of *Women's City Club Magazine*: "Here then, in Indian ritual are things which are beautiful and true—they are also good in the sense that they seek a harmony of the Indian with the forces of nature with which he believes himself to be one. With prayer, in song and in the dance, he binds his life and his spirit with the moving spirit of that cosmos which he knows."[73]

In similar vein, government-commissioned anthropologists described Diné religion as possessing "a complexity, an intellectual quality, and a mysticism that suggest an oriental religion."[74] While these descriptions do not indicate actual understanding of Zuni and Diné spiritual beliefs, they do convey them to a non-Native audience as bona fide established *religions*—using familiar language such as "prayer" and "harmony" and appealing to intellectualism. This depiction of viable, organized, admirable Indigenous religions marked a sharp departure from the rhetoric of earlier commissioners and BIA personnel, who emphasized "superstition," "sorcery," and barbarism.[75] And it contrasted the Meriam Report, which dismissed participation in "primitive dances and festivals" as fatalistic escapism from poverty, while also invoking alcohol and narcotics—hardly a positive appraisal of Indigenous cultures.[76] As Vine Deloria Jr. argued in 1984, "Collier's provisions for the revival of Indian cultural practices seem naïve today; in 1934 they were exceedingly radical because few people saw any value whatsoever in reviving Indian culture, let alone giving it an aura of academic and educational respectability."[77] The contemporary academic respectability stemmed from the government's employment of anthropologists, such as Scudder Mekeel and Ruth Underhill, to advise on BIA policy, to produce schoolbooks and teaching materials, and to offer teacher training. As advocates of cultural relativism rather than civilization hierarchies, these individuals advised that existing (traditional) community organizations, societal structures, and cultural values should form the basis for any reforms and adjustments in the life of Native American communities on the reservations and that traditional cultures should not be condemned purely because they were different to Euro-American culture.[78]

Both through the removal of restrictions on religious ceremonies and the emphasis on appreciating Indigenous cultures, the New Deal architects went further than the Meriam Report, at least on paper. Indeed, Circular 2970 suggests that, in theory, the New Deal Indian Service was promoting cultural pluralism, by which minority groups could participate in the dominant society/nation but also have the right to maintain their cultural heritage and values. Collier affirmed Native Americans' right to exercise religious freedom and professed acceptance ("appreciation") of Native American cultures while simultaneously advocating tribes' adoption of US democratic political structures. In this, he appeared to follow Horace Kallen's pluralist model by which ethnic groups have the right to maintain their sociocultural heritage yet must also accept a common political democratic culture as practiced by the dominant society.[79] Interestingly, policymakers rarely used the term "cultural pluralism" to describe BIA policy in the 1930s and 1940s, preferring instead to speak of "cultural tolerance" or to urge Native Americans "to choose wisely a scale of values for living in two cultures."[80]

Circular 2970 was merely a letter. Like Burke's anti-dance circulars of the 1920s, it held no statutory power. Yet it generated a significant backlash based on concern it promoted the artificial preservation of Indigenous cultures—the glass-case scenario feared by Meriam. Some missionaries, congresspersons, and tribal council representatives denounced the New Deal as an attempt to force Native Americans into a retrograde existence, segregated from the rest of US citizenry. This was forcefully argued in a 1943 report by Senators Elmer Thomas, Dennis Chavez, and Burton Wheeler:

> While the original [federal government] aim was to make the Indian a citizen; the present aim appears to be to keep the Indian an Indian and to make him satisfied with all the limitations of a primitive life. We are striving mightily to help him recapture his ancient worn-out cultures which are now hardly a vague memory to him and are absolutely unable to function in this present world. We non-Indians would not try, even to recapture our glamorous pioneer culture though it might be done without sacrifice, and though the adjustment in attitude and desires could be made with far less difficulty than the Indian would have in holding on to his rapidly receding past, to say nothing of his ancient past.[81]

The senators therefore not only placed all traditional Indigenous cultures firmly in the past but they implied those cultures were dead and scarcely remembered—thus accusing Circular 2970 of artificial cultural preservation, even resurrection. They then went one further by attacking Native American identities as incompatible with contemporary existence and calling upon the federal government to "eliminate the rehabilitation of Indians as Indians."[82] The report advised the abolition of the BIA and the immediate transfer of all Native children to the US public school system to hasten their cultural and societal assimilation. The missionary and author Elaine Eastman concurred, accusing Collier of "an official drive to 'revive' outgrown customs and ceremonies for the benefit of white tourists and sight-seers"—a sweeping judgement that wholly disregarded the Pueblos' determined fight to defend their ceremonial dances just ten years earlier.[83]

Some Native leaders and spokespersons also feared artificial cultural preservation and segregation from US society, notably the Kiowa delegate, Delos Lone Wolf, who denounced the IRA with the statement "I would rather pay taxes and be a man among men, than a useless Indian forever."[84] Seneca activist Alice Lee Jemison, a staunch defender of Seneca sovereignty, lambasted the IRA for its apparent disregard of existing treaty rights and tribal council structures. She was also a cultural assimilationist who, at a congressional hearing in 1937, informed senators that "it has been the policy of John Collier, since he became Commissioner, to train the Indians *to be only Indians* and to try to locate them in national parks under Government control, where they will be *forced* to live in that way."[85] Jemison thus raised the issue of consent, arguing that the majority of Native Americans did not wish to practice traditional customs and lifestyles and that the BIA sought to force these cultures upon them. Her tone also implied that Indigenous cultural identity was somehow lesser than American identity—"only Indians." This point was reinforced by Senator Chavez (New Mexico), who argued that the Diné "want to be Americans. They feel that they are going down. They do not want to dance with feathers on."[86] Again, the contrast was drawn between a positive, integrated, American identity and a negative, antiquated caricature of Indigenous cultures. Traditional cultures were depicted as not merely outdated but as actively threatening Native peoples' ability to thrive in modern America.

Contemporary critics of the Indian New Deal therefore interpreted it as a preservationist policy that sought to encourage, and even impose, traditional cultures upon Native communities. Historians writing in the 1970s and 1980s shared this view. According to Kenneth Philp, "Collier had a poetic insight into Indian culture and wanted to preserve it," while Robert Fay Schrader argued that "preservation rather than destruction of Indian life and values became the guiding principle behind official policy."[87] Brian Dippie concluded that Collier committed "the assimilationists' error in reverse"—thereby supporting Jemison's view that cultural preservation was a coercive policy based on non-Native whims.[88] More recently, scholars have adopted the opposite stance—charging that the Indian New Deal was a clandestine government attempt to control and assimilate Native communities, politically and economically, while paying lip service to cultural tolerance.[89] Indeed, this interpretive split reflects, in part, the frankly confusing and contradictory messages sent out by Collier and leading New Dealers throughout the New Deal.

Collier may have published laudatory and romanticized descriptions of Tesuque and Taos ceremonies while lifting the dance bans, yet he also spoke frequently of the need for Native communities to "adjust" to the "modern" world. In a 1936 essay he attempted to summarize current BIA policy: "To help him [the Indian] preserve the vital things of his old life, including the usable part of his institutions, is plainly a duty of Indian service. But is not 'assimilation' also a duty; and indeed is it not a necessity if the precious Indian heritage is to survive?"[90] Collier then suggested, somewhat confusingly, that Native Americans could safeguard their futures "by choosing not assimilation and not heritage, but by ardently and skillfully choosing both."[91] He advised that "necessary adjustments to the modern world should be carried out with the least possible dislocation of their traditional life," and he urged Native communities "to guard the valid old and build the valid new."[92] This was hardly a mandate for total preservation of traditional cultures—indeed, the New Dealers extolled the virtues of "modern science" and "new technologies."[93] Rather, the policy was one of selective adaptation, as advocated by Yale professor of education Charles Loram, who wrote a 1934 article for the Indian Service bimonthly journal *Indians at Work* promoting ethnological training for BIA employees. Loram, a specialist in colonial education programs involving Indigenous communities in South Africa and a future researcher on the Phelps-Stokes Fund's 1939 investigation into New Deal policy on the Navajo Reservation, advised the bureau to "adopt the policy of 'adaptation,' that is to retain either in its present or in a modified form what is of permanent present day value in the indigenous cultures while deliberately introducing important elements (that is, health, sanitation, use of land, cooperative societies) which are working better on western civilizations."[94]

Selective adaptation—a "best of both worlds" scenario—did not represent total cultural preservation. And it raises significant questions for the concept of cultural tolerance—not all aspects of traditional cultures would be tolerated or promoted by the federal government. Loram's proposal, while envisaging a permanent role for *aspects* of Native cultures, rested on non-Native assumptions of what was "working better" in the present day and implicitly devalued Indigenous land use and medical knowledge. These would have important implications for the BIA's education program in the 1930s.

New Deal Education Policy

The Indian New Deal promised major changes for the on- and off-reservation BIA schools. The IRA, however, made only one brief reference to education: the annual congressional allocation of $250,000 for loans to individual Native Americans "for the payment of tuition and other expenses in recognized vocational and trade schools," of which a maximum $50,000 was available for high school and college loans.[95] The emphasis on vocational rather than academic education differed little from earlier policy, although the 1930s witnessed increased promotion of rural job training, reflecting the New Deal's reservation-centric approach.[96] Yet in a 1933 *Indians at Work* editorial, Collier indicated a major curricular and pedagogical overhaul was imminent.[97] The new policy included the prioritization of day schools for the younger grades; an emphasis on vocational education that was to be locally relevant to a child's employment prospects; and the phasing out of military-style marches and harsh punishments.[98] In part this resembled the Meriam Report's recommendations—hardly surprising given that Carson Ryan served as director of Indian Education from 1930 to 1935. Both Ryan and his successor, Willard Beatty (1936–52), were prominent PEA members, and their rejection of the Uniform Curriculum marked a key change from previous practice.

Circular 2970 also had an impact on the education program, as demonstrated in the draft proposal of the Wheeler-Howard Bill presented in February 1934. Under Title II, labelled "Special Education for Indians," Collier laid out his apparent rejection of monocultural education:

> It is hereby declared to be the purpose and policy of Congress to promote the study of Indian civilization and preserve and develop the special cultural contributions and achievements of such civilization, including Indian arts, crafts, skills and traditions. The Commissioner is directed to prepare curricula for Indian schools adapted to the needs and capacities

of Indian students, including courses in Indian history, Indian arts and crafts, the social and economic problems of the Indians, and the history and problems of the Indian Administration. The Commissioner is authorized to employ individuals familiar with Indian culture and with the contemporary social and economic problems of the Indians to instruct in schools maintained for Indians. The Commissioner is further directed to make available the facilities of the Indian schools to competent individuals appointed or employed by an Indian community to instruct the elementary and secondary grades in the Indian arts, crafts, skills and traditions.[99]

While the final text of the IRA only referred to vocational education and funding, the draft proposal (coupled with Circular 2970's concern that schools continued to eschew Native cultures and arts) revealed an intent to broaden the curriculum to include "Indian culture." True, this appeared restricted to history, arts and crafts, and unspecified "traditions," with no mention of religion or cultural perceptions. Yet the draft did envisage the continuation of Native cultures, presented this survival as a positive step, and seemed to promote community control (in other words, employment) of cultural instructors. While the draft does not indicate that these steps were implemented, it does suggest an intentional disconnect from the monocultural curriculum of previous administrations.

The New Deal witnessed significant practical changes to the Indian Service school system, notably day school construction and, to a more limited extent, boarding school closure. Day school education was particularly promoted for the Diné, Pueblo, and Lakota nations. In the period 1933–43, seven off-reservation and nine on-reservation Indian boarding schools were closed across the United States, while eighty-four new day schools opened, reaching a total of 216 day schools by 1943. Day school enrollment rose from 6,836 students in 1933 to 21,559 a decade later—though daily attendance figures were often considerably lower.[100] Reflecting the closures, enrollment at off-reservation boarding schools fell from roughly 12,000 in 1933 to 5,500 in 1943; however, at the close of 1941 a total of forty-nine Indian Service boarding schools were still operational, revealing their continued importance.[101] As stipulated in the IRA, the civil service examinations were altered in a bid to recruit more Native American teachers and school personnel. But in practice, few Native teachers were hired at the bureau schools—Native staff tended to be housekeepers, matrons, and bus drivers, although each school on the Navajo Reservation was meant to employ at least one "Indian Assistant" to aid classroom management and to advise on cultural issues. Despite the increase in day schools, education provision remained inadequate. Native parents and state education boards expressed concern at failing academic standards at some schools; the prioritization of vocational education and experimental progressive education techniques came at the expense of the academic curriculum, seriously curtailing Native students' chances of college and university places.[102] The arrival of World War II then stripped schools of personnel and funding, leading to the closure of nineteen day schools and six boarding schools on the Navajo Reservation alone. Indeed, by 1945 an estimated fifteen thousand school-age Diné children had no access to school facilities.[103] Furthermore, by the late 1940s federal policy reverted to an ethnocentric, nationalist stance. Congressional opposition to reservation-based programs and to any vestige of cultural tolerance crystallized by 1945, culminating in reduced appropriations and Collier's resignation. Tribal sovereignty itself was threatened in the 1950s and 1960s by "termination" policy which sought to dissolve the federally recognized status of some nations in a bid to hasten the assimilation of Native Americans into the US cultural and political mainstream. The apparent cultural tolerance of the Indian New Deal was thus short-lived, and formal government-sponsored schooling for Native American children reverted to monoculturalism until the advent of tribally run schools in the late 1960s.

The changing attitudes of policymakers towards Native American cultures clearly had an impact on government policy. Education policy is a key area in which policymaker attitudes can be tested, as it targets the younger generation and intentionally plays a strong role in shaping pupils' worldviews. Education policy therefore reveals much about policymakers' aspirations for pupils' futures: economic, social, and cultural. All three of the approaches outlined above (assimilation; Meriam Report; New Deal) contained elements of assimilation and cultural tolerance—albeit the tolerance permitted in schooling before 1930 was sporadic and limited to the point of invisibility. The key differentiator was the attitude taken under each approach to the *future* of Native American cultures. Leupp and Estelle Reel may have permitted lullabies and marketable crafts, yet "lullabies," as they understood them, aren't expected to outlive childhood, and the crafts were divorced from their cultural context and intended for consumption *outside* Native communities. Indigenous ceremonies, dances, languages, and cultural values were not included in the assimilationists' vision for Native futures. The Meriam Report accepted Native Americans' right to choose their cultural identity, and its authors emphasized cultural sensitivity over coercive assimilation. However, it relegated Native cultures largely to the past and to the realm of superstition, destined to fade away naturally once communities had been shown the wonders of modern technology and healthcare. The New Deal presented a more complex stance, blending Meriam's promotion of scientific and technological adjustment (and perceived superiority) with a new promotion of religious freedom and a professed acceptance of the value of Indigenous cultures—an acknowledgment that they would, and should, continue. On paper, the New Deal education program promised to include Native "traditions," as well as histories and arts, on the government school curriculum—a considerably closer step to pluralism than either Meriam or Leupp had envisaged. In theory, the New Deal seemed to offer a different approach to what had gone before. In practice, the reality proved far more complicated, limited, and confusing.

PRESENTING NATIVE "PASTS" IN THE CLASSROOM

2

In 1934 Director of Indian Education Carson Ryan informed Diné of his intentions concerning BIA schools: "You should have Navajo literature and history. Your children should know your history and the relation of that history to the rest of the world. They should help you in the preservation of your arts and crafts. The schools should be real Navajo schools."[1] This statement raises several issues—not least the glaringly paternalist suggestion that Diné parents needed bureau assistance to transmit their histories and art to their children. However, Ryan's choice of language is also significant: he repeatedly used the word "history" to describe the Diné past, rather than the characteristically fantastical terms ("myth," "legend," and "folklore") favored by earlier policymakers such as Francis Leupp.[2] And Ryan's statement, despite its pronounced condescending overtones, does suggest that with the New Deal, the BIA intended to include Native histories and cultural heritage on the government school curriculum—the emphasis on "your history" distinguishes the new program from the exclusively Euro-American history taught previously.

Yet despite Ryan's enthusiastic directive, some of the courses taught in the 1930s bore little resemblance to Native histories or to balanced explorations of a community's past. K. Tsianina Lomawaima and Teresa McCarty argue that the "Indian lore" courses introduced at Haskell and Chilocco boarding schools were merely extensions of the BIA's "safety-zone," by which the federal government "veered and tacked between shifting notions of safe and dangerous cultural difference." To this end, the Haskell course emphasized Native societies' distant past, focusing on "origins" and "early locales" rather than specific events or more recent history, while topics such as "stories" and "games" suggest educators reduced Indigenous histories and religio-cultural beliefs to fantastical or recreational pursuits. In addition, Lomawaima and McCarty argue that the history and lore courses had scant extension beyond Haskell and Chilocco and were considered too radical for the day schools.[3]

This chapter explores this interpretation by examining how Indigenous histories, pasts, and cultural heritage were treated at the New Deal government boarding and day schools. By analyzing student compositions, history lessons, history textbooks, arts and crafts instruction, and a government-sponsored history pageant, it assesses the extent to which Indigenous histories were included on the New Deal curriculum and shows the tensions between Euro-American and Indigenous conceptualizations of history and the past.

Heritage, Storytelling, and Tales of "Long Ago"

Lomawaima and McCarty have rightly noted the flimsiness of the Haskell history and lore class.[4] However, some Native teachers who had been secretly incorporating Indigenous cultures into the school curricula for years did notice greater cultural freedom in the classroom from the mid-1930s onward. Esther Horne, a Shoshone teacher at Eufala Indian Boarding School, Oklahoma, and Wahpeton Indian Boarding School, North Dakota, described the 1930s as "a time when the policy of the government was to affirm rather than destroy Indian values and culture." Despite the aggressive monoculturalism of the Assimilation Era curriculum, Horne had skillfully included Native histories and cultures in her lessons, such as focusing on the Trail of Tears in discussions of Andrew Jackson's presidency and the pivotal role played by Sacajawea in the Lewis and Clark expedition. She recalled the New Deal as a time of curricular change: "We were now encouraged to include American Indian materials in the curriculum, and so we began to combat the negative stereotypes of Indian people so pervasive in school textbooks." Horne consequently established an Indian Club at Wahpeton and actively promoted Native dances to her pupils: "We discussed the fact that Indian dancing is the true folk dancing of the

Americas and that it is a part of our unique heritage." Students made traditional costumes, practiced and held tribal dances at Wahpeton, and gave public dance and drum performances at local schools and churches. Horne recalled the 1930s with enthusiasm: "Those days were so exciting! Finally, we no longer had to hide the fact that we were incorporating our cultural values into the curriculum and student life." In other words, the New Deal gave breathing space to Horne's *existing* commitment to teaching Indigenous cultural heritage and histories.[5]

The curricular changes wrought by Ryan and his successor Willard Beatty were also noted by non-Native teachers. Marguerite Bigler Stoltz worked as an English teacher in five government-run Indian boarding schools between 1928–37. Accustomed to the Uniform Curriculum of the coercive Assimilation Era, in 1933 she abruptly found herself charged with delivering "Indian" topics in class. Her pupils at Carson Indian School, Nevada, and the Seneca Indian School, Oklahoma, initially demonstrated scant interest in what she tellingly described as "their folklore." Indeed, Stoltz felt her Oklahoma students "did not seem much like Indians. . . . They felt they should do the same things that were done in public schools. Being Indians should make no difference. This was a modern world and they were a part of it. The past was not too important. . . . Only when I made assignments of stories told them by older people would they mention anything Indian."[6]

This observation reveals more about Stoltz's own preconceptions of what constituted "Indianness" than anything else, yet it also indicates that the new lessons were devised with scant input from pupils or communities—the very people the school was supposed to serve. The new program was undeniably ambitious in scope. According to Stoltz, the Carson School was to have traditional arts and crafts instruction, a pageant and Indian dance program, and a wildflower show featuring traditional medicinal plants—activities she described as "worthwhile projects" which "bolstered our jaded spirits."[7] Teachers "were to encourage the children to write Indian stories," reflecting Ryan's bid to make education relevant, or at least familiar, to a child's background and home environment. Indeed, the 1931 Annual Report of the Commissioner of Indian Affairs (ARCIA) had recommended that day-school teachers "urge them to write about their own Indian life, and to depict their own customs, their own legends, their own economic and social activities."[8]

Stoltz initially found her boarding school charges less interested in

"Indian stories" than she was, perhaps reflecting that, by the 7th, 8th, and 9th grades, many of the pupils had experienced several years of assimilationist residential schooling and may have regarded the "Indian" themes as alien to the classroom environment. They may also have been unwilling to disclose culturally sensitive or private material to an outsider. However, Stoltz found greater enthusiasm for a weekly written assignment, "a story of long ago, one that perhaps their grandmother had told them." The historicized stories therefore differed from the descriptions of contemporary home life advocated in the 1931 ARCIA. While some pupils were initially unenthusiastic, Stoltz claimed that "after a while they seemed to enjoy the weekly assignment of 'A Story of Long Ago,' and took pride in the collection we made."[9]

The stories produced by the Seneca and Carson School pupils are poignant, emotive, and sometimes humorous.[10] They are characterized, above all, by variety. Some are Coyote stories, featuring heroic, unlucky, or mischievous Coyote protagonists. Others could be described as Creation narratives, while some are personal, family accounts and others more general tribal histories. Some stories combine multiple categories. Stoltz did not detail the pupils' research methods: some compositions may have been exercises in creative writing, while others appear to reflect conversations with grandparents, parents, and "old folk." The majority of the Carson writings from 1935 included in Stoltz's memoir are Coyote stories, cautionary tales, and origin/explanation stories (for example, "Why the Rabbit has a Short Tail"), whereas the majority of the Seneca School assignments (1933) feature family or tribal histories. Although the exercise in written storytelling was an imposed one—set by the teacher and using her conceptual framework of "A Story of Long Ago"—the compositions represent the pupils' own words and choice of plot, offering insights into how some Native students in the 1930s negotiated the demands of school and identity. Stoltz offers no information concerning the name, tribal identity, religious affiliation, gender, age, or family background of the storytellers, which prevents meaningful contextualization—however, the content of the stories reveals important themes and student perceptions. As Farina King reminds us, student compositions "offer glimpses into the classroom."[11] They represent fleeting instances of Native voices often missing from school records.

One of the most striking features of the Seneca and Carson compositions is the pupils' respect (implicit and explicit) for older generations, notably grandparents and parents. True, one author describes their grandmother as "kind of superstitious, as most old people are," and another, after recounting the bringing of pine nuts to Nevada by a brave ancient mouse, confesses, "I don't know if it is true or not. It is the old folk's story and I've heard it many times."[12] Yet most of the Seneca School stories are attributed to grandparents, and some praise their particular skills or achievements—for example, catching a fifteen pound catfish with a pole; establishing a lucrative gold mine; and bravely facing down Confederate soldiers during the Civil War.[13] Genuine affection for deceased grandparents and elders is a recurrent theme: as one pupil poignantly notes of her grandmother, "Since she is gone, things aren't the same. Life is duller. She took care of me for about eight years while Mother was working away from home."[14] Some of the Coyote and cautionary tales present grandparent characters in a worthy light: in one Carson tale a headstrong young Coyote disobeys his grandmother's warning to avoid a hill and ends up fatally smothered by bears. His conscientious grandmother looks everywhere for him and then mourns for years.[15] In a tale which explains why young deer have white spots, kindly Grandfather Crane ingeniously saves orphaned deer from a murderous bear.[16] And a student recounting the death of their grandfather's childhood friend who had recklessly killed an owl concludes, "That is why I don't kill owls," demonstrating respect for grandfather's advice.[17]

Some of the compositions describe traditional cultural practices. Some place the practices firmly in the past: a Carson student described how parents prayed to the "Yellow Old Lady in heaven who made good teeth" to provide strong teeth for their children and concludes, "But now Indians think it is just foolishness to do that."[18] A Seneca School student outlined how their grandfather performed snake dances to bring rain for the corn: the author employs the past tense to detail "how they used to make rain when they needed it" yet suggests the dances were effective, bringing rain within a day.[19] The composition "How the Indians Get Power" describes in the present tense the transmission of vital information from elderly medicine men and women to their grandchildren, noting that the young must "listen to whatever is told them by the old folks. If they don't listen to what is told them, they sometimes get sick." The author then switches abruptly to the past tense when describing medicine training—ending on the sentence, "Lots of Indians *used* to go to the cave on the other side of Dayton."[20]

Some compositions, however, appear to describe practices which students had directly experienced. A Seneca School student began a composition on "Indian War Dancers" with the statement, "Indian dance is the way we worship God, just like white people go to churches." The author employs the present tense to describe war dances, stamp dances, Quawpaw, and Cherokee dances, and they detail their grandmother's popular "cook shack." The reader is left in no doubt as to the author's pride in the dances.[21] A similar sense of pride is evident in a Carson essay, "The Making of Baskets." The author praised basket makers' skills, pointedly noting, "Although many of them did not even go to school they can still make better things than some of the well-educated Indians." Basketry is presented as an authentic "Indian" skill, and the student notes the significance of the designs as "stories which are shown in a kind of Indian sign language."[22] It is possible that this student, recognizing the recent addition of arts and craft instruction and an Indian pageant to the Carson curriculum, offered a positive portrayal of traditional basketry in order to please Stoltz—yet this doesn't explain the jibe against "well-educated" Indians who had forsaken the crafts.

The stories written by the Seneca and Carson students in 1933 and 1935 were not part of a formal history curriculum, as Stoltz's retrospective use of the term "folklore" implies.[23] The lesson's main aim was to hone pupils' prowess in written English, not to provide an analysis of historical experiences. Yet the stories demonstrate pupils' attitudes to their family's or community's past and to aspects of both historic and contemporary cultures such as the figures of Coyote and Wolf. The respect accorded to grandparents' achievements and advice reveals a connection to family and the past which the schools' recent assimilationist ethos had singularly failed to extinguish. The pupils also knew of Indigenous experiences of the American Civil War, the Trail of Tears, and the execution of the outlaw Cherokee Bill, despite having not had the opportunity to cover their own history in school—clearly many grandparents, parents, and elders had taken it upon themselves to instruct children in their past.[24] And even accepting that Stoltz pushed the students into writing about "long ago," the tone of many of the stories is neither disinterested nor scornful. Indeed, the students expressed pride in the exploits and "brave" demeanor of Cherokee Bill; in the courage of the grandmother facing down Confederate soldiers; and clear sympathy for those who endured the Trail of Tears.[25]

That Stoltz's students preferred to write about events of "long ago" rather than present-day activities could suggest a disconnect from traditional community identity, yet the absence of information on the pupils' background and personal beliefs prevents any accurate conclusions. The pupils' preference for "stories of long ago" may have had a strong cultural basis: the link to didactic practices of storytelling, a feature of many Indigenous cultures. Some Native teachers in the Assimilation Era had already adapted the storytelling tradition for the classroom. Susie Reyos Marmon, who graduated from Carlisle Boarding School and taught at Laguna, devised her own bilingual curriculum including written English-language translations of Laguna stories.[26] Indeed, the incorporation of storytelling into the curriculum was more recently advocated by Vine Deloria Jr., who advised that "storytelling with the further requirement of being able to recite the story accurately after hearing it several times would make the accumulation of knowledge fun again" and could also reduce the culture clash experienced by many Native pupils at government and public schools.[27]

Preservation, "Origins," and History Books

It wasn't just pupils who were tasked with presenting "the past" in the New Deal schools. Preservation of heritage, ranging from arts and crafts to music and performative expression, received official government support. From 1940 to 1952, ethnomusicologist Willard Rhodes was sponsored by the BIA to record the music and songs of fifty Native American nations, and copies were supplied to government school libraries. Esther Horne utilized the recordings in her classes, describing them as "invaluable." In her assessment, "The traditions and memories that those records captured were so important to the students and to those of us who were teaching these kids the importance of remembering their past."[28] Horne's active usage of the recordings countered the fears expressed in the Meriam Report that preservation of traditional heritage would only benefit academics and tourists. The recordings were used both as teaching aids for historical tradition and as a soundtrack for dance and music lessons: they became a living experience for the school children. A similar fusion of preservation and active learning was experienced by Stoltz at the Carson School. Pupils and teachers were instructed "to collect seeds and Indian medicinal plants, and information as to how they were used" and to exhibit the findings in a wildflower show. Stoltz indicates it was the pupils who possessed the knowledge for this exercise, suggesting that the rubric's use of the past tense ("how they *were* used") was misleading. Stoltz would drive her class into the desert and let the children "disappear in the sage. After a while ... they would emerge from the brush with flowers."[29] Just as Rhodes learned that Indigenous music was "not a relic of the dead past but a vital, dynamic force functioning in contemporary Indian life," so Stoltz realized that her students knew the plants and their medicinal heritage.[30]

Preservation of songs and botanical awareness, however, did not mean that Indigenous *knowledge* and historical *understanding* formed the basis for school lessons during the New Deal. Reports received by Director of Navajo Education George Boyce in June 1941 suggest the ethnocentric nature of the new historically inclusive curriculum. Teacher Fred Richards detailed at some length the "Navajo history" unit he had devised for his 8th grade pupils at Fort Defiance. The module commenced with Columbus and the Pilgrim Fathers—Richards defended this flagrant anachronism by claiming that "identical elements in the history of the Pilgrims and the early settlers helped us to piece together the fragmentary information we found in legends, clan names, archaeological discoveries." His next statement is particularly telling: "Largely because there is no recorded history of the Navajos until recent years, our prehistorical discussion on Hosteen had to be based on our imagination."[31] The notion of inviting Diné historians to discuss Diné history was clearly not contemplated. Richards taught his pupils the Bering Strait theory concerning Native American origins, rather than Diné Origin narratives, which are valued as historical sources as well as moral guides by many Diné.[32] As historian Jennifer Nez Denetdale explains: "Traditional Navajo perspectives on the past are grounded in the creation narratives that contain within them Diné beliefs and values. The creation narratives are a vital part of our oral tradition and are the foundation in which Navajo historical perspectives are embedded. For many Diné, they remain the authoritative explanations for the cultural and social transformations in our communities."[33] "Origins" may have been included on the Fort Defiance curriculum, but Diné Origin narratives sadly were not.

What also emerges from Richards's report is a dual interpretation of the Navajo history unit's didactic purpose. According to Richards, the unit's central aim was "to help my pupils in the eighth grade develop the power of correctly expressing their thoughts and to help the students organize informative data in preparation for oral report to the class," yet he admitted that "the immediate aim of the students was to learn about Navajo history." Clearly the Diné students were interested in their community's past and wanted to explore it in class. Richards's didactic approach did not, however, permit community involvement: he prioritized the printed academic word, referencing archaeologist Richard Van Valkenburgh's *A Short History of the Navajos* as the key source for post-1846 Navajo history.[34] The recourse to "imagination" in the case of "prehistorical" (pre-European colonization?) Diné history suggests that, for Richards, the authentic and retrievable past existed solely in manuscript form, not in the knowledge of living custodians or in the Diné Origin narratives.[35] This New Deal–era approach sits oddly with Collier's later characterization of history as "continuing, cumulative biological and social history, which reaches into the present."[36]

The Fort Defiance School history unit reflects a further characteristic of New Deal Indian Service attitudes towards Indigenous histories. As Richards acknowledged, he devised the history unit as a means of facilitating spoken English and teaching oral presentation and research skills, rather than as a bona fide history class. The education chapter of the Meriam Report, coauthored by future director of Indian Education Carson Ryan, also advocated the use of Indigenous histories as a medium through which to convey other skills and lessons. According to the report, schools should include "Indian history as a means of understanding other history and for its own importance in helping Indians understand the past and future of their own people." Tribal history, according to Ryan, was needed to give the Native American "an understanding of his place in modern society," rather than a detailed appreciation of a community's *own* conception of its past achievements, struggles, and identity.[37]

History did, however, appear on the curriculum as a subject in its own right during the later stages of the New Deal. In 1937, Director of Navajo Schools Lucy Adams outlined her plans for the Navajo junior vocational schools, which, in addition to the vocational and health programs and "tool subjects" such as English and math, were to offer "a program of civic education which would provide knowledge of Navajo history, geography and resources."[38] A year later she admitted that history and geography classes had been hampered by "an unfortunate lack of reading and reference materials for teachers and students."[39] To mitigate the problem, Willard Beatty commissioned a series of texts entitled "Indian Life and Customs," which originated from anthropologist Ruth Underhill's 1935 summer training program for Indian Service teachers.⁴⁰ In Beatty's words, the series aimed "to furnish an understanding of Indian life and customs before the coming of the White man" and was "written primarily to satisfy the questioning of Indian children who desire to know about their tribal history."⁴¹ More specifically, Underhill was tasked with "telling the whats and whys about a number of Indian tribes: who they were, where they lived, how they lived, what they lived in, what they wore, what they ate, how they fought, what they made, what their family life was like, and what their religious beliefs were, so far as anthropologists have been able to reconstruct the story."⁴²

The texts marked a departure from earlier policy in that they focused on the history and the historic living practices of Native American communities—albeit from a resolutely non-Native and academic standpoint. Underhill's acknowledged sources for one of the earlier books in the series, *The Papago Indians of Arizona and Their Relatives, the Pima* (1941), reflect the New Dealer zeal for established academic expertise: the Bureau of American Ethnology, the Southwest Museum (Los Angeles), and the Laboratory of Anthropology (Santa Fe) appear to have supplied most of the material, although the Zia artist Velino Herrera created the illustrations.⁴³ At several points in the text Underhill asserts that no knowledge now exists of particular customs and practices—thereby implying that contemporary Tohono O'odham communities retained no memory of key aspects of their past.⁴⁴ However, she does make one reference to community knowledge, noting with regard to tribal government, "This was the way it was in very ancient times, according to the old men"—which suggests that living memory did play some role in her research.⁴⁵ It is possible that Tohono O'odham elders did not wish to share details of their ceremonies and knowledge with Underhill, especially in light of Assimilation Era government attempts to ban summer rain ceremonies. What Underhill didn't mention is the lengths Tohono O'odham communities went to defend their ceremonies, which hardly indicates forgotten or extinct practices.⁴⁶

The content of the *Papago* textbook is varied. Underhill devotes considerable space to meticulous descriptions of historic Tohono O'odham and Akimel O'odham practical skills, notably related to arts and crafts, weaponry, and agriculture successfully tailored to a desert environment. Unlike the Meriam Report, Underhill found something positive in nomadism, noting that "in the centuries of wandering over hills and valleys, the Indians had found that every cactus has some sort of fruit."⁴⁷ The reader learns that the historic Tohono O'odham possessed awareness of astronomical phenomena such as constellations and used them to calculate the time for planting, harvesting, and feasts; that they knew how to treat colds, indigestion, and rheumatism using medicinal herbs; that they were good parents; and that they "did well" at fighting and made "fairly good" weapons.[48] In other words, readers found that they were skilled, capable people, well adapted to life in a difficult natural environment. And Underhill also assures her 1940s audience that the Tohono O'odham were not aggressively bellicose but were pushed into retaliatory conflict by sporadic Apache raids: "The People did not really like to go to war. They were too busy cultivating their fields and hunting for food to care to go out fighting."[49] This appears calculated to satisfy contemporary Euro-American perceptions of good citizenship, industriousness, and righteous self-defense.

Underhill also details traditional Tohono O'odham and Akimel O'odham methods of recording historic events. She outlines how, from "the year the stars fell" (1833) until recently, an elderly man in each village would make marks on a long stick "to remind them of the things which had happened every day." In Underhill's view the marks are "not real writing" as they varied according to the person recording them, but the chronicler "could lay his thumb on mark after mark and recite the history of his village for eighty years or so." Tellingly, she dismisses this impressive demonstration of knowledge as "a kind of history," suggesting that it did not quite measure up to the efforts of an academic chronicler.[50]

Ceremonies and religious beliefs were similarly subjected to an odd mix of sympathy and condescension. Underhill spent much space describing Tohono O'odham creation beliefs and ceremonies, adopting a neutral tone and offering detailed factual description of proceedings and dances.[51] Most ceremonies are described in the past tense, although Underhill concludes the book by stating, "There are many who still tell the old stories, carry on old ceremonies, and sing the old songs."[52] The epithet "old" jars somewhat with the message of cultural survival—rather than portraying a *living* belief system, Underhill appears to be suggesting the practices are static relics, although she does fleetingly acknowledge that "they even make new songs, as beautiful as the old."[53] A 1940s anthropological study of Tohono O'odham communities reported that while some ceremonies were declining in frequency, overall "the old [traditional] culture is still strong"—indicating this was more than the occasional practice that Underhill's book implies.⁵⁴ Also striking is Underhill's apparent need to present *pragmatic* origins of traditional ceremonies; she argues that most ceremonies were designed to bring rain and food "since there was no running water in the land and lack of rain would mean starvation."⁵⁵ The persistent use of the term "magic" to describe religious beliefs also carries a sense of dismissiveness—war recitations, prayers, and visions are all categorized under what would be, in the author's eyes, a fantasy.⁵⁶

Underhill's textbook on historic Pueblo life, *Workaday Life of the Pueblos*, while published a few years later, contained similar themes to its predecessor. Again, she favored academic sources (the Denver Art Museum, the Laboratory of Anthropology at Santa Fe, and "specialists" at Columbia University) over Pueblo oral histories—though additional "information was given and crafts demonstrated by Pueblo Indians of today."⁵⁷ She does very briefly acknowledge the existence of Pueblo Origin narratives, again using such descriptors as "legend," "mythology" and "poetic," but focuses more on what they do *not* tell us about origins and farming: "We do not know where the pueblo people came from, or when."⁵⁸ The main thrust of the chronological history account until the seventeenth century reflects archaeological research by "trained people": "Little by little they [archaeologists] are working out a history of the Southwest" using pottery fragments and tree ring data. To be fair, Underhill does accept that the archaeological data has limitations: "The earth does not tell us where this [farming] knowledge came from, anymore than the Indian stories do." The text covers an ambitious scope (all Pueblo communities) and a vast time frame, from the Anasazi through Spanish occupation and the Pueblo Revolt ("the first American Revolution") on to the late nineteenth century, where much of the social history (village life, farming, family) is based. Like its *Papago* predecessor, *Workaday Life of the Pueblos* portrayed the historic communities as hardworking, skilled and adaptive farmers, hunters, architects, and craftspersons. The narrative explicitly steers clear of describing present-day religious activities, but Underhill did emphasize the preeminent role of religion in Pueblo life, likening the communities to "religious settlements, like the early colonies of Puritans and Quakers in New England." In similar vein, she likened the ceremonial origins of traditional Pueblo sports games to Heracles's invention of the Olympic Games—a possible bid to reassure non-Pueblo readers by equating Pueblo tradition with familiar old-world heritage.⁵⁹

In contrast, the final text in the Indian Life and Customs series, the 1953 book *Here Come the Navaho!*, begins by telling the origins of the Diné from their creation narratives. Noting that she had used a variety of sources "published, unpublished and oral," including contributions from over thirty Diné "informants," Underhill declares that the Diné "have several origin stories, full of poetry and miracle, which we may call the Navaho Bible."[60] She then outlines the narrative of the arrival of the First People; the story of Changing Woman and her sons, the Twin Heroes, who rid the land of monsters; and ended with the creation of the clans and their journeys. For Underhill, "This tale sounds very much like history. Indeed, if we leave out the miracles, the whole Navaho story presents a clear picture of possible early wanderings." However, she then points out limitations—primarily the lack of dates and written documentation. To Underhill, the metaphysical elements of the narratives were embellishment, not fact: "When they did not understand something or could not remember, they said there must have been a miracle, performed by the spirits." She likens the Origin narratives to old-world mythology, including Arthurian tales, Greek legends, and Viking Sagas, as largely fictional sources with historical value—"Even our oldest stories are memories of things that really happened." Just as the city of Troy had been found through archaeology, so too, Underhill muses, might the locations of the Diné narratives be traced by the "diggers" of the present. *Here Come the Navaho!* therefore marked a break with the earlier texts in the series by not merely mentioning Origin narratives but claiming them as semihistorical sources. However, in the process of affirming the potential *historical* nature of the narratives, Underhill dismissed their *metaphysical* content—an integral aspect of traditional Diné history. And the chapter on the Origin narratives was swiftly followed by one detailing the migration of Diné and Apache ancestors from Canada and beyond, in effect the Bering Strait model taught by Fred Richards in the early 1940s. The reader is left in no doubt as to which explanation of Diné Origins Underhill (and the contemporary academic establishment) accepted as historical truth.[61]

The Indian Life and Customs series was, despite its clear limitations, a breakthrough in the treatment of Indigenous histories and cultural practices in the government school environment. Designed for both pupils and teachers, the texts represent a pioneering BIA attempt to depict tribal histories in a factual and positive manner—a sharp contrast to many

Assimilation Era school superintendents who, according to John Gram, felt that "the past was the last thing they wanted to understand or preserve."[62] In 1936 anthropologist Scudder Mekeel had criticized the government schools for utilizing American history books that, in their brief references to Native Americans, perpetuated negative, "savage" stereotypes. Aside from fleeting (but repeated) references to "wild" and warlike Apaches, the Underhill texts avoided these tropes.[63] The Indian Life and Customs series didn't focus purely on origins and the distant past—the Pueblo and Navajo texts charted chronological history up to the present day. And they all included sections on contemporary community life, which served to situate Native communities and cultures in the present rather than the past. Witness the concluding chapter of *Workaday Life of the Pueblos*:

> Yet the old pueblo life still goes on. The same men who sit, one day in their blue overalls, discussing a cattle program with the government expert, may be dancing the next day in the beautiful handwoven garment worn a hundred years ago. The pueblos long ago decided upon a way of life and developed it to suit their needs. Now they may change the unimportant things, like clothing and crops, but their life as religious settlements goes on.[64]

However, the content of the books overwhelmingly represented Western anthropological interests, with little thought given to Indigenous interpretations of history. With the exception of the later *Navaho* text, Underhill prioritized Western academic knowledge over Indigenous knowledge and perspectives. Even the titles are suggestive: despite Beatty's claim that children of the represented nations were the key intended readership, non-Native names such as "Navaho," "Pima," and "Papago" are applied throughout; indeed, Underhill acknowledged that the "modern" names "Pima" and "Papago" "were given in fun" by the Spanish.[65] That a Spanish joke could supersede a nation's right to be referred to by their own name in a BIA-produced text suggests the bureau's inability to move beyond established academic terms and subject-specific boundaries.

Arts and Crafts Education: Primacy of the "Past"

A second range of school texts commissioned by the Indian Service under Beatty's direction—the Indian Handcrafts series—also focused on

Indigenous pasts and cultural heritage. While not history books per se, they focused on the artistic traditions of certain nations, with an emphasis on *historic* designs, materials, and production techniques. Like the Life and Customs series, the Handcrafts authors primarily based their research upon American academic sources, including the Smithsonian Institute, Denver Art Museum, and the American Museum of Natural History, rather than on consultation with contemporary Native artists and artisans, although one author did spend "much time ... in the homes of the Ojibwa Indians" while preparing her text.[66] Strikingly, no named Native persons appear in the lists of acknowledgements. While many New Deal crafts initiatives were aimed at adults and were overseen by the Indian Arts and Crafts Board (IACB), the Handcrafts series was designed for use in the government schools. As Beatty noted, the texts sought to "enable teachers and pupils to visualize clearly the various steps and the practical carrying out of these ancient crafts" and thus "where practicable to stimulate a revival of them among the people to whom they historically belong."[67]

Despite this present-day aim, the Handcrafts texts tended to promote historic designs and techniques based upon museum collections as opposed to encouraging artistic innovation amongst teachers and pupils. A key theme is the repeated contrast drawn between contemporary tourist tat and the superior craftwork of historic, noncommercial artists: as associate supervisor of home economics for the Indian Service, Carrie Lyford noted in 1943, "The early Ojibwa kept their handicrafts at a high level of excellence and honored good workmanship." In contrast, she denounced the work offered to tourists as "hastily and poorly made in the eagerness of the craft worker to secure profit from the contemporary market."[68] Tourist curios aside, Lyford suggests many craft techniques had been largely forgotten and so should be retaught to youth and adults alike through the government schools using historic designs and methods to ensure quality. Interestingly, she did acknowledge the reality of artistic evolution: "At no time within the historic period has the practice of the crafts been static, always it has been subject to change as new conditions have influenced the lives of the craft workers."[69] This tepid acceptance of organic artistic change contrasts with a more enthusiastic appraisal of some developments in "Sioux" beadwork. Lyford may have claimed that "by 1900 the great period of beadwork was over," yet she acknowledged "workers who realize the variety of shapes and colors now at their disposal have an interesting opportunity to develop the traditional style in new directions and for new purposes."[70] However, the author's tolerance of artistic innovation only went so far: "The present day handicraft worker can develop attractive patterns, *confining herself to the accepted geometric forms*."[71] In other words, design evolution was permitted but only if it subscribed to historic design models.

Lyford's texts contain numerous photographs of craft items and of contemporary craftspersons, and each book offers detailed pattern diagrams for students to follow. An unwavering theme of her writing was high praise for the skill of "ingenious" historic Native artists and artisans. When describing "early Ojibwa" crafts, she notes, "The ancient curvilinear designs and the simple geometric quilled patterns done in soft colors carefully combined, show a love of beauty and an artistic restraint that make their old handicraft articles worthy of study."[72] For Lyford this detail invariably (though not always) contrasted with present-day deterioration—for example, "The quills used in much of the birch bark work are coarse, and the work is not so fine as that done in the early days."[73] Likewise, she decries the "increasing elaboration" in "Sioux" beadwork since 1875, lamenting that the "strong, simple quality of the early work in small beads has given way to overcrowded patterns."[74] A further theme of the Handcrafts series was the risk of craft extinction; Lyford acknowledged that many traditional crafts were still in production in the 1930s, yet she often ascribed this survival to a few elderly artists, hence the need for schools to stimulate a craft revival.[75] Notably, she did admit the role played by government education policy in craft decline, recognizing that boarding schools disrupted—and often prevented—the transmission of craft skills from parent to child.[76] This was also touched on by Ruth Underhill in her contribution to the series, *Pueblo Crafts*. The boarding schools are described as places "where some young people spend their time when they might be learning crafts at home," requiring school crafts programs taught by Native teachers.[77]

Pueblo Crafts differed slightly from Lyford's texts, largely in its emphasis on the crafts as "living arts, developed to fill practical needs." Underhill stresses that Pueblo crafts *continue* to play vital roles in modern Pueblo life—notably for ceremonial purposes and for revenue through sale—and that craft "revivals," especially in pottery, have been ongoing since the early 1900s. The theme in *Pueblo Crafts* is change. The crafts "are in all stages of change," reflecting their practical uses—for example, weaving for ceremonial purposes; plain cooking pottery ware for home consumption; and decorated pottery for sale outside the community. Indeed, Underhill refers to forty existing pottery styles developed by twelve Pueblo communities, noting, "New ones are constantly appearing or old ones are being revived." And the evolution in styles is no recent occurrence: "Indian art is moving and the pottery scraps show that, although the change is slow, there has always been change."[78]

Underhill was clearly at pains to present artistic innovation as a natural and positive phenomenon, with a long pedigree confirmed by archaeological evidence. After detailing traditional production methods and some historic designs, she included a brief section on modern variegated pottery styles. The differences in her appraisal of the innovations are suggestive. Tesuque potters' use of "commercial poster colors" draws Underhill's unmitigated scorn: "In contrast to the [traditional] earth colors, these are of violent bright shades and, since they are applied after the pot is fired, they soon wear off. This venture has no historic derivation and it is unfortunate that it is encouraged by the tourist trade."[79] Contrast this negative review with her appraisal of San Juan potters' addition of a band of slanting marks around the shoulder of buff-colored clay pots: "This style is said to come from ancient pottery found in neighboring ruins. Women have added variations of their own to this ancient style."[80] Clearly the San Juan innovations, rooted in discontinued ancient designs, appealed more to Underhill than the wholly modern Tesuque designs that pleased the tourists. She didn't, however, include the potters' *own* appraisal of their wares. Underhill's dismissal of tourist wares ignored the opinions of Pueblo artisans, and with Lyford, she missed their ability to adapt and to negotiate market demands. As Jennifer McLerran reminds us, "In denying the value of tourist arts, we deny the value of the native artists' ability to perform complex acts of cultural translation."[81]

Like Lyford, Underhill believed that museums and art collections had an important role to play in *guiding* Native artisans in their choice of styles. Despite her emphasis on Pueblo pottery as a "Living Art," she feared some designs had been forgotten, leaving aspirational craftspersons without any guidance. According to Underhill:

> It is not so simple as might be thought for an Indian craft worker to know about the art of her own people. Suppose she is a potter. There

may have been no potters in her family or, perhaps, in her whole village for a generation. Or there may have been a period of poor design after the new, cheap goods came in. She might have a hard time finding out about the beautiful things in her own native tradition were it not for the museums. For White collectors have been buying up the pots since 1879 and now there are more good ones in a museum than in almost any village.

The Indians go to see them and they ask questions. They get explanations of the sketches and notes which the Whites have had time and money to make while the Indians have not.[82]

This passage, while undeniably paternalistic, does reflect Underhill's recognition that non-Native collectors, acting from a position of wealth privilege, had effectively bought up and rehomed many physical embodiments of the Pueblos' craft heritage, thus preventing new potters from learning of their art's past. The picture she builds is of Pueblo potters proactively seeking out the museum staff and artifacts to learn from the historic styles. This did not necessarily imply replication of the old designs but suggests the museums were being used by the potters as part of the learning and creating process. However, while Underhill accepted artistic innovations, her comments on the Tesuque pots indicate she favored those developments which constituted additions to, or variations on, a historic design root. The "tradition" was the building of new onto the firm foundations of the old, not the crafting of pots per se.

The concept of craft "revival" played a key role in New Deal policy and was a cornerstone principle of the IACB.[83] In 1936 Beatty stated that "increased emphasis within our Indian schools is being given to instruction in the older Indian crafts and toward a revival of Indian art," echoing Harold Ickes's earlier hope "that revivals of near-lost crafts may be brought about."[84] Lyford's tendency to favor older craft designs was therefore reflective of wider BIA sentiment—many of the craft lessons taught at government schools in the 1930s and early 1940s featured historic methods and patterns. Day-school pupils at the pueblos of Paraje, Santa Ana, San Ildefonso, San Juan, Taos, and Tesuque were encouraged to prepare "ancient earth color" paints for use in art lessons. The production process, described by Supervisor of Elementary Education Rose Brandt as "long and tedious," had been largely forsaken by many contemporary Pueblo artists who preferred commercially prepared pigments. Brandt, however, lauded the beneficial impact of the traditional process upon Pueblo pupils' artistic flair, arguing that

> The arduous and protracted labor involved in the conversion of crude earth materials into pigments did not diminish the children's enthusiasm for their own colors. In fact, they prefer not using the commercial colors formerly provided. This enthusiastic confidence in their own materials doubtless contributes in a measure, at least, to the thoroughly unconscious self-assurance and the freedom and dash of Pueblo children's earth color paintings on simple brown paper.[85]

The children may have enjoyed the paint-making process, but Brandt doesn't seem to consider whether adult artists would welcome the "arduous and protracted labor" she enthusiastically extolled.

Promotion of the past was also evident in Navajo day and boarding school craft classes in the 1930s. By 1936 the Navajo School Service had implemented a program "to induce" a return to traditional patterns in Navajo weaving for commercial purposes. Examples of "traditional" Diné rug designs were provided by the Laboratory of Anthropology (Santa Fe), and the program architects sought to direct a move away from the so-called modern style of weaving, which produced heavier cloth for floor coverings and saddle blankets, encouraging a return to the softer robes of the nineteenth century. Teachers such as Fern Harris of the Charles H. Burke Indian Boarding School in Fort Wingate were, however, forced to admit slow progress, particularly concerning designs. Many Diné weavers rejected the use of set, recyclable patterns, instead adhering to the long-standing concept of visionary design, by which patterns are created through vision and memory.[86] The Indian Service, seeking to replicate historic designs, was contradicting authentic Diné design processes.

The Diné dye project and its associated publication, *Navajo Native Dyes: Their Preparation and Use*, differed slightly from other New Deal craft revival projects. The publication began in solid pro-historic style, lauding "the unique achievements of these ancient art-craftspeople" (the historic Diné weavers of the seventeenth and eighteenth centuries) and "desiring to perpetuate their art" through a project "to revive interest" in traditional plant-based dyes. However, while the foundational dyes were based on traditional recipes, lead investigator Nonabah Bryan—the Diné weaving instructor at Wingate Vocational High School—also created new ones: "Many new shades and tints have been developed through experimentation with different plant combinations." This spirit of experimentation and development contrasts with the deification of historic designs promoted by Lyford. The project clearly envisaged an active usage; a wide variety of plants were used "in the hope that Indians from all parts of the reservation could find satisfactory products close enough to their homes to make this method of dyeing practicable." In a further departure from the Lyford and Underhill crafts books, Bryan was named as project leader in the published text—although the introduction was written by non-Native home economics teacher Stella Young.[87]

Despite the Diné dye project's experimentation, the majority of 1930s government-sponsored craft ventures prioritized historic designs and techniques. Replication of museum specimens was not a purely New Deal initiative, but it reflected a long-standing belief amongst art experts and anthropologists in the superiority of artistic and cultural "purity" over so-called hybrid products. Contact with other communities, notably Euro-American tourists, was deemed by academics to have weakened and bastardized tribal arts, hence their desire to "revive" and "restore" them to their former pristine state. Such thinking informed the Indian Arts Fund in its bid to "revive" San Ildefonso pottery in 1924 and also influenced Seneca anthropologist Arthur C. Parker in his promotion of the WPA-funded Seneca Arts and Crafts Project (1935–41). Through this project, Seneca artists and artisans were hired by the Rochester Municipal Museum of New York to replicate items and patterns from the Lewis Henry Morgan Collection of Iroquois Art.[88] As Parker noted in the BIA's *Indians at Work*, "Instead of cheap and tawdry souvenirs that have nothing of the old art in them our workers will now make objects that have ethnological value. They will be typical of the days when Indian art was original and pristine."[89] Cephas Hill, the Seneca project supervisor at Tonowonda, confirmed the emphasis on replication, stating that Seneca project employees were "duplicating skirts and leggings which are now only in museums. The reproductions are faithful to old models and drawings both in design and workmanship."[90] Significantly, both Collier and Henrietta Burton, Indian Service supervisor of home economics extension, enthusiastically approved of the Seneca and San Ildefonso art restoration projects, and Burton advocated a similar preservationist approach for Washoe basketry.[91]

Replication may have been implemented in the schoolroom and in adult education classes, but it wasn't always popular within Native communities. By the 1930s many Diné silversmiths produced "Baroque" designs, which were deemed "unaesthetic" and inauthentic by IACB art experts. In a bid to encourage a return to older, less ornate styles, the Indian Service only promoted historic designs at the Navajo school silver shops. Diné master craftspersons such as Ambrose Roanhorse were charged to instruct the younger generation of smiths in the simpler styles of previous eras and indeed to revive the earliest silver forms such as filed bracelets. Anthropologist John Adair noted that while the school silver shops produced "in my opinion the best of the silver that is being made today for the white consumer," Diné customers preferred the more ornate products, particularly those with multiple sets of turquoise. Adair recalled that the old-style bracelet and ketoh made at his request by master smith Tom Burnsides did not go down well with Burnsides's relatives and prospective Diné patrons:

> I showed the filed bracelet with no turquoise sets that Tom made to his aunt, Mary Burnsides, and I asked her what she thought of it. She said, "It looks old-fashioned; it ought to have some turquoise in it." The ketoh which Tom made was offered for sale by the trader, Bill Stewart, to Mr Blacksheep, who wanted one. But he didn't like it, and said that he wanted one with more stones in it.

Ironically, what the Indian Service and non-Native art experts considered to be authentic and pristine Diné design was viewed by contemporary Diné as undesirable and unfashionable.[92]

In similar vein, Indian Service teacher and textbook writer Ann Nolan Clark's attempted revival of "oldtime" Tesuque pottery styles proved unpopular with both Tesuque potters and their customers. Clark initiated the reversion to older styles after being "beseeched on every side by interested Santa Fe friends of the Tesuques to see if we could raise the standard of Tesuque pottery which is poor judged from aesthetic values." The old-style wares failed to sell at the Tesuque Fair, a result that was embarrassing for Clark and potentially ruinous for the potters, prompting the teacher to "wonder if it could possibly be true that Indians know best what is best for Indians?"[93] Although Clark's account lacks a date, it seems likely these events preceded Underhill's 1944 criticism of contemporary Tesuque pottery—suggesting that the potters had successfully reverted to the prerevival styles.[94] Yet again, neither account presents the views of the potters as to which style they preferred.

Not all the arts and crafts promoted at the government schools during the New Deal were traditional, however. Spinning and weaving were introduced to the curriculum at Little Wound Day School and Oglala Community High School on the Pine Ridge Reservation, with weaving hailed as a "new craft" for Lakota women and girls, and in 1940 teachers Nellie Star Boy Menard (Sicangu Lakota) and Flora Goforth introduced flatbed loom weaving to the schools on Rosebud Reservation. Pupils, both junior and adult, were encouraged to make blankets with a view to marketing the surplus.[95] In contrast, an attempted revival of traditional belt weaving at Tesuque Pueblo was aborted due largely to a doubtful market, and traditional San Ildefonso basketry received no bureau encouragement following its depiction by Indian Service observers as "a slow and poorly paid occupation."[96] Community wishes do not appear to have held much sway with policymakers in such cases: as Burton commented in 1936, at San Ildefonso "the Indians still speak of the vanished art of basketry with deep regret."[97] Commercial returns therefore played a key role in determining which historic arts would be promoted to the school curricula. As noted in 1946 by former social worker and historical writer Evelyn Crady Adams, "Instruction is intended to improve both quality and quantity in order to swell monetary returns. Native skills and techniques are preserved but the products themselves are frequently modified to meet modern demand and practical usage."[98] This reflected Beatty's view that the arts instruction at the schools "has not only a fundamental cultural value, but it also has a distinct economic value."[99] Historical authenticity was not, therefore, the sole aim of the New Deal crafts program; rather, the program was viewed as key to enhancing product quality, signifying true Indigenous origin, and increasing market value. But if historical "authenticity" was prized as a signifier of potential market quality, cultural significance—despite Beatty's statement—wasn't prioritized by the craft booklets or the IACB more generally. The *continued* cultural value of products was rarely acknowledged in the government publications, and the transfer of craft instruction to the schoolroom environment often ignored the cultural and spiritual aspects of the traditional design and production processes.[100]

The Pageant of Navajo History (1940)

The treatment of Indigenous histories and cultural traditions at the government schools was uneven, veering from formal textbooks on the historic past to selected historic craft patterns and designs and the recording of family histories and traditional songs. One event combined all of these ideas and powerfully illustrated the competing New Deal themes of authenticity, selectivity, and control of the presented past. In 1940 Superintendent E. R. Fryer issued a memorandum to "All Navajo Service Personnel" urging their support for the annual Navajo Tribal Fair which that year would feature "the presentation of a Pageant of Navajo History."[101] Fryer described the 1940 tribal fair as "this unmatched opportunity for mass education of the people for whom we work" and labelled it "a major factor in the Navajo Service program of education"—thereby confirming the BIA-controlled nature of the event at that time.[102] The Navajo Service discussions surrounding the pageant offer an insight into bureau concepts of the role of history and culture in the education program and also the bureau's continued bid to promote Western soil conservation and healthcare ideals. It also reveals interesting comparisons with the tradition of Euro-American historical pageants so popular in towns across the United States in the 1910s and 1920s.

Using the theatrical device of an elderly grandfather describing events of the past to his young grandchildren, the pageant sought to depict the history of the Diné from 1625 to 1940, taking in such events as the 1846 US treaty; the 1863 Long Walk; the 1868 treaty and return to Dinétah; and culminating in 1940 with the Navajo Tribal Council's resolution pledging military allegiance to the United States.[103] It featured an all-Diné cast, largely drawn from the school population but also including "non-pupil" members of each school community in "mass scenes"—indeed, pageant organizer Earl Raines sought a "hearty response on the part of non-pupil Navajos."[104] In essence the pageant was intended to be a community affair and a significant, "ambitious" event.[105]

The official aims for the Navajo Pageant appear to have been twofold. Raines hoped it would boost "moral [sic] and pride"[106] and that the pageant was "something for the welfare of the tribe." He also expected it would "create a favorable interest in contemporary and historic Navajo life that will extend not only to thousands of Navajo people but far beyond the reservation as well."[107] To Raines, therefore, the pageant's key aims were to make Diné proudly aware of their ancestors—a celebration of selected aspects of "Navajo history"—and to stimulate an interest in Diné life amongst the wider public. This didactic function reflected the aim of the early-twentieth-century American Pageantry Association (APA), which claimed that "pageantry is a useful art in the same sense that the schoolhouse is useful, teaching something [community history] that everyone ought to know."[108] Raines's paternalistic, and inaccurate, belief that pride in—and accurate knowledge of—Diné history was in limited supply on the reservation is shown by his continued reminders for staff to consult academic sources rather than present-day Diné concerning authentic nineteenth-century costumes and hair styles. "Authenticity" appears to have been a driving principle for Raines, as his memorandum to the Pageant Committee demonstrates:

> No one needs to be reminded of the ludicrousness of someone's wearing an old-type squaw dress with oxfords and anklets in impersonating Navajo women of the 1800s. Costume is as great a factor as any other in presenting a well-rounded performance. You should not depend too strongly upon the pupils or even an average middle-age Navajo to tell you what were authentic costumes of nearly a century ago. You, yourself, have probably already found much material in studies that have been made.[109]

The prioritization of academic studies over community knowledge is striking. It strongly indicates that the "delegitimization" of Indigenous perspectives by Euro-American academics, identified by Lomayumtewa C. Ishii in his research on early-twentieth-century anthropologists in Hopiland, continued well into the 1940s.[110] Interestingly, by dismissing the Diné community as a source of Diné historical knowledge, Raines distanced himself from the APA's earlier recommendations, which had urged local pageant directors to interview older community members and thus obtain information "not to be found upon the printed page, but genuine, homely, and traditional history."[111] Similarly, the Lakota author and educator Luther Standing Bear had recently urged Native Americans to become their own historians in order to give a more balanced narrative—"fairer and fewer accounts of the wars and more of the state-craft, legends, languages, oratory, and philosophical conceptions."[112] This perhaps did not fit with Raines's rather grandiose pageant narrative: a story of great military and political events with prominent (and exclusively male) leaders.

Raines did seek some Diné input. He requested that council members Howard Gorman and Chic Sandoval read over the script a day after academic Richard Van Valkenburgh had given his assessment. However, whereas the latter would provide "the standpoint of an historian," Gorman and Sandoval's advice was to form "the standpoint of a Navajo"—apparently, Raines didn't recognize the existence of Navajo historians. The presentation of the advisory membership of the Pageant Committee continued the paternalist approach: Gorman and Sandoval, the sole Diné representatives, were listed last, after Adams, Norma Runyan, and teacher Orpha McPherson.[113] As well as translating the script into Navajo, Gorman did propose an amendment—that the elderly grandfather character should not encourage the children to go to bed.[114] In July Raines went even further in his zeal for historical "accuracy" by urging that schools give preference in casting to descendants of the figures portrayed. However, in the same communiqué, he stipulated that all roles—Diné, Euro-American, Zuni, Santa Clara, and Mexican—be played by Diné. It is here that Raines appears to have cast "authenticity" by the wayside: rather than involve Zuni and Santa Clara dancers, he argued that "Navajos can and should learn these dances and songs and present them." No concern for any possible religious or cultural significance of these unnamed dances is evident in his letter.[115] Clearly, for Raines, the principle of mass participation could override the principle of authenticity.

The content of the pageant is also revealing. Episode one describes the origins of the Diné—yet, like Fred Richards's history module, it stages only the Bering Strait theory rather than Diné Origin narratives, which as Lloyd Lee notes, "represent the identity of the people, the land, and the universes."[116] In episode two, which depicts the 1846 treaty and Diné raids on US military supplies, the grandfather asks his grandson the date of the treaty. In an unsubtle promotion of book learning, the boy replies, "Grandfather, the books tell us it was 1846." The US military is portrayed as honorable throughout: when speaking of General Carleton, the narrator notes, "He told the Navajo chiefs he was tired of treaties *they* did not keep." Kit Carson is introduced, without a trace of irony, as "famed Indian fighter and frontiersman." In the aftermath of the Carson campaign, kindly soldiers provide war-weary Diné with food and blankets, while Carson and Chief Barboncito shake hands in the foreground; indeed, Carson commiserates with the Diné leader, saying, "It has been hard on all of us," before urging him to "think of the American soldiers as friends."[117] The horrors of the Long Walk are dealt with but briefly—reflecting Raines's expressed desire to avoid a "sob story all the way."[118] While the grandfather-narrator acknowledges that many Diné died before reaching Bosque Redondo, the US soldiers are once again portrayed as thoughtful and compassionate, "kindly" allowing an elderly woman to ride with them in a wagon. In contrast, Carson's Zuni allies are cast as the villains of the piece, dehumanized as "wolves" wildly reveling in the Navajos' defeat. Moreover, both Barboncito and Carson appear scornful and dismissive of the Ute, Zuni, and Mexican soldiers: the audience is left in no doubt that the US soldiers possessed the moral and military authority.[119]

The remainder of the pageant depicts the return to Fort Defiance, the role of traders on the reservation, and, finally, the Indian New Deal. Unsurprisingly, the federal government is portrayed in a favorable light throughout. The 1868 treaty appears as generous, with leader Ganado Mucho extolling its benefits: "Let us remember that Washington is kind to all of us. Look at that old billy goat.... He butts against something he can never conquer. We must realize that we were doing that—butting against something that we could not break. Let us never do that again." Further, the grandfather-narrator notes of the 1880s, "The government helped us, too," in particular the "good agent" Dennis Riordan, who introduced profitable merino sheep to the reservation. No mention is made of Diné weavers' concern that merino wool produced inferior rugs. Traders are shown giving candy to Diné children, while Manuelito, earlier described as one of the "wild Navajos" who "wanted war," appears sporting a plug hat which he describes as "a Washington hat fit for a chief!"—an image of harmonious reconciliation. His wife Juanita, however, does not appear as a named character in the script.[120] In the epilogue, staged in the present-day, the narrator hails the benefits of irrigation, day-school education, improved roads, and coal mines, declaring that "soil conservation and good land management are fattening our sheep and restoring our land and saving it for our children."[121] Indeed, Lucy Adams stipulated that "the floats should all emphasize what is being done now and the opportunities open for Navajos."[122] The future for the Diné and the reservation, as presented in the pageant, was bright.

Yet not everyone was included in the happy denouement. The "medicine man," a stalwart of the earliest episodes, does not appear in the epilogue as a named character, suggesting his total absence from the scene and perhaps—by implication—from the BIA's vision of the ideal Diné future. This relegation of the "medicine man" to the past resonates with earlier American historical pageants, such as the "Pageant of the Old Northwest" (1911), which used generic "medicine man" characters to lament the "inevitable" passing of Native Americans and the concomitant rise of Euro-American settlement and "modern" technology.[123] However, whereas the earlier depictions were largely passive characters whose brief function was to announce Indigenous peoples' supposedly natural decline, the Navajo History Pageant medicine man functions primarily as an instigator of war. In one scene he prepared Diné warriors for battle with the Americans by painting snakes on their moccasins and asserting that bullets cannot strike them. The next episode begins with their military defeat to Carson, demonstrating to the audience the apparent folly of the medicine man's efforts. Following this, active expressions of traditional Diné cultural practice in the pageant are relegated to a three-minute dance sequence and two instances of Diné music played in the background.[124] The message seems to have been that while traditional music, clothing, and dances have a future, Diné medicine and some aspects of ceremonial belief belong to the unhappy past, as obsolete and as ultimately damaging as raiding and warfare.

The Navajo Pageant was hailed a success by its organizers, attracting large crowds to the 1940 Navajo Tribal Fair; it featured in the promotional material advertising the 1941 Flagstaff All-Indian Powwow, which claimed one thousand Diné had participated in the pageant.[125] Tribal chairman Jacob Morgan requested that a segment be performed for the council members—unfortunately, his reaction has not been recorded in the BIA records.[126] The pageant was supported by many Diné, including the school children and their communities and members of the tribal council. Howard Gorman not only translated the script into Diné bizaad but also took the role of the grandfather-narrator. Children brought clothing and jewelry from home to use as costumes, despite Raines's misgivings. Clearly people at the time felt that there was something in the pageant which they could call their own or which they could refashion to their own interpretation.

And the pageant did represent a bureau attempt to depict actual events in Diné history, albeit largely restricted to Diné-US relations. In this way it differed from earlier BIA-sponsored historical enactments at Indian schools, which tended to celebrate generic colonial-era events, such as the arrival of Columbus and the first Thanksgiving, or romantic fictional tales—notably Longfellow's *Hiawatha*—which bore scant relevance to the pupils and communities who performed and watched them.[127] Indeed, just four years prior to the pageant, Diné pupils at Crownpoint Boarding School had to participate in a highly insensitive Thanksgiving "playlet" which featured child protagonists narrowly avoiding ritual sacrifice by sinister, forest-dwelling "Indians."[128]

The Pageant of Navajo History was not a generic "first contact" tale, nor was it the static portrayal of the past permitted by Commissioner Daniel Browning at the 1895 Fort Wayne centennial celebration. Rather than "mannequins frozen in history" or a description of the "safe" distant past, the Navajo Pageant depicted recent history in motion and traced its relation to the present.[129] Throughout the performance, the historic Diné are depicted as honorable, if perhaps misguided, in their pursuit of raiding, and Barboncito and Ganado Mucho are characterized as politically astute, eloquent leaders motivated by a love for their people. Manuelito may be portrayed as an enthusiastic warrior in his youth, but his role in the pageant is by no means villainous. It's not just soil conservation and day schools that get championed in the script—Diné community and identity are, too.

Yet the exclusion of the medicine man character from the present-day act, and the prioritization of American academic interpretations of tribal history and authentic dress, betray the selective nature of New Deal cultural tolerance. The presentation of a federal government–friendly past and present, and the continued elevation of US academic authority over Diné historical knowledge, both suggest the unequal government-Indigenous relationship that characterized the New Deal era. The whitewashing of an uncomfortable past was indeed something of a feature of education in the wider New Deal; schoolkids at the government's flagship Subsistence Homestead project in Arthurdale learned nothing of their community and region's involvement in slavery, despite the on-site presence of a historic plantation cabin used by the enslaved. Rather, they were taught an idealized version of West Virginian and Kentuckian "pioneer" history that emphasized the exploits of Daniel Boone and the industrious communitarianism and resilience of early homesteaders—a narrative of the past that promoted community spirit and a proud regional identity over an understanding of ethnic conflict and exploitation.[130]

Of perhaps greatest significance, however, was the framing of the pageant as a "Pageant of Navajo History," when it reflected a historical perspective that was not intrinsically Diné. By focusing on great men, military events, and treaties all involving the United States, the pageant positioned Diné history within an overarching metanarrative of US-tribal relations, reflecting Euro-American concepts of history and the past. In this sense, the pageant, despite its effort to tell actual Diné history, perpetuated the ongoing colonialist American history paradigm identified by historian Susan Miller.[131] As Jennifer Nez Denetdale has noted, "Western senses of past have been privileged and Native perspectives either dismissed or ignored"—the 1940 pageant, with its focus on Diné-US relations and the "documented" past, did just that.[132] And the pageant authors' focus on depicting peaceful US-Diné coexistence (and federal government benevolence) may have foreshadowed what social scientists have since identified as the mainstream representation of non-white histories as selective, "White-washed products that reflect beliefs and desires of the White American actors whose preferences disproportionately shape everyday realities."[133]

Indigenous Teachers' Curricular Contributions

The BIA's assumption that many Indigenous traditions were nearing extinction and that non-Native academic experts were needed to teach Indigenous peoples their histories and arts often did not match the reality of community life. Further, it downplayed the role of Indigenous educators in preserving knowledge. Sicangu Lakota teacher and future National Endowment for the Arts National Heritage fellow Nellie Star Boy Menard did much more than introduce flat loom weaving to the day schools of the Rosebud Agency in 1940.[134] She also established the Rosebud Arts and Crafts cooperative and shop in 1937, which helped members refine and market traditional Lakota craft products. Building on the beadwork, quillwork, needlework, and tanning skills she had learned from her grandmother and mother, Menard and her cohorts produced objects "sewn in the old way" and then evaluated each other's work, with Menard explaining market retail concerns to the cooperative members.[135] In her capacity as community art teacher she also taught Lakota artwork to Rosebud day-school teachers, thereby ensuring the transmission of authentic Lakota arts and crafts skills to the next generation. Yet despite this pivotal role in the BIA's education program, Menard wasn't mentioned by name in Lyford's 1940 textbook

Quill and Beadwork of the Western Sioux. She possibly appears anonymously as the "skilled Sioux woman whose training came from her grandmother" who was teaching the popular beadwork elective recently introduced at Oglala Community School.[136] This lack of recognition is all the more striking given the strong likelihood that Menard collated many of the Lakota designs Lyford included in her text—the only vestige of an acknowledgment is the author's note that museum sources were "supplemented by such information as could be provided by the older Indians on the reservations."[137] Incidentally, given that Menard was born in 1910, she hardly fit the elderly beadworker image that Lyford presented in the text.

Nonabah Gorman Bryan also played a key role in perpetuating traditional crafts in the 1930s. Described by her colleagues as "an artist" in weaving, she taught traditional weaving to around 150 girls a year at Wingate Vocational High School. Bryan was instrumental in perfecting the dye recipes, drawing upon traditional formulae, and devising her own. While she did receive credit for her work on the Indian Service publication, Bryan raised significant concerns to IACB and BIA personnel, which were ultimately disregarded. She informed IACB researchers that the students needed much longer at the loom than the seventy-five minutes permitted per lesson. She also conveyed Diné concerns regarding public dissemination of the dye recipes outside the classroom, which could contravene the spiritual requirements observed by Diné weavers in the plant-gathering process. Unfortunately, the Indian Service took the view that, since the project received government funding, the booklet was government property and so could be distributed (and sold) to all. Despite Bryan's leadership of the project, her advice fell on deaf ears.[138] For general superintendent E. R. Fryer and Wingate superintendent Herman Bogard, the dyes were a product, a commodity, stripped of any religio-cultural significance or concerns.

Menard and Bryan were not alone in using their existing expertise to enrich the New Deal government school curriculum. Esther Horne had learned beadwork from her mother and aunt and so was able to draw upon her own knowledge to teach pupils at Wahpeton School. Indeed, she only used Lyford's book if she didn't know how to make a particular item.[139] Horne actively sought the contributions of parents and community members rather than relying on academic texts. Charged with teaching a fourth-grade demonstration course at a summer school at Pine Ridge, Horne invited a pupil's father to talk to the students about his ancestor Red Cloud. She was initially surprised that the man "felt comfortable enough... to share some of the family's and tribe's oral traditions," but after the success of this first visit, "Many of the parents and relatives of the children that I taught during the demonstration session that summer came to visit our classroom and share their native expertise." The relatives clearly considered their contribution to be didactic and valued the opportunity to show pupils and teachers their "artifacts" and discuss "Indian food" such as pemmican, fry bread, and wojape to "reinforce the fact that a traditional Indian diet was nutritious."[140] Horne continued to use Native sources for her classroom teaching when she established an Indian Club at Wahpeton "as a teaching tool for the students, staff, and anyone else with whom we might share our music, dance, philosophy, and way of life."[141] Acknowledging that she lacked both the knowledge and the experience necessary for teaching the variety of dances and costume making reflective of the different nations the school represented, Horne's solution was practical and effective: she asked for help from the surrounding communities and from Native colleagues such as dormitory worker Martha Voight (Hidatsa) and bus driver Albert Houle (Turtle Mountain Ojibwe).[142] Non-Native teacher Marion Dreamer, at Day School Number Five on Pine Ridge, also sought the assistance of the local Lakota community who "brought me some Indian things to use in the school room" and built a tepee for class use.[143] The input of Indigenous communities in shaping Horne's costume making and dance classes, and the provision of materials for Dreamer's lessons, indicates that historic traditions were very much alive outside of the schoolroom, contrary to bureau assumptions.

Horne did not eschew academic sources entirely. She made full use of BIA staff summer schools, attending Native art classes run by Frederick Douglas, curator of the Denver Art Museum, and Ruth Underhill's ethnology course on the Plains nations. The relationship between Underhill and Horne illustrates the competing concepts of authority, knowledge, and authenticity inherent in the New Deal education program. Horne recalled that Underhill reacted defensively when she challenged her on an aspect of Dakota culture: "She was offended and a bit indignant that I would question her authority and not just believe everything she said." Interestingly, "Sioux" students in the class supported her challenge, prompting Horne to reflect that "I did learn a great deal from her [Underhill], but I learned a lot more from our Sioux students who were in this ethnology class with me."[144]

And this incident perhaps reveals a crucial difference in teaching styles between Horne and the academic experts employed by the BIA: whereas the latter believed they were imparting authoritative, irrefutable historical truths to their students based upon a narrowly defined range of sources, Horne approached the topics of "history" and "culture" almost from the standpoint of a student. In order to teach the histories and cultural traditions of other communities, she asked people from those communities for help, and she sought out opportunities to learn more. For Horne, teaching was a fluid and ever-evolving enterprise; for the New Deal academic expert, the teaching process was static, based upon the findings of research already undertaken, processed, and verified.

The treatment of Native histories and traditional cultures on the BIA school curriculum during the New Deal reveals several issues. Ryan and Beatty did seek to include Native histories and elements of traditional cultures on the curriculum, although implementation varied considerably from school to school and the inclusion was highly selective. Histories featured an artificially favorable portrayal of federal government policy; historic arts were based largely on collated, and therefore academically verifiable, museum specimens. Narratives and presentations of the past were often constructed with little involvement (or acknowledged involvement) of the communities concerned: authenticity, so valued by New Deal bureau policymakers, was deemed to be the preserve of the dead (and by extension those who studied them) rather than the living. The Native past was seen to be in danger of receding into oblivion, of being forgotten by communities buckling under the oppression of past government policies and contemporary economic crises. But the living did have their own interest in, and opinions on, the past. Just as Diné parents confounded Raines by supplying historic costume items and jewelry for the Pageant of Navajo History, so too did elderly Seneca residents at Tonowonda visit the Seneca Arts Project to "offer suggestions and criticisms to the younger workers," supplementing the official museum sources with living memory.[145] The attempted control wielded—consciously or subconsciously—by government personnel over Native cultures and histories was never absolute in practice.

History and heritage lessons also reflected contradictions inherent within wider New Deal Indian Service policy, notably the conflicts between tribal sovereignty and government paternalism and between preservation and assimilation. The BIA often elevated the past over the present:

arts and crafts lessons demonstrated policymakers' tendency to conflate historicity with cultural authenticity, and textbooks portrayed a community's ancestors as better managers of their natural environment than their descendants. Indeed, this suggests the "repressive authenticity" narrative identified by Patrick Wolfe as a facet of settler colonialism, whereby settlers construct "authentic" indigeneity as a "frozen precontact essence" rather than an evolving and dynamic phenomenon.[146] True, Ryan and Beatty (although not always their staff) expressly used the term "history" to describe Indigenous pasts in contrast to the repeated reference to "legends," "myths," and "folklore" by earlier commissioners and officials. At the same time, non-Native academic experts, appointed by the BIA, controlled the construction of history textbooks, arts manuals, and craft projects, and they generally proved unable to move beyond established Euro-American boundaries of evidence, verifiability, and naming. The New Dealers may have seen a value in Native pasts that their BIA predecessors had not—yet they seemed unwilling to entrust the narrative construction or the interpretation of that past to contemporary Native Americans themselves. Instead, they promoted a version of history based upon the artifact collections and documented observations of non-Indigenous scholars and collectors, a history that was largely celebratory of *past* Indigenous achievements. This narrative ultimately reflected Euro-American interpretations of the past, skill, morality, and artistic value, revealing a paternalistic belief that Native histories needed Euro-American protection and guidance in order to survive and be retold. What governed the New Deal attitude to Native histories wasn't so much safety—the presentation of a distant past, far removed from present tensions—but a Eurocentric mindset that prescribed the very definition of history and that assigned its guardianship and dissemination to Euro-American academics and educators. This was a shift from Assimilation Era salvage ethnography, which had sought to "save" knowledge and artifacts by removing them from Native communities, to a "salvage curriculum" of sorts, which sought to instruct communities in their own history and artistic traditions.

SOIL CONSERVATION, SCIENCE, AND HEALTH ON THE CURRICULUM

3

The New Deal school curriculum included selective versions of Indigenous pasts and traditional arts and crafts. Yet it simultaneously promoted Western science, notably in lessons on ecology and healthcare. This chapter examines the close links between school curricula and the government's soil conservation program on the Navajo Reservation, and it also explores the tension between Diné traditional medicine practices and the BIA's healthcare policy. The Indian Service's failure to reconcile, or even to acknowledge, the clash between the conflicting belief systems of Western science and Diné metaphysics offers a sharp rebuke to BIA claims of a pluralist curriculum.

The federal government's disastrous stock reduction program imposed on the Navajo Nation, 1933–47, has garnered widespread and justified condemnation both from contemporary critics and in the decades since its creation.[1] A divisive policy from the start, its underlying rationale highlighted a stark disconnect between government-appointed experts and Diné communities. True, all parties recognized that the reservation faced a grave environmental threat by the early 1930s: as with swathes of the US Midwest, drought conditions and soil erosion threatened major desertification across Arizona and Utah, which could prove catastrophic for a rural economy. However, federally appointed soil conservation specialists and Diné leaders disagreed as to the cause; whereas the Soil Conservation Service (SCS) diagnosed the problem as erosion caused by overgrazing, many Diné ascribed the aridity to drought caused by lack of rainfall, which had resulted from spiritual disharmony (*Hochxójii*). The proposed solutions were antithetical in the extreme. Diné communities sought to restore harmony and balance (*Hózhójii*) by holding sings, paid for with livestock, which would reenact creation through prayer and song, bringing rain.[2] SCS scientists, through their focus on eliminating overgrazing, mandated extensive culls of stock animals. The BIA threw its full support behind the scientists and subsequently instigated a series of unpopular and poorly managed culls. The scale was substantial: by 1947 the number of goats under Diné ownership had plummeted from 173,000 to around 56,000; the number of sheep fell from 570,000 to 358,000; and the number of horses dropped by 9,000.[3] The slaughter caused significant outrage and distress amongst the Diné for whom livestock is a gift from the Holy People and so must be nurtured—culls were interpreted as a violation of *Hózhójii* which then ushered in damaging *Hochxójii*, thereby perpetuating the drought.[4] The cultural insensitivity of stock reduction, coupled with the economic hardship it caused poorer families, sparked concerted opposition to the policy.[5] To combat this, the BIA sought the help of the newly inaugurated day schools, as well as the reservation boarding schools, in promoting its soil conservation vision to the next Diné generation, a vision which rested squarely upon the acceptance of Western science and ecology as primary environmental creeds.

Significantly, the federal government's unwavering belief that erosion was due solely to overgrazing rather than meteorological conditions stemmed from flawed evidence. SCS scientists adhered rigidly to ecologist Frederick Clements's "climax theory," which stipulates that colonies of mature vegetation remain intact unless catastrophically disturbed, for example by chronic overgrazing. According to Clements, the pristine, mature state of the Colorado Plateau was grassland, not the sagebrush scrub prevalent by 1930—indicating a catastrophic, unnatural intervention.[6] SCS scientists bolstered this argument using mid-nineteenth-century descriptions of the land by Euro-American travelers, often military expeditions. These emphasized a grassy landscape with little obvious grazing and no arroyos, appearing to support Clements's theory of human-generated despoliation. However, as historian Marsha Weisiger has noted, the travelers' accounts didn't represent the entire landscape but focused largely on watering holes and riparian areas.[7] Neither the SCS nor BIA consulted Diné sources concerning the historic landscape.[8] The SCS also rejected the argument posited by American geologists Herbert Gregory and Kirk Bryan, which ascribed the increase in arroyos to climatic alterations and "long-term geological processes," with overgrazing as accelerant rather than instigator.[9] This disregard was an error: tree ring data has since revealed a cycle of changing and extreme weather in the decades preceding 1930 that weakened plants, including severe droughts in the 1880s and between 1899–1904, followed by an abnormally wet period (1905–20) that created arroyos and a lowered water table. While the 1934 and 1936 droughts were less severe, the tree ring data indicates the earlier climatic conditions (droughts, heavy rainfall, floods) were the catalyst for soil erosion in nondesert areas, which was then accelerated—but not created by—grazing.[10]

In effect, while drought wasn't the sole cause of the environmental crisis, contemporary Diné were right to look to meteorology for an explanation. In similar vein, government scientists were right to note the *cumulative* impact of grazing on the already-damaged land—yet by focusing solely on grazing and on Eurocentric misrepresentations of the historic landscape, they missed the chance to develop a shared strategy with the Diné that addressed the entirety of the problem. The failure to consider tree ring data is particularly striking considering that contemporary archaeologists were using it to date the ancient histories of Pueblo and Diné communities, as outlined approvingly by Ruth Underhill in her history texts commissioned by Beatty for government schools.[11] Instead, the SCS and BIA adopted a strategy in isolation that excluded the Diné from the decision-making and data-gathering processes; dismissed Diné knowledge and experience of the land; disregarded Diné cultural beliefs and practices; and indeed blamed the Diné for the erosion crisis. This monocultural framing and management of soil conservation and ecology was then replicated in the school curriculum, with predictably negative results.

Schools as Stock Reduction Propagandists

Soil conservation, or "range management" as it was often termed, rapidly came to occupy a central position in the Navajo Service education program. In a policy report for the Appropriation Committee of the House of Representatives in December 1935, Collier wrote of the "re-orientation" of government-directed Native education to meet the needs of soil conservation: "Substantial progress in this direction is already being made at the new day schools and community centers of the Navajo reservation and among the Pueblos elsewhere."[12] He had previously informed Ickes, "It is to be the primary function of the local centers and schools to arouse, enlist and direct the active cooperation of all Navajos in the vital, basic task of restoring and maintaining the productiveness of their homeland." This aim, in Collier's view, made the school program "the keystone of the Navajo project."[13] Indeed, the "Primary Objectives for Indian Schools," which comprised part of the civil service exam for Indian Service teachers in the late 1930s and early 1940s, listed "intelligent conservation of natural resources" as a key educational aim, preceded by the need "to aid students in analyzing the economic resources of the reservation and in planning more effective ways of utilizing these resources"—tellingly, these objectives were listed above vocational education and health improvement. Teachers were also exhorted "to aid [students] in achieving some mastery over their environment."[14] The concept of taming the natural environment was alien to traditional Diné concepts of the balanced relationship between humans and nature, and this clashed with another school objective promoting "appreciation of . . . tribal lore. " The discrepancy appears to have passed unnoticed by BIA authorities.[15] As social scientist Manley Begay Jr. has noted, "A purpose of Navajo life is to maintain balance and respect between the individual and the universe and to live in harmony and beauty with nature, the social milieu of family and community, and the Holy Ones."[16]

"Mastery" of nature hardly fitted with Diné concepts of balance and respect. However, it did chime with the civilization hierarchies still promoted in geography and history classes at US public schools in the 1920s and 1930s, which hailed Western colonizers' adaptability to climate variation (via technology) as a marker of advanced civilization.[17] The New Deal BIA, despite its professed cultural tolerance, clearly believed the Diné should adopt this aspect of Western "progress."

For range management to assume a central place on the school curriculum, teachers had to be equipped to deliver it. In 1935 Clyde Blair, the first director of Navajo Education and a former superintendent of Albuquerque Indian School, feared that SCS would "usurp the administration of the schools," given that many new day schools were short-staffed and existing personnel lacked ecological expertise. Collier was quick to reassure that no SCS takeover was imminent, but he did anticipate some conservation personnel might be needed at the day schools. In his view, "If Soil

Conservation can find and hire the sort of talent that we need in the Navajo schools and we are without the funds or the authority to hire such talent, no jurisdictional dispute should be allowed to prevent getting the necessary result."[18] In a private letter, Collier reminded Blair that "Soil Conservation is dealing with the central and urgent problem of Navajo life." If SCS could supply personnel during this "emergency" and could take "an intellectual responsibility in it," this would be an "intensely desirable" result. While he spoke of the "enrichment" which SCS personnel could bring to the Navajo school program, Collier's primary motive appeared pragmatic: "We are having much difficulty in finding the right talent on our civil service registers."[19] The BIA had put the cart before the horse in devising an ambitious environmental education program without first finding staff who could teach it. Collier's proposal also held ominous implications for the schools' professed cultural pluralist stance by drawing upon staff who had zero experience or understanding of Native American cultures and lives.

By 1936 the BIA had realized the necessity of providing conservation training to its own teaching staff. A summer school for teachers and Indian assistants was held at Wingate Vocational High School so that, according to a somewhat mollified Blair, schools could "take their full part in education and guidance of the Navajo people toward full cooperation with the land management program of the government." He drew a link between education and anticipated Diné acceptance of range management: "Problems of water, soil, and livestock can be more easily solved as the Navajo is given greater opportunity to understand them."[20] In 1937 the bureau newsletter *Indians at Work* advised that a two-week accredited course on "school application of soil and water conservation" would become part of the regular staff summer school held at Arizona State Teachers' College: it aimed to "meet the definite need of teachers throughout this section for more basic information in instructing their pupils in the vital problem of soil conservation and proper land use in the Southwest region."[21] The role of the schools as unabashed promoters and intended facilitators of range management was therefore well understood by BIA education staff by the mid-1930s. However, soil conservation gained an even stronger scholastic presence in 1937 with Blair's replacement as director of Navajo Schools by Lucy Wilcox Adams. Adams had transferred to the Indian Service from SCS in 1936. Her appointment was championed by General Superintendent E. R. Fryer, an avowed soil conservation enthusiast and former Forest

Service employee.[22] Indeed, Fryer's initial support for Adams was linked to her SCS credentials: he informed Beatty that "her background in Soil Conservation Service would make her especially valuable in the adoption of curricula in this jurisdiction to meet the economic and environmental problems of the people."[23] As he noted approvingly a few months later, "Mrs Adams is anxious to emphasize, as early as possible, land management education."[24]

Adams quickly affirmed the primacy of range management in the Navajo education program. In August 1937 she secured the transfer of Clay Lockett from SCS to the Indian Service specifically to develop soil conservation education. Even more telling was the "Program for Navajo Schools" issued December 1937. "Land and Economics" occupies a primary position on the first page, based on Adams's belief that the "Navajo problem" was economic in nature (the need to make a living) and could be solved by "proper" land use. In other words, she believed the majority of Diné would participate in a reservation-based pastoral and agricultural economy which necessitated a healthy land range. With this cornerstone principle established, Adams outlined the schools' key aims:

> The principal task of the educational system should be to give the student the knowledge and skills necessary for a better control of his environment and so raise his economic standards; to establish health habits and provide opportunity for the correction of physical defects; to develop understanding of and participation in a conservation program, in its broad sense; and to create in the new generation public opinion favorable to such a policy.[25]

The schools' remit therefore exceeded mere education in soil conservation theory and techniques—schools were actively enlisted as propaganda agents for the federal government's range management policy.

The curricular prioritization of range management even led Beatty to consider segregating Diné children from other Native nations at the government schools. He believed that the "problems" experienced by Diné communities could be best solved "by educating their young people in schools where it is possible to emphasize problems of Soil Conservation, Land Use, Range Management, Agriculture, and other problems of vital concern to the Navajos." Beatty felt that Albuquerque Indian School (AIS) and Santa Fe Indian School (SFIS)—"essentially the high schools of the

Pueblo area"—did not offer a curriculum that catered to Diné needs. He consequently directed Fryer to "discourage" enrollment of Diné children at "non-Navajo High Schools," excepting individuals who were "especially gifted in arts and crafts" and so might benefit from specialized training at SFIS. The directive not only reveals Beatty's emphasis on regionally relevant curricula but also suggests the BIA's perception of education as a problem solver. Further, key issues in Diné contemporary life, including land use and agriculture, were seen as "problems" needing urgent rectification.[26] Interestingly, Collier opposed the segregation bid, noting that Diné children were needed to boost enrollment at AIS and SFIS and vital to the economic operation of both schools. Pragmatism aside, he recognized that both Pueblo and Diné communities farmed and raised livestock and so had "the total problems of land use in common," in addition to being "in contact all the time," which meant the "basix [sic] educational material, growing out of land use etc, would be more or less interchangeable." He consequently discouraged attempts to confine Diné children to Navajo Reservation schools.[27]

By 1940 soil conservation was firmly entrenched at all levels of the Navajo school program. According to the 1940 *Annual Report to the Secretary of the Interior*, BIA education policy's key aim was "teaching Indians to make wise use of their own resources." It went on to chart the application of range management principles throughout the school program, even for beginners. With SCS cooperation, "Simple conservation facts have been incorporated into the teaching of the fundamentals of reading, writing, arithmetic, particularly in the semi-arid Southwest." For the higher grades, "The study of conservation and the land is correlated with the study of American history and the geography of the country as a whole"— demonstrating not only the omnipresence of soil conservation throughout the curriculum but also the presentation of ecology/range management as a wider *American* problem to be overcome, as it had apparently been in other parts of the country.[28] Any concept of Diné Bikéyah as a spiritual homeland, or of a cultural relationship between land and people, was ignored in favor of a national contextualization. Despite the confident tone of the report, some day-school teachers actively strove to avoid even the mention of soil conservation for fear of alienating Diné communities.[29]

Irrespective of individual teacher's or community concerns, the vocational high schools on the Navajo Reservation soon adapted their curricula to meet the soil conservation prioritization. The Tuba City Vocational High School catalog claimed, "Special stress is placed upon sheep production, range management, and soil erosion."[30] Shiprock Agricultural High School's catalog reiterated the "Primary Objectives of Indian Schools" and confirmed that "the general program of the entire school centers around rural life" on the reservation.[31] Wingate Vocational High School went further, offering specialized instruction in sheep rearing. Indeed, the Southwestern Range and Sheep Breeding Laboratory was established at the school in 1936, with the aim of "improving" the local churra sheep to enhance their marketable worth. Under the direction of John Cooper, the laboratory crossbred a foundation flock of churras with other breeds in an ultimately unsuccessful attempt to create a hybrid that combined churra hardiness, long-stapled wool, and milk quality with an increased mutton yield and uniform fleece fiber. The bid to retain the churras through scientific breeding was in part motivated by Diné weavers who valued their wool which required less carding and produced higher quality blankets and rugs than the increasingly dominant rambouillet hybrids. As Wingate weaving instructor and dye expert Nonabah Bryan had informed IACB field researchers, merino wool was too short and too hard for rug weaving—the old churra sheep were the best.[32] In this respect, the sheep laboratory sought to protect, rather than replace, something intrinsic to Diné life: "our Old Navajo sheep."[33]

Other aspects of sheep rearing education did not, however, build upon Diné knowledge, traditions, or practices. The SCS rigidly ascribed soil erosion to what it perceived to be archaic and irresponsible Diné sheep grazing methods, essentially accusing the Diné of inadvertently harming the range. This mirrored British colonial officials' response to environmental decline in South Africa in the same period. They blamed denudation of the land on "overstocking" and other allegedly "backward" African pastoral practices, with scant thought for the colonial state's constrictive pressure on land and Indigenous economies.[34] This stance did not invite a solution based upon exchange of ideas—for the BIA, the immediate replacement of existing Diné pastoral practices was the sole goal. Pastoralism education at the reservation schools therefore involved teaching *new* methods of sheep care and breeding. Note the Wingate program in animal husbandry proposed by Lucy Adams in 1937: "Breeding, feeding, care and marketing of livestock and livestock products, principles of range management and erosion control, with supplemental work in agriculture and farm management."³⁵ The implication was that Diné pastoralists, whose families had spent decades sheep farming on the reservation, did not know how to breed, feed, or care for their livestock appropriately. A similarly dismissive attitude appeared in a report on a sheepshearing demonstration to "local women" at Hunter's Point Day School. According to observer Walter Stepp: "Mr [John] Cooper showed the group how to properly tie the wool after shearing for marketing. He explained that Navajo wool had been penalized on the market because of improper tieing [sic] and mixing of the grades of wool. A little more care in keeping the wool clean plus this proper tieing [sic] would do much to increase the market price of their product, as he pointed out."³⁶ While the shearers might have found advice on US public taste useful in terms of exploring new retail markets, references to "improper" tying and to unclean wool suggest lack of respect for existing Diné techniques; Cooper and Stepp appear to have conflated *difference* in tying technique with *inferiority* of technique. In contrast, while sheepshearing demonstrations were encouraged in non-BIA, government-directed rural projects in the New Deal era, they emphasized transmission of local knowledge rather than its replacement. At the Arthurdale (whites-only) community farm project in West Virginia, school pupils visited local farms to observe sheepshearing and carding—community members' skills were presented as the correct procedure for pupils to adopt.³⁷

The Hunter's Point shearers weren't the only Diné adults to receive instruction in pastoralism at the BIA schools. In December 1939, fifty-five Diné men and women enrolled in a twelve-day adult short course at Wingate Vocational High School. This included a half-day visit to the sheep laboratory, including a tour of the building, a two-hour "discussion and demonstration" session on the suitability of different wool types for handweaving, a half hour's instruction at the feeding pens, and ninety minutes on the range to discuss flock management and land use. Participants were encouraged to "closely inspect" the sheep used in the breeding program, to observe the breeding methods, and to ask questions. The tour leaders and instructors were all Diné—they answered questions and led the discussions. According to Animal Husbandry Assistant Herbert King Jr., the visitors asked many questions and showed "a great deal of interest in all operations"—especially "the fact that young Navajo men were actively engaged in all phases of the work." The short course, on the whole, seems to have been an interactive experience, with visitors invited to contribute their opinions, and sheep lab was no different. However, King Jr. ended his report on a telling note, stating that the adult students left "with the feeling that the work being done was beneficial for them and their people," while the laboratory personnel "felt that they knew these people and their problems a little bit better, and that the work in which they were engaged was really worthwhile."[38] The spirit of cooperation and friendliness is cheering, yet the choice of language betrays the one-sided nature of the discussions for at least the personnel. The visitors apparently learned to appreciate the range work, while the staff gained a greater understanding of Navajo *problems*—not ideas or skills—and thus found their soil conservation mission (and the worldview upon which it was based) reinforced.

The perceived need to refashion and improve Diné pastoral techniques became an accepted mainstay of the New Deal education program. Adams's successor as director of Navajo Schools, George Boyce, proposed a textbook for day-school teachers that "would, of course, be devoted to economic and environmental activities on the Navajo [reservation], as trading, the way to shear sheep, the way to raise, the way to irrigate."[39] Again, the implication was that, in BIA eyes, traditional Diné methods of shearing, irrigating, and stock raising were incompetent and needed to be replaced. The methods utilized to teach children and adults range management also portrayed Diné practices as actively harmful to the land. A series of didactic dioramas constructed by SCS employees in 1938 offered a graphic illustration of federal government attitudes to Indigenous economic systems. The dioramas depicted the Navajo Reservation in a "before" and "after" format, and the message was uncompromising: traditional Diné land use was branded "improper use," which created desert conditions "through misuse or overuse of the area." In contrast, "proper use" involved "correct" numbers of sheep, "proper" use of timber, and "proper" farming practices, which were vaguely defined as "man in complete harmony with nature." Contemporary Diné pastoralism was categorized as a "problem," involving "meager" land development and the "abuse" of natural resources. The diorama promoters did not mince words when describing the apparent negative results of Diné land use: "Too many sheep, many of poor quality; range crowded with horses and cull steers; wethers conspicuous in sheep bands (Navajos do not dock tails of wethers); total range area overgrazed; no thought given to seasonal use; sheep returned to hogan each night; many very smallherds [*sic*]." "Proper use" was presented as the opposite of the existing system: Diné were to practice seasonal use of the range area; horses, goats, "aged steers," wethers, and hogan corrals were "conspicuously absent" from the scene; small herds were consolidated. The "Future" scene was accompanied by the following caption:

1. Development of crafts and industries.
2. Intelligent assignment of agricultural land.
3. Wide-spread [*sic*] development of reservation resources.
4. Proper use of range land.
5. Good livestock management and good stock.
6. Education—health facilities.
7. More equitable distribution of use of land resources.
8. Government and Navajos working in complete harmony.[40]

The preponderance of negative terms in the Diné (or "past") section, when contrasted with positive language such as "development" and "intelligent" in the SCS-mandated "future" section, is striking. This dismissive approach was not one employee's opinion—it permeated the entire range management education program. In February 1939, an Agricultural and Range Management Training Conference was held for education personnel, featuring a presentation entitled "Problems of Navajo and Pueblo Economy and Their Demands on the Schools." While the presenter opened with a fierce criticism of previous education policy which "has worked strenuously to make an urban white man out of a complete rural-minded Indian," they then denounced the Diné livestock industry as "unquestionably the most inefficient in the United States." This wasn't presented as the fault of the Diné but rather the result of poor education and federal government negligence; still, they were described as slow to search out or accept new concepts. The solution, according to the conference speakers, was the adoption—via education—of "long accepted white livestock practices." This was envisaged as a one-sided education process, where the only learners would be the Diné:

> The Navajos must understand that one good sheep on good grass is worth three half starved inferior animals. They must understand that ewes bred at the proper season by good type well fed bucks will bring

uniform readily marketable and heavier lambs. They must understand what is meant by proper shearing practices and that these practices, if followed, mean several cents a pound difference in wool income.... The Navajo must understand the use of water and land to get the most from their cultivated acreage.[41]

If the BIA and SCS felt some paternalistic sympathy for the Diné for having hitherto received little "white" assistance in managing their farming, they clearly held no respect for Diné agrarian techniques or skills and instead mandated their total replacement with Western science-based methods. As Diné representatives from Indian Wells protested, "Many, many years of experience have taught the Navajos how to herd and care for stock in our beloved land of Arizona."[42] Their words fell on deaf ears. Indeed, the BIA's insistence on viewing Diné pastoralism as problematic suggests the settler colonialist trope whereby ostensibly benevolent intervention is presaged on the concept of Indigenous dysfunction.[43]

The federal government's belief that the Diné were directly, albeit inadvertently, harming the land spilled over into government-sponsored publications and school textbooks. Anthropologists Clyde Kluckhohn and Dorothea Leighton acknowledged that a "natural erosion cycle" had played a role in the crisis, but they blamed "uncontrolled and abusive land use, primarily overgrazing" for exacerbating the soil depletion.[44] The 1940s bilingual school primer series *Little Herder*, while largely sympathetic to Diné culture and society, expressed this theme more baldly. In *Little Herder in Spring*, the child protagonist (a young Diné girl who herds her family's sheep) ponders the ecological crisis and what she can do to help. The words are telling:

Earth,
They are saying
That you are tired.

They are saying
That for too long
You have given life
To the sheep
And The People.

They are saying
That the arroyos
Are the hurts we have made
Across your face,
That the moccasin track
And the sheep trail
Are the cuts we have given you.

Earth, my mother,
Believe me when I tell you,
We are your children,
We would not want to hurt you.

I am only little.
I cannot do big things,
But I can do this for you.
I can take my sheep
To new pastures.

I can take them
The long way
Around the arroyos,
Not through them,
When we go to the waterhole.

This way
Their little feet,
Their sharp pointed feet,
Will not make the cuts
Across your face
Grow deeper.[45]

The cultural insensitivity of the text is startling. Although the narrative emphasizes unintentional damage, the message that the Diné had inflicted wounds to the earth's face remains emotive and brutal, especially considering both the primer's youthful readership and the cultural mandate of maintaining *Hózhójii*. True, the earlier story in the series, *Little Herder in*

Autumn, appears to acknowledge the prevailing Diné explanation of the crisis—drought through lack of rainfall—yet the section "It Is Dry" is significantly shorter than Little Herder's later reflections on the damaging sheep trails.[46] The remainder of *Little Herder in Spring* focuses on her parents and their discussions of stock reduction policy. The Euro-American author, Ann Clark, attempts to convey the father's concern and confusion over the soil crisis: he attends meetings that last days on end, consisting of people "talking, talking, talking. Some this way. Some that way." The father has faith that the meetings will provide a solution so that he will know whether to reduce his flocks or to continue as before. Yet the meetings only leave him confused, with no sense of resolution. As the mother character notes, "Big talk, too much, is like a flood taking things of long standing before it." It is unclear from the narrative whether this is a rebuke against government officials for failing to explain the policy fully and convincingly or against Diné pastoralists for clinging to "things of long standing" instead of embracing radical change. The primer's one clear message was the gravity of the ecological situation.[47]

The final entry in the series, *Little Herder in Summer*, steers clear of stock reduction and erosion but features a lengthy promotion of another controversial government initiative: sheep dipping. Clark acknowledges it is not a traditional practice:

> Sheep must be dipped
> In medicine-water.
> There is no pollen.
> There is no Holy Song.
> There is no Trail of Beauty
> In this medicine-water.
>
> But my father says
> It is good for the sheep.

Although Little Herder's mother dislikes the dipping, reflecting widespread sentiment, the narrative presents it as necessary to protect the flock from ticks and lice and also as a fun community occasion with singing and eating. The primer therefore instructed its young readers that government advice on pastoralism and soil conservation was a positive thing to be followed for the good of all.⁴⁸

The BIA-commissioned Life and Customs textbook published in 1946, *Workaday Life of the Pueblos*, also promoted the government's soil conservation program, albeit as a brief add-on at the book's end rather than a key theme. In contrast to *Little Herder*, the depiction of range management on the United Pueblos Agency (UPA) emphasized full cooperation and harmony between "government experts" and Pueblo farmers:

> The soil of the Southwest was cracking and washing away as the result of overgrazing. Government experts had to educate the Indians and White ranchers alike as to the way it must be used and no ranchers gave greater cooperation than the Indians. The government helped by digging new wells, reservoirs and ditches so that the fields could spread into land never used before. The pueblos themselves bought new tools.... Pueblos are planning livestock programs, with careful treatment of the soil and scientific care of the animals, advised by government experts.⁴⁹

The ubiquitous "government experts" resurfaced in a passage describing the introduction of wheat and alfalfa to the UPA, hailed (by Underhill) as contemporary equivalents to the "wanderers whom some legends call 'Dew People,'" who had taught the early Pueblos to raise corn.⁵⁰ The message was clear: the federal government, backed by its scientific advisors, cast itself as the Pueblos' new protector, guiding them to save themselves from an environmental apocalypse by transforming their agrarian and pastoral systems. Indeed, Collier proudly promoted Laguna and Acoma on the international stage as conservation success stories who had rescued their land by cooperating with government initiatives.⁵¹

It wasn't just Indian Service personnel who accepted the government's vision of range management and farming. The authors of the 1940 New Mexico Association on Indian Affairs report, despite criticizing the implementation of BIA and SCS policy on the Navajo Reservation, staunchly supported range management, stating that "proper training in the conservation and cultivation of the soil, and the actual daily handling of farm tools can not [sic] begin too early in the education of the Navajo for life on the soil."⁵² The Phelps-Stokes Report, while also cataloging the limitations of the education program, lambasted the "embarrassing and emotional criticisms" by those "friends of the Indian" who decried the BIA's failure to consider Diné customs and heritage. According to Phelps-Stokes, "Such friends seem to have failed to understand and appreciate the imperative necessity of saving the soil of the Navajo Reservation." Such a result could, so the report concluded, only be attained through "the achievements of modern science and the best American ideals."[53] So what we see by 1940 is a largely united front of government and non-Indigenous philanthropic bodies, demanding the substitution of a Western land management narrative for Diné and Pueblo narratives. While the New Deal did not seek a classic (physical) settler colonialist land grab, it did strive to wrest control of the narrative of land stewardship and maintenance—an attempted dispossession of Native knowledge systems and socioeconomic sovereignty.

Primacy of Western Science on the Curriculum

Science played an integral role in the dissemination of the soil conservation program at the reservation schools. At the day schools, beginners and young children were taught about local flora and fauna. Teacher Valentine Salomore devised an elementary science curriculum for his 5th graders that featured nomenclature of plants and local animals, plant reproduction, the keeping of class snails, lizards, turtles, caterpillars, and "facts about Nature." This bid to teach pupils "many of the interesting things in the world around them" reflected the Ryan/Beatty emphasis on locally relevant education.[54] However, nature classes could rapidly become fraught and contested spaces given the unfamiliarity of many teachers with Diné culture. Norma Runyan, who began teaching at Tuba City Boarding School in 1937, sought to enliven her nature lessons by introducing a stuffed owl to the classroom. The pupils, confronted by a taboo animal, "either voiced objection or 'shut me out' by maintaining a stony silence"—a description that likely underplays the children's sense of horror and affront. It was left to Diné teacher George Hood to salvage the situation by assuring the students that Runyan simply "had not known any better."[55] What appeared to non-Native teachers as harmless animals and objects could have a very different significance to the children and communities served by the schools.

Flora and fauna weren't the only subjects on the elementary science curriculum. Gertrude Giesen devised a science unit for her beginners' class at Fort Defiance boarding school that included "elementary water cycle—water forms—erosion—irrigation—growing season—resting season."[56] This was a clear attempt to correlate the school and soil conservation programs. In similar vein, Fred Richards taught an 8th grade unit entitled "Desert People and Their Water," which included a survey of dryland areas of the world; other nations' solutions to dryland problems; the relationship between agriculture and water; the water cycle; and desert soil and vegetation. According to Richards, the topic was selected because it represented "a real life situation" and involved such locally relevant material as family water supply, community water supply, wells, springs, and pumps. He noted that the lessons sprang "out of the interests and needs of the Navajo ways of life," although his follow-up statement that "since my pupils do not know exactly what they need and want, I have to want for them" suggests the demand did not originate from his students.[57] The water cycle and weather continued to feature prominently in school curricula. Norma Runyan, promoted to assistant supervisor of Indian Education six years after her rocky start at Tuba City, advised teachers that "additional elementary science should include observations of and activities designed to build toward the understanding of natural phenomena, such as: causes of cloud formations, of changing seasons, of what becomes of rain that falls, of causes of snow, of the workings of the water cycle ... of how the time of day changes and why."[58]

Runyan appeared oblivious to the cultural implications of this one-sided curriculum.[59] By teaching the children only Western scientific explanations for natural phenomena and disregarding metaphysical interpretations, the schools risked plunging their charges into debilitating cultural conflict of the sort noted by Anishinaabeg writer Basil Johnston. He recalled the "family schism" created when "a young scholar" fresh from science lessons at a Canadian residential school in the 1940s challenged his father's spiritual interpretation of lightning.[60] As Vine Deloria Jr. observed in the early 2000s, "One of the most painful experiences for American Indian students is to come into conflict with the teachings of science that purport to explain phenomena already explained by tribal knowledge and tradition. The assumption of the Western educational system is that the information dispensed by colleges is always correct, and that the beliefs and teachings of the tribe are always wrong."[61]

Yet back in the 1930s some educators did recognize that the monocultural science curriculum could create problems, and at least one raised the alarm. In November 1938, while employed by the BIA as a "curriculum specialist in the field of mathematics," future director of Navajo Schools George Boyce conducted a series of research trips across the United States with a view of devising "a program of scientific education" for the Navajo Service.[62] Boyce at that time had little practical experience of Indian Affairs—Beatty privately commented to Lucy Adams, "It is my present feeling that we need not expect any very concrete results from Mr. Boyce's visit immediately. While he is accustomed to analyzing situations in terms of their mathematical implications he is, of course, completely foreign to the Indian Service and to Indian problems."[63]

Despite such low expectations, Boyce perceived something that apparently Beatty and Adams had not: endemic contradictions within the BIA education program. He issued a prescient warning:

> The policy of the government, as the agent of society, seems to me to be aimed at a preservation of the inherent cultural values where they still persist in a given group. Many of these may be preserved. In many instances, desirable new values may be introduced or absorbed which are both desirable and inevitable. At some points, however, there is a direct conflict. For example, the introduction of the "scientific" explanation of various phenomena. When this happens, there is no driving force which would hold together the main reason for Navajo ceremonial and spiritual life as it has traditionally existed. What substitute values may be added to take the place of the older spiritual values, I am not prepared to say. The point which I note here is that a carefully-thought out philosophy of education, requiring considerable discussion, seems to be rather urgently needed.[64]

At that point in his life, and perhaps reflecting his unfamiliarity with Diné culture and religion, Boyce demonstrated Eurocentric and ill-founded pessimism concerning the future of Diné "spiritual values." Yet salient is his perception, despite being an outsider, that science lessons were in direct conflict with Diné traditional worldviews and religio-cultural values and that education directors urgently needed to resolve this. Beatty's reply to Boyce's warning is unfortunately not included in the archive.

Far from ignoring the potential for cultural conflict, some contemporary commentators outside of government welcomed the science onslaught. Note the tone employed by the Phelps-Stokes Report authors when describing what they viewed as "The Navajo Problem": "The Navajo problem is a most perplexing combination of Indian heritage, Indian customs and Indian ways of life in conflict with modern scientific programs of soil conservation." The report didn't merely acknowledge the existence of culture clash, it actively took sides—branding the Diné "a rural people who are exceedingly primitive and who place superstitious interpretations upon natural phenomena." Despite criticizing the Navajo Service education program for reliance on progressive education methods and the poor quality of some teaching personnel, Phelps-Stokes applauded the imposition of elementary science, arguing it should occupy "an important place" on the school program. Indeed, the authors depicted the "Navajo problem" as a clash between primitivism and modernity, a stalemate arising from "the failure to reconcile the tenacious and anxious devotion of the Navajo people to their customs and their language with the aggressive determination of able and devoted soil conservationists to save the soil elementally necessary to the very existence of the Navajos." The language is telling: while the Diné are dismissed in negative terms implying irrationality and agitation, the soil conservation personnel are hailed as not merely competent but as the only possible saviors of the land.[65]

The report went further in later chapters, casting Diné culture as an agent of active harm which could only be corrected through science education: the authors tasked the schools with eliminating "the dangers and limitations of the hogan, the hostility and ignorance of superstitious heritage, the determined opposition to soil conservation."[66] Indeed, Phelps-Stokes queried "whether many of the customs are a help or a hindrance in the adjustment of Indian life with American standards of living."[67] In this, the report reflected wider contemporary educators' concern at the ongoing impact of "superstition" in rural, non-white communities. Columbia University scholar Mabel Carney, an influential advocate of progressive education and cultural relativism, believed that natural science had an important role to play in rural African American schools; she described African American life in the 1930s as "not only predominantly rural but widely influenced by crude superstition requiring the searching rays of scientific knowledge for its eradication."[68] Decades earlier, home economics educators in New York had railed against what they perceived as harmful Eastern European and Italian superstitions concerning immigrants' pregnancy, birth, and childcare—as one reformer summarized, "The educator frequently finds herself confronted with superstition."[69] The battle lines between science and "superstition" in American educators' thought were longstanding and had evident racial and ethnic community targets.

Indian Service personnel in the 1930s generally refrained from attacking Diné culture in such overt terms, at least in writing. Words such as "primitive" and "superstition" rarely appear in official reports or correspondence from the period.[70] Nevertheless, references to positive and less positive aspects of Diné tradition were made by successive directors of Navajo Schools. Clyde Blair criticized the practice of abandoning homes following a death, which he felt accentuated a "tendency to move about" that "prevented better homes and the attendant accumulation of personal property other than livestock."[71] His successor, Lucy Adams, professed to accept Diné culture in principle but cautioned against apparent detrimental elements. She urged teachers to recognize that important learning took place in the home and community, not just the classroom. Yet she also advised that the school "should concern itself principally with strengthening and supplementing Navajo culture at those points where it is failing its own people, or where it does not control the knowledge necessary to manage its resources."[72] Somewhat unhelpfully for new Indian Service teachers, Adams did not explain what "failing" cultural aspects were. A similar vagueness permeated teacher Fred Richards's outwardly uncompromising claim that "the practices which are inimical to their [Diné] welfare ought to be discouraged." While he listed what he perceived to be valuable elements of Diné cultural heritage ("games, songs, arts, dances, history, customs, and folklore"), he didn't give a single example of "inimical" practices.[73] Rather than explicit attacks on Native cultures, as executed by earlier administrations, New Deal Indian Service personnel appear to have simply omitted from the curriculum anything they disagreed with, in effect replacing the assimilationists' active condemnation with silent dismissal.

Health Education

Elementary science lessons, in addition to promoting soil conservation, were extended to health, hygiene, and medicine. Indeed, the teaching of mathematics and English was secondary to health education in the government's list of priorities: the BIA supervisor of secondary education, Allan Hulsizer, described these subjects as "outgrowths" of sanitation education at the Navajo schools.[74] According to the Phelps-Stokes Report, the government schools were "the necessary allies of the medical service."[75] The Fort Defiance classroom outline for 1940–41 proclaimed, "We want them [the Diné] to have healthy bodies, adequate medical care, healthful hogans, and a chance for recreation."[76] Teacher Gertrude Giesen listed health as a specific objective for her beginners' class, with the aim "to have children living a wholesome life, with a minimum of nervous strain, in which good health practices (not too foreign to hogan procedures) become a part of daily life."[77] The emphasis on making hogans healthier environments did not waver: Assistant Supervisor of Indian Education Norma Runyan advised day-school teachers to incorporate health-related lessons in the elementary science curriculum, such as identifying and eliminating harmful insects within the home and imparting "some understanding" of indoor air currents and the necessity of ventilation. She was particularly concerned that children be taught "why it is very bad practice to entirely close up the 'smoke hole' in a hogan as some people do when a stove is installed."[78] In this last point Runyan appears to have been critiquing recent innovations in home facilities rather than traditional hogan design which incorporated ventilation.

Ora Medley, 6th grade teacher at Fort Defiance, went further in her health lessons towards a dismissal of traditional Diné home maintenance. She not only championed fresh air but also the importance of a clean hogan, which would make "home a healthier and happier place in which to live." The implication was that Diné children needed to be taught this at school because they could not learn this from their parents and that hogans were viewed as unsanitary environments. Medley instructed her pupils that "cleanliness is the foundation for Good Health" and taught them the importance of drainage, garbage disposal, and the dangers of flies. This education was intended for community as well as pupil ears: as Medley noted, "My main idea is to teach the child how to help his family... how to share what he has learned with all in his Community; make the lessons simple so that the child will understand how to tell others."[79] Ruth Underhill, in her history textbook for the Navajo schools, cautioned that "the earth-floored hogan, with its cosy fire and its scent of juniper smoke, would always be a good hiding place for germs."[80] Continuing this crusade against dirt floors, Phelps-Stokes observed that the schools sought to transform the hogan environment by promoting hard floors (easier for sweeping) and furniture which would serve the "fundamental" need of getting the occupants off the floor.[81] An article in *Indians at Work* by Dr. W. Peter, medical director of the Navajo-Hopi area, explicitly linked dirt floors, lack of ventilation, and multigenerational room occupancy to the spread of TB, charging that a typical Diné head of household "builds the kind of a family shelter which any aggressive tubercle bacillus, looking for new victims, must acclaim as the finest imaginable breeding place for tuberculosis." Indeed, Peter claimed, "In this respect Hosteen Navajo is his own worst enemy."[82] The Navajo Service thus strove to change existing Diné home practices and attitudes by replacing them with Euro-American views on health and homemaking.

And not just replacement. The impression given in many of the teachers' curriculum plans is that Diné healthcare did not exist, that health and hygiene were somehow alien to Indigenous communities. Diné practices simply did not appear in lessons and in staff correspondence. Time and again teachers proclaimed that "health habits must be formed," that the children must "develop good health habits," and that rudimentary healthcare, including care of the eyes, nose, hair, feet, nails, and skin, needed to be taught at school. Dolls were used to teach beginners dressing and bathing of infants, feeding, and first aid.[83] The notion of parents and family as primary healthcare providers does not seem to have been recognized; the teacher's role was to fill the apparent medical void by creating an awareness and appreciation of essential "health habits." Historian Donald Parman, writing in 1976, appeared to reflect this belief in 1930s Diné hygiene incompetence, arguing, "The Navajos' ignorance about sanitation also caused many illnesses. Their lack of outhouses, use of contaminated drinking water, and failure to wash cooking utensils and dishes properly all led to typhoid, diarrhea, and other intestinal disorders."[84] And the emphasis on healthcare education extended beyond the Navajo Reservation. Tohono O'odham children at BIA day schools began the school day with toothbrushing and face washing, while McCarty's Day School (UPA) attempted to stamp out impetigo through hygiene lessons, claiming, "We are trying to teach the children and through them the parents."[85] McCarty's even held a community "Health Day" in June 1938, which was scheduled for a Saturday so as to maximize attendance by men and boys who were at SCS camps and sheep tending during the week.[86] While healthcare provision for Diné, Pueblo, and Tohono O'odham communities was an important federal government obligation, and any practical bid to eradicate conditions such as impetigo, trachoma, and tuberculosis must have been welcome, the health education program was predicated on the paternalist assumption that hygiene was an alien concept to Indigenous cultures. As researcher Alice Joseph noted in her government-sponsored study of Tohono O'odham communities in the early 1940s, the schools' incessant promotion of Western hygiene rules "must often seem to the children an implicit criticism of home conditions."[87]

The condescension demonstrated by the Indian Service and medical researchers towards Indigenous communities' health and homemaking skills did not occur in a vacuum. Rather, it mirrored earlier attitudes towards immigrant communities in American urban centers. Progressive Era reformers, representing philanthropic organizations such as the New York Association for Improving the Condition of the Poor, were scathing regarding what they perceived to be immigrant women's ignorance of "American standards" of health and hygiene. A statement issued at a 1913 conference on immigrant education offers important parallels to the Indian Service's New Deal health program:

> The immigrant woman is ignorant of the value of fresh air, and in our campaign of education we have to make the mother of a family realize that ventilation prevents sickness and that sickness means expense before she will attempt to ventilate her home. The educator has to create a horror of flies by drawing attention to the flies on the filth in the street, and then showing how they convey germs into the house. Such a thing as ventilating clothing or comforters or pillows is unknown, and the educator shows that unheard of things are possible by assisting at the first bed cleaning.[88]

The contributor accused immigrant women of a profound ignorance of basic personal hygiene and antenatal care, claiming, "Personal service on the part of the educator is necessary to demonstrate *the methods* of personal cleanliness."[89] This indicates the prevailing faith in one correct (American) standard and practice over an acceptance of differing approaches to health and care—not to mention an apparent blindness to the impact of economic privation. Strikingly, the conference proceedings were prefaced by a letter from the commissioner of education, proclaiming tolerance for aspects of immigrants' "Old World" cultures: "For the enrichment of our national life as well as for the happiness and welfare of individuals we must respect their ideals and preserve and strengthen all of the best of their Old World life they bring with them."[90] As with the New Deal BIA, such cultural tolerance apparently didn't extend to respect for non-American healthcare and homemaking practices if they clashed with prevailing Western science-based beliefs.

Healthful homecare and sanitation education were also a feature of wider New Deal rural policy in the 1930s. Home Economics Extension agents sought to improve rural healthcare and raise living standards by instructing farm women in the latest canning, garbage disposal, and "New Housekeeping" techniques, urging them to relinquish such "antiquated methods" as washboards and brooms. Reflecting predominant 1930s Euro-American gender norms, this attempted uplift positioned women firmly in the domestic sphere, as homemakers and mothers, and discouraged farm women from participating in agricultural production and stock raising, which was viewed as a male preserve.[91] This "family wage ideal," reflecting primarily middle-class, Euro-American values, permeated Indian Service education policy as well—notably in the gendered vocational training and the emphasis on women as guardians of health and home. Indeed, this may explain the New Dealers' ignorant disregard of the key role of Diné women in the pastoral economy along with policymakers' focus on explaining stock reduction to male representatives.[92]

If "modern" hygiene was promoted as the vanguard in the fight against infection, diet constituted the preserver of health and formed another essential ingredient of the New Deal curriculum. Teachers taught the importance of a "balanced diet" to their charges—one that championed nontraditional (and unpopular) food such as lettuce.[93] Poultry, too, was promoted as a desirable addition to Diné meals: according to Howard Roberts of the Tuba City school agriculture division, "A few hens on many of the Navajo farms would not only be a step toward greater independence but a stride toward securing a better balanced diet which is sorely lacking in the Navajo menu."[94] Roberts may have been referring to economic privation stemming from the Depression and soil crisis, but the implication is that, once again, government personnel viewed existing Diné practice as deficient. Anthropologist Alice Joseph was even more scathing in her dismissal of the traditional Tohono O'odham diet, deeming it "inadequate" and so lacking in vitamin C as to damage children's gums and general health.[95] This contrasts with the approach depicted by Collier in the 1940

Annual Report to the Secretary of the Interior, in which he claimed, after careful study, "native" foods were being included on some boarding school menus. The message appeared to be that, following official (presumably government-directed) research, *some* traditional foods were worth keeping and that Native children had the right to choose their diets.[96]

This approach was translated into practice, at least at Fort Defiance boarding school. Traditional Diné foods secured a place on the curriculum—albeit at the end of a long list of "specific learnings" associated with daily lunch. Gertrude Giesen used lunch to teach beginners a formidable array of lessons:

> English—politeness—proper ways of handling foods and utensils, conversation during meals—proper ways of eating and of sitting at the table—cleaning up after eating—washing before eating—values of foods—contents of foods—where various foods come from—gardens and orchards in relation to foods—what other animals enjoy same foods—Navajo foods—ways of preparing and eating Navajo foods—careful dishwashing, rinsing and wiping—care of sick people's dishes.[97]

This active teaching of Diné foods and food preparation at a government school marks a clear break from earlier BIA attitudes towards Native traditional diets and culinary techniques. However, the unfortunate proximity in the list to utensil hygiene and illness, and the absence of positive descriptors such as "proper," suggests a perceived dietary hierarchy; in the educators' minds, Diné cuisine occupied a lower tier than Euro-American diets. This blended tolerance and condescension reflected the tone of the aforementioned *Annual Report to the Secretary of the Interior*, which stated that studies of Indigenous foods and food preparation techniques had been undertaken "in the belief that it is neither necessary nor desirable to change the dietary habits of Indian children simply because these do not coincide with our own tastes." These foods were added to boarding school menus, "thus giving dignity to native customs and encouraging children to evaluate their own practices before discarding them for new ways." On the one hand, the Indian Service was promoting Indigenous foods at the schools, yet in the same breath it was suggesting that students might well be rejecting them in favor of "new ways." Once again, the *tone* suggests a perceived dietary hierarchy, even if the *practice* (food inclusion) did not.[98] Interestingly, what the report didn't mention was the vital support sometimes provided by parents and grandparents who delivered much-needed mutton, pumpkins, and corn to the Navajo boarding schools—less a case of school tolerance of Native foods than a reliance upon them when school supplies and gardens failed.[99]

Unhealthy Schools

Despite the emphasis on "proper" health and dietary and hygiene standards, Navajo and UPA school records from the New Deal era are replete with references to pupil illness. Taos Day School, one of the larger and better-equipped UPA plants, reported attendance problems due to a protracted mumps "epidemic" from April to June 1937 and an influenza "epidemic" in March 1938.[100] Influenza outbreaks also struck Nutria Day School in spring 1937 and Cochiti Day School in spring 1939, while twenty-five pupils were incapacitated with flu at Huerfano Day School in fall 1943.[101] A "light epidemic" of whooping cough was reported at San Juan Day School in May 1943, while an attack at Picuris Day School was blamed for poor attendance rates in fall 1937.[102] Cochiti Day School appears to have suffered prevalent outbreaks of serious illness, including mumps in September 1936, a typhoid epidemic in spring 1937 which "greatly reduced" attendance, and whooping cough in May and June 1938, followed by a "colds epidemic" in spring 1940.[103] These illness bouts evidently caused sufficient harm to attendance rates that teachers recorded them in their quarterly reports. They also alarmed parents, who understandably began to associate the schools with the spread of disease. Following a meningitis outbreak in the area served by Teec-nos-pos Day School (Navajo), the local school board representative, Chester Tso, visited all families with school-age children to find out why they had stopped sending them to school. He reported that "these people refuse to send their children to school until this disease has disappeared or to their mind been controlled."[104] While the school may not itself have caused the outbreak, the parents clearly believed that their children were at risk of contracting meningitis at the school and so withdrew them accordingly.

None of the attendance reports cited above lists the source of the outbreaks. However, facilities in some schools in the 1930s and 1940s left a lot to be desired. A note added to the bottom of the November 30, 1941, quarterly attendance report for Laguna Day School stated, "Extremely cold school room responsible for numerous colds among 2–4 grades."[105] In this case, the school itself—far from being a haven of healthful education—was actually making the children ill. Other reports, while not going so far as to link the schools to illness, did note conditions which actively contradicted the health lessons they promoted, such as this 1937 communiqué from teacher Miguel Trujillo of Paraje Day School: "I am forced to complain again about our water supply for the school. We have been out of water for the entire plant—children's toilets, toilets in our quarters and for other domestic purposes—for three days. . . . We would also like to have a sanitary drinking fountain or water cooler as the children are now drinking from buckets." Trujillo's exasperated tone is hard to ignore—indicating the water failure was no anomaly.[106]

And sanitation problems persisted across the day school network in the Southwest. Isleta Day School had no working bathrooms in September 1937; teacher William Shoop reported that while the old ones had been removed, no new bathrooms had been built which meant the children had to use outdoor privies without handwashing facilities.[107] The reply from UPA superintendent Sophie Aberle was hardly reassuring: low funds rendered help impossible.[108] The bathhouse and toilets at Mesita Day School were condemned as "unsanitary" in October 1938 due to "improper" installation and drainage. Assistant Supervisor of Education Louise Wiberg advised teachers against using the bathhouse, thereby acknowledging the health risk—yet again the BIA pleaded lack of funds.[109] Taos Day School had reported a similar predicament in March 1936: Principal Leroy Jackson denounced the failure to build new toilets in the grade-school building following the condemnation and razing of the old ones. In addition, sewage from the hospital had flooded the school garages and created a "dangerous" hole—a double risk for the children's health.[110] In a possibly related development, teachers reported a major fly problem in September 1937, worsened by the absence of external screens for the school doors.[111] Flies were high on the curriculum's list of health enemies, so one wonders how the teachers were able to promote the BIA's wellbeing agenda to the children while the BIA school so flagrantly failed to follow it. Ruth Underhill, in her history textbook *Here Come the Navaho!*, may have dismissed Diné traditional measures concerning flies: "Their myths said nothing about keeping flies away from food."[112] Yet some government schools were conspicuously doing nothing to keep the bugs at bay. The screens advocated by Western science were apparently as elusive as any religious or cultural intervention.

Unhealthy and dangerous environments at some schools weren't the only obstacles to the health education agenda. Collier promoted the day schools as local health centers where medical personnel could administer inoculations and treatments and where teachers could cater to pupils' and parents' basic health-care needs—he claimed the schools were "bringing both children and adults into closer and continuous contact with health objectives."[113] In practice, though, not everyone benefitted from medical attention. In her report on Red Rock Day School (Navajo) dated February 1943, Norma Runyan noted there was still no thermometer on the premises. Incidentally, she urged the teacher to place "greater emphasis on health habits" in the lessons.[114] The predicament at Sanostee Day School in early 1936 was particularly concerning. In a report denouncing the dangerous state of the recently renovated school buildings, secretary of the Sanostee School Chapter, James Cohoe, also condemned the absence of a local doctor. Cohoe asked:

> When we are going to have the doctor, whom we were promised to have here at all times to help us in emergency cases, this promise was made when the agreement was made in having a day school here, we certainly do need a doctor here at all times, for such cases as we had on Jan. 16 1936 when a student of this school was hit on the head with a bat while playing.[115]

Cohoe and the Sanostee community therefore wanted the school to fulfil its obligation to provide medical care for pupils—a service already offered at the boarding schools. The reply from the superintendent of the Navajo Reservation, Chester Faris, was disappointing. Faris made no reference to any promise of resident medical personnel at the day school; rather, he believed that the nurse based in neighboring Newcomb was making regular visits to Sanostee. Faris did promise to talk with the director of health, Dr. W. W. Peter, about the possibility of increased doctor/nurse visits, yet this hardly squared with what the Sanostee community was expecting from their school.[116] Delegate Robert Martin raised similar concerns at a Navajo Tribal Council meeting: "We are also much concern [sic] about health conditions among our people. We have very little help in this matter. Mr. Collier promised our people that he will establish a field nurse at every day school and a doctor to hold a clinic at all day schools. Where are they, we do not see them."[117]

As Wade Davies has noted, the BIA did "rely heavily" on schoolteachers to provide medical care for pupils, notably the hated trachoma treatments, yet Martin and Cohoe's statements show the need, and indeed community demand, for trained medical personnel at the day schools.[118] This was a long-standing concern. In 1928 the Meriam Report had warned that the medical attention given to children at government day schools was "below a reasonable standard."[119] In May 1931, testimony from Picuris Pueblo representatives before a Senate subcommittee revealed that the government doctor, based at Taos, had only visited Picuris three times in the past year (acknowledged by Senator Lynn Frazier as "not often enough") and was frequently unable to get through in winter when roads were blocked for "weeks at a time." Consequently, teacher Miguel Trujillo supplied the Picuris community with medicine and basic "remedies"—indeed, his multitasking prompted them to request his salary be increased, "because our teacher serves as teacher and at other times he serves as doctor and as taxi cab driver."[120] Despite the concerns expressed in the Meriam Report and at the Senate hearings, the complaints levied by Martin and Cohoe reveal that medical provision at the more remote Navajo and UPA day schools remained resoundingly inadequate through the 1930s. That many participants in the Wingate adult short course in December 1939 utilized the boarding school's dental and medical facilities also suggests the day schools were hardly fulfilling their promised role as community health hubs.[121]

Attitudes Towards Diné Medical Practitioners

New Deal Indian Service attitudes towards health education cannot be separated from their attitudes towards Indigenous spiritual healers, also known as "singers" and "medicine men" or "medicine women." Diné traditional medicine views illness as an expression of disharmony, so traditional healers seek to restore harmony through both ritual and pharmacological treatment. Traditional medicine has a spiritual dimension; one scholar describes the Diné healing system as "sacred, the very core of Navajo religion."[122] In the first decades of the twentieth century, government officials and philanthropic observers reacted unfavorably to traditional medical practices, branding them mere superstition that was at best ineffectual and at worst harmful to patients.[123] However, scholars of government healthcare policy have noted a change in Indian Service attitudes to Diné healers in the mid-1930s, as Collier urged medical personnel to demonstrate sensitivity to Diné religious and cultural beliefs.[124] Collier's attitude towards Native medicine stemmed largely from his belief in religious freedom. His analysis of Indian healthcare in his 1940 report to the secretary of the interior contained a defense of religious liberty—"essential to a democracy"—and a portrayal of Native American "curing ceremonials" as "an essential part of their faith."[125] He argued that the "modern methods" of healthcare workers "must continually be adjusted to the ancient beliefs, ceremonies, traditions, and taboos of the many Indian tribes"—in other words, that Western medicine had to take Indigenous religio-cultural considerations into account.[126]

This defense flew in the face of contemporary Christian missionary medicine on the Navajo Reservation, notably the efforts of Dr. Clarence Salsbury, director of the Sage Memorial Hospital. From 1934 to 1938, Salsbury held an annual four-day chautauqua at the Presbyterian Mission at Ganado which featured gospel teaching, dry farming and tanning lectures by boarding school graduates, and a medical and dental clinic. The event proved popular, attracting hundreds of Diné attendees each year, perhaps in part from the impressive staffing levels: twenty-five doctors and fifteen nurses operated the clinics. Salsbury publicly linked Western medicine with Christianity as the twin embodiments of progress, and he railed against what he perceived to be damaging Indigenous religious practices such as the use of peyote by the Native American Church. Indeed, an external sign at Ganado bore the legend "Tradition is the Enemy of Progress," which countered Collier's claim that sings posed no threat to Diné healthcare.[127] Future tribal chairman and missionary Jacob Morgan, writing in September 1934, hailed the first chautauqua for its promotion of Christianity and simultaneously criticized the Indian Service for acting "to encourage the Indians to keep their own paganistic practices."[128] In response, Collier discouraged BIA personnel from attending the chautauquas, and in 1938 the Indian Service established an annual tribal fair at Window Rock, which featured clinics run by government doctors, without Christian proselytizing.

Greater tolerance of Diné healing beliefs was demonstrated by Dr. W. W. Peter, who was appointed supervisor of the government's Navajo medical program in 1934. Peter's immediate concerns were to expand the TB immunization program and to increase the number of field nurses working on the reservation, with a view to preventing the spread of infectious diseases, notably TB and trachoma. Despite this concerted promotion of Western medicine, Peter did not seek to eliminate Diné healing ceremonies. In fact, he requested a Blessing Way ceremony to dedicate the new Fort Defiance Medical Center in 1938. Far from being ignored or challenged, practitioners of traditional Diné medicine were being invited to practice publicly at a BIA-sponsored institution. Collier claimed the government extended the invitation "as evidence that it by no means wished to interfere with or belittle the Medicine Man's religious role in tribal life."[129] Yet the dedication ceremony, as important as it was, did not in itself represent Peter's acceptance of non-Western medicine. The occasion was, to the BIA and Health Service, one of commemoration, honoring, and festivity—not an endorsement of the ceremony as a medical treatment.

Anthropologists also influenced the debate over Diné traditional medicine—and actively sought to mold the attitudes of BIA and Heath Service personnel. In 1944 Alexander and Dorothea Leighton, psychiatrists who blended Western medical knowledge with anthropology, published *The Navaho Door*, which Collier's preface described as "a study of Navajo healing institutions," intended initially for Indian Service workers.[130] Following a four-month visit to the Navajo Reservation, the Leightons accepted that healing occupied a key role in Diné religion; they also appreciated that medicine, education, religion, economics, agriculture, industry, and societal norms were interlinked and so could not be addressed or altered in isolation.[131] Significantly, they moved beyond a recognition of the public relations value of tolerating healing ceremonies and praised the surgical skills of singers who knew much practical medicine (as the Leightons viewed it) such as bone setting and abscess treatment.[132] They also professed potential respect for singers' expertise in pharmacology, postulating, "It is possible that some of their herbs have medicinal properties that are unknown to us"—though this phrasing suggests conjecture rather than acknowledgement of skill.[133] The Leightons were at pains to stress to their readers the benevolent and conscientious nature of singers, noting they did not impose their services on patients: "To suppose that the Singer is a wily charlatan is... to do an injustice to his character."[134] This challenged unfavorable US public perceptions of "medicine men" as exploitative charlatans.

For example, the Jesuit priest Louis Goll had publicly denounced Lakota spiritual healers as "clever and cunning men ... [who] wielded a baneful influence over the people, making them believe that they had seen visions or had had significant dreams after going through certain rites of fasting."[135] The trader Sallie Wagner, who operated the Wide Ruins trading post on the Navajo Reservation in the 1940s, continued this theme of self-interested shamans in her memoirs. She detailed her outrage at being informed by a Diné "medicine man" that if she wished to attend a sing as spectator she must "Pay or Stay Away." Wagner felt "hurt and angry and embarrassed" at this treatment and devoted a page and a half to outlining her discontent—while making no mention of either the patient's condition or the outcome of the ceremony.[136]

The Leightons did not view the pecuniary aspect of sings as an indication of the singer's moral corruption or fakery. Rather, they argued that the "very considerable investment" by a patient's family merely indicated that "the Navajo like ourselves are prone to develop strong faith in anything that has cost them time, money and thought." Indeed, they equated the singer with an American "country doctor" who imparts "good, sound, practical advice based on his knowledge of his people."[137] This, together with their assessment of singers as "usually an intellectual type," contrasted sharply with earlier non-Indigenous depictions of "primitive," corrupt, and incompetent medicine men.[138]

According to Wade Davies, the Leightons urged government medical staff to treat the Diné healers as colleagues, not rivals.[139] Yet despite their bid to present healers as sincere and competent health workers, the overriding thrust of the Leightons' work appears firmly to position the singers as *junior* colleagues rather than as peers. They urged government doctors to treat them "as colleagues *to some extent*," which involved permitting singers to witness surgical operations at the hospitals.[140] The healers, when faced with Western medicine, were therefore to occupy the position of observers and not active participants in the medical process. The Leightons appear to have valued the psychological benefit of traditional Diné healing, rather than its actual curative power or practical efficacy beyond what they viewed to be basic care. In their view, "Navajo religion offers powerful suggestive psychotherapy which can certainly aid states of anxiousness and render the physically ailing better able to bear their illness."[141] A researcher working with Tohono O'odham communities shared the view that medicine men's work had strong psychotherapeutic value, reporting that "government doctors on Indian reservations are coming to see this point and to make use of the medicine man rather than to decry him."[142] This chimes with Collier's 1934 statement that "their functions in the sphere of mental healing are important," which he immediately followed with the claim that singers "do not offer any significant resistance to modern medicine."[143] Again, the singers were presented as subordinates and not peers, whose value lay in easing psychological stress, posing no barrier to the vital implementation of Western medicine.

Anthropological thought in the New Deal era tended to emphasize cultural tolerance as a prerequisite for successful cultural adaptation. As John M. Cooper, president of the American Anthropology Association, wrote in 1940, "A knowledge of native health concepts and practices is, as a rule, a necessary first step toward efficient medical service in many of its important phases."[144] Alice Joseph, in a BIA-commissioned anthropological study of Tohono O'odham communities, claimed that acceptance of Western medicine was linked to the physician's sympathetic attitude to traditional culture: "Much depends upon the white doctor's attitude toward Indian beliefs. If he does not openly condemn the medicine man and gives due credit to their effectiveness, if he is willing and able to answer a call under any circumstance, he begins to gain the respect and co-operation of the people. But if he seems dogmatic and unsympathetic to the Indians, they mistrust and fear him."[145] The Leightons also advised that non-Diné medical personnel should acquaint themselves with Diné cultural beliefs and language in order to transmit medical knowledge more effectively. Their statement to this effect is illuminating:

> If our medicine is to help and not harm the Navajo, we must avoid clean sweeps. We must get them to accept and use our pertinent, practical knowledge without undermining their faith. That faith must grow and adjust also, but it must not be ruthlessly attacked simply because it offers some obstacles to medicine. Instead, white medicine should be expressed to the Navajos in terms of their own culture, in ways that fit into their understanding of the world and their scale of values. The physicians who have contact with the Indians could do much if they knew some of the fundamentals of the Indian's outlook and religion.... If one wins the friendship of a few Navajo and takes time to listen, he

will learn much that will be of practical value when it comes to managing therapy.[146]

In other words, understanding Diné religion was the key to securing Diné *acceptance* of Western medicine—a goal which implies the latter's curative superiority. Secondly, the statement, while seeking to protect Diné "faith" from being "ruthlessly attacked," does describe some aspects as "obstacles to medicine," thereby contradicting Collier's earlier pronouncement.

The depiction of Diné faith as a potential barrier to the progress of Western medicine was no isolated reference in the Leightons' work. In *The Navaho Door*, published four years after their plea for cultural understanding, they argue that the singers' treatment of contagious diseases and complex surgical cases was ineffective; indeed, they suggest that many people delayed hospital treatment until after a sing had been performed, with negative results. To combat such practices, the Leightons urged government doctors to assume the role of "health-educators" to teach the Diné health and hygiene. They insisted that Diné religion should not be attacked in the process ("It will not be necessary, nor desirable, to try to do away with Navaho religion") but that "the people and the practitioners [singers] will have to come to recognize the difference between the sort of illnesses that need hospital care at once and those they can care for at home, and to learn how to use their resources to produce better health." This education extended to cultural modification: in addition to delaying sings until after hospital treatment, singers were advised to adapt the ceremonies to minimize the level of exertion for patients—for example, waiting four months before holding a sing for TB sufferers who had been hospitalized.[147]

This limited cultural tolerance towards Diné traditional medicine was also reflected at the highest echelons of the Indian Service. Despite defending the religious basis of Native medical systems in his 1940 report to the secretary of the interior, Collier seemed most interested in reassuring his superior that Diné healers posed no threat to the Health Service program. His praise for traditional medicine was largely limited to "the mental stimulus produced by the powerful songs" and an acknowledgement of the curative benefits of certain herbs, massages, sweat baths, and cauterizations performed by traditional healers. While the defense of religious freedom was a welcome departure from earlier policy, Collier, by largely confining Diné medicine to the religious sphere (which in Euro-American thought was distinct from the scientific/medical sphere), failed to accept medical value in Diné curative practice beyond the spiritual/psychological and the rudimentary treatment realms. He proclaimed that healers' participation in the dedication ceremonies "demonstrated a reciprocal appreciation and *realization of their own limitations* in the face of modern science."[148] This indicates a perceived knowledge hierarchy in New Dealer thought, which elevates Western medical practice over Diné curative religio-cultural practice.

The division between "religion" and "medicine" was made explicit in discussions over content for the proposed 1939 Indian Service Summer School training program. The course featured a segment entitled "Courses in Subject Matter Related to Basic Indian Service Problems"—tellingly, this included such topics as "Water, Soil and Livestock," "Health Education," and "Navajo Medicine Men and their Cures."[149] The latter was taught by anthropologist Ruth Underhill. Superintendent Fryer and John Provinse, an anthropologist involved in range management planning on the Navajo Reservation, expressed concern that Underhill's course should "not deal too specifically with Navajo medicine men and their cures."[150] This wasn't motivated by concern for protecting sacred knowledge. Provinse advised that Indian Service personnel should learn only the cultural and spiritual context of Diné medicine, rather than curers' empirical knowledge. In his opinion, "I think this medical lore, whether good or bad, should not be presented without a rather complete presentation of the spiritual and social organization out of which it arises. To present it otherwise would seem to me to allow either for an undue glorification of the native medicine man or misunderstanding of the medical problem on the Reservation, which goes much beyond mere cooperation with the native curers."[151] He urged Homer Howard, supervisor of in-service training, to "stay away from the presentation of too many facts of Indian diagnosis, prescriptions, and cures, and only draw on the available information for illustrative material to complete the broader background of Indian 'medicine' as a part of the religious experience." The main aim was to inform school and medical personnel of the "social and spiritual world" of their pupils and patients and so imbue them with tolerance of Diné cultural values and beliefs.[152] By treating Diné medical beliefs and practices as purely religious, Provinse implied he did not recognize them to be medically effective. Indeed, he did not believe anyone could legitimately advise Health Service personnel "of the nature and efficiency of some of the native prescriptions."[153] In response to this argument, the lesson title was changed to "Indian Religious and Curing Concepts," removing any reference to medicine.[154]

The distinction drawn by Provinse (and Collier) between "religion" and "medicine" is significant. It shows that while leading New Dealers understood that Diné medicine had a spiritual foundation, and that religious beliefs should not be actively denigrated or prohibited, they themselves did not view Diné medicine as *actual medicine*, capable of effecting diagnoses, treatments, and cures. Instead, they saw it as esoteric and intangible. This reflects sociologist Clayton Dumont Jr.'s argument that Western scientists, when defending their theories and approaches, have tended to depict Native arguments and viewpoints as "rooted in the 'irrationality' of 'myth,' 'superstition,' and 'religion.'"[155] Collier may not have viewed Native religious beliefs as irrational, but he did not see them as equal to scientific knowledge in the fields of medicine and ecology. And even this limited cultural tolerance was missing in some jurisdictions. Anthropologist Laura Thompson concluded that "the policy of the Indian Service medical officers in the Hopi jurisdiction is to make no concessions to native custom. Deviations from established medical practices in favor of the native way are not allowed." Non-Hopi doctors' rigid insistence on hospital diets that contradicted Hopi customs, and their demand upon hot cereal baby food rather than traditional cornmeal gruel, inspired many Hopi women to reject the government health program altogether. This was the early 1940s—yet "cultural tolerance" amongst Indian Service medical staff towards Hopi beliefs and practices was clearly in very short supply.[156]

What can we learn from the science education in BIA schools in the 1930s and early 1940s? The soil conservation and healthcare elements of the BIA's education program on the Navajo Reservation certainly bore little resemblance to biculturalism. Schools were charged with promoting the federal government's range management policy and therefore had to instill an acceptance of Western science—which they taught to the total exclusion of Diné metaphysical interpretation and experiential knowledge. Scientific knowledge was highly valued in federal government and academic circles in the 1930s: as Kluckhohn and Leighton approvingly noted, "Whatever its defects, the government program has been without a doubt one of the closest approaches yet achieved to an intelligent, planned, and integrated application of scientific knowledge to the practical affairs of a whole people."[157] Their positive appraisal contrasts sharply with the view expressed by Indian Wells chapter officials before a senate subcommittee: "Soil erosion is important but must recognize the Navajo people, not be allowed to dominate the situation. Those in charge of it are more concerned with the scientific aspect of the matter than with the human side."[158] Whereas Diné representatives offered the possibility of a shared strategy that recognized the threat of erosion but wasn't science dominated, New Dealers valued science alone. Just as with history, the New Dealers subscribed to a knowledge hierarchy: science was assumed to hold the best answers to problems of an ecological, agricultural, or medical nature, whereas Diné pastoral knowledge was assumed by non-Diné to be inadequate and ripe for replacement with the latest American techniques. Significantly, in the arena of ecology and farming, the bureau did not seem to value traditional Diné beliefs or even recognize that these policies could conflict with Diné religion.

Yet in the healthcare sphere, the government's approach was slightly more nuanced. Diné health habits, diet, and even childcare techniques were assumed to be inferior to Euro-American practices. Federal healthcare teams were, however, urged to value both the psychological benefits of traditional Diné healthcare and the ceremonial aspects—in other words, the acceptance of the performance of ceremonies as religious rites. This did not, however, extend to the acceptance of traditional healing practices as equal to Euro-American medicine. A Shiprock School science report is particularly telling in this respect. Recalling a lesson on disease and digestive enzymes, the teacher noted, "We made no derogatory statements about the Navajo medicine man, but some of the students were thinking of this problem and doubted their efficiency, but praised their use of various herbs to cure sickness."[159] In this Eurocentric knowledge hierarchy, the singer had a foot on the knowledge ladder several rungs below the Indian Service doctor. New Dealer attitudes towards Diné traditional medicine also have implications for the "safety zone" concept. Take, for example, this passage from *The Navaho Door*, which was intended as a guide for Indian Service personnel: "Beliefs can and do become cumbersome, bringing their owners handicaps and inabilities to meet changing circumstances, but in helping people adjust themselves, one must be sure he is not attacking beliefs and practices *vital* to their welfare."[160] The perceived need to jettison only those practices deemed "cumbersome" by government employees at first glance suggests the safety zone: the tendency of the federal government to distinguish between "safe" and "unsafe" cultural practices while permitting those it deemed innocuous. Yet the language used doesn't indicate safety. The Leightons—approved by Collier—described the beliefs and customs to be saved as "vital" to communities' welfare. Vital, as opposed to harmless. However, the government reserved itself the right to decide what was "cumbersome" and what was "vital."

The simultaneous and seemingly antithetical promotion of Western science and defense of Indigenous religions reflects the New Dealers' insistence on viewing the "scientific" and "religious" as two wholly separate spheres, as evidenced in Collier's florid reflections on the Taos Pueblo community in the early 1920s:

> These tiny communities of the red man, archaic, steeped in a non-rational world-view of magic and animism and occult romanticism—it seems a wild if alluring fantasy that they might live on, that they might use the devices of modern economic life, and pragmatically take over the concepts of modern science, and yet might keep that strange past of theirs, that psychic and social present as it truly is ... so human and so mystic.[161]

The New Dealers therefore confidently prioritized "modern science" while erroneously imagining it could easily be separated from Native religions and treated as noncultural—as an impartial truth to be accepted by all. They viewed religion and culture as enduring entities founded on knowledge and ritual preserved from the past, which could be separated from lifestyle developments (health, economic, agricultural) in the present-day environment. Ritual could continue, while daily life underwent changes in line with modernity. While claiming to appreciate and admire Diné cultural "tenacity," Collier and his colleagues blithely imposed their own model of a compartmentalized society upon the Diné and so missed the opportunity to develop a shared, pluralist strategy to tackle ecological and medical challenges.

"Teacher and students in day school classroom," ca. 1940, Navajo Area Office. Source: Bureau of Indian Affairs, National Archives and Records Administration.

"Teacher with students learning sanitary kitchen practices in day school," ca. 1940, Navajo Area Office. Source: Bureau of Indian Affairs, National Archives and Records Administration.

(facing page) Top: "Young female day school student concentrating on spelling work book," ca. 1940, Navajo Area Office. Source: Bureau of Indian Affairs, National Archives and Records Administration. Bottom: "Male student dramatizing story," ca. 1940, Navajo Area Office. Source: Bureau of Indian Affairs, National Archives and Records Administration.

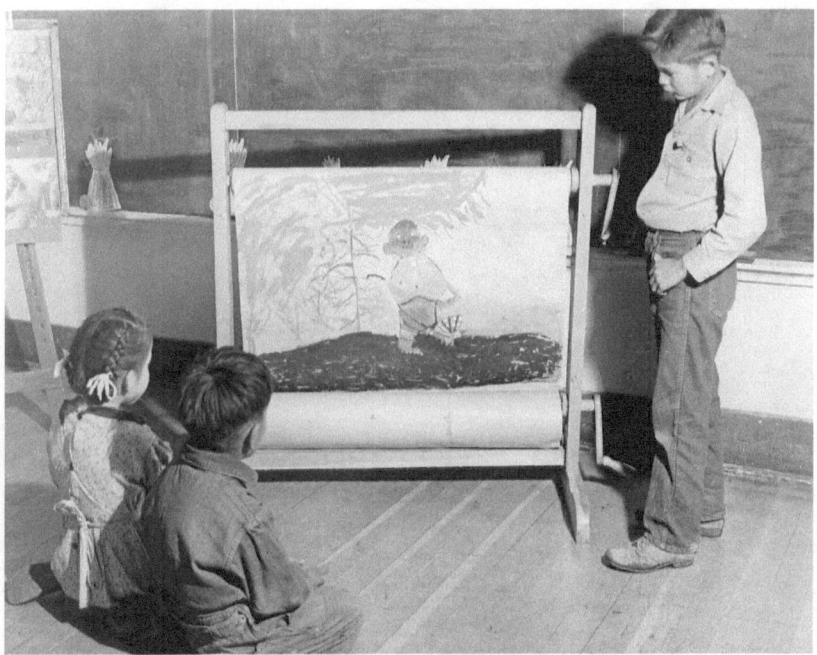

"Older students learning penmanship in day school," ca. 1940, Navajo Area Office. Source: Bureau of Indian Affairs, National Archives and Records Administration.

INDIGENOUS RELIGIONS AND THE INDIAN SERVICE SCHOOL PROGRAM

4

Indigenous religions and languages had been, with very limited exceptions, decidedly unwelcome in bureau schools before the 1930s.[1] Assimilation Era policymakers viewed Christianity and the Protestant work ethic as bringers of "civilization" and thus demonized traditional religions as pagan and "outmoded," while dismissing religious expression as a wasteful distraction from economic production.[2] Successive commissioners of Indian Affairs strove to prevent boarding school students and graduates from even attending traditional ceremonies and dances, with Circular 1665 (1921) and its Supplement (1923) seeking to restrict spectatorship of such events to those above fifty years of age. This indicates a bid to sever the younger generation from the religious and cultural practices of their elders, with a view to achieving eventual cultural extinction. In similar vein, up to the early 1930s BIA schools operated a rigid "English-only" policy which saw children harshly punished for daring to speak their Native languages. Religio-cultural expression and language constituted prime targets in the long-running assimilationist campaign; therefore, a key test of the New Dealers' cultural tolerance is how they treated them and whether they envisaged an active future for them, apart from the gradual cultural die-out anticipated by the Meriam Report.[3] This chapter explores the New Dealers' attempt to restrict unsolicited missionary (Christian) proselytization at the government schools. It then turns to the new policy of granting pupils leave of absence to attend community ceremonies before examining the extent to which teachers and BIA personnel displayed sensitivity to, and acceptance of, Native religions and cultures in the classroom and beyond.

The Order on Religious Instruction in the Indian Schools

Christian missionaries had embarked on concerted conversion efforts since the earliest days of European colonization of North America, establishing praying towns, churches, and schools for the purpose of Christianizing and "civilizing" Indigenous communities. In 1869 however, the relationship between missionary organizations and the federal government became more formalized as a part of President Grant's ill-fated "Peace Policy." Seeking to counter widespread corruption in Indian Affairs, Grant encouraged the aggrandizement of missionary influence on the reservations in the belief that Christian workers would be immune to such vices as cronyism and pecuniary greed. The result was the dividing of reservations between missionary denominations and the unfettered influx of missionaries to the government-controlled schools, where they exercised considerable spiritual influence over pupils. The marriage between Christian evangelization and assimilationist government policy appeared to be complete.

In January 1934, Collier issued a challenge to this symbiotic relationship between church and state. His Order on the Treatment of Religion in the Indian Schools immediately attracted accusations of anti-Christian and anti-assimilationist intent. By stipulating that missionary teaching at government schools could continue "as a privilege but not as a right" and stating that "intentional proselytizing in the Indian boarding schools is prohibited," Collier indicated that religious instruction in the classroom would be subject to regulation. On paper, the order clearly intended to restrict the untrammeled influence of missionaries at government schools: Christian teaching was permitted only if "there are children who by personal or parental choice seek the services of such missionary denomination." Likewise, compulsory attendance of church services and Sunday school was prohibited, except by parental consent.[4] While there is little evidence to suggest Collier canvassed support for this regulation from Native communities, some Diné leaders had previously expressed concern about the degree of influence exercised by missionaries. At a meeting of the Navajo Tribal Council in July 1926, Chairman Chee Dodge denounced missionaries' influence in education, exclaiming, "It looks like the missionaries drive our children away and drive us; we don't want to be driven; we want to have our own way."[5] His successor, Tom Dodge, also considered missionary influence a "topic on which we should take some definite action." In 1933 Dodge, himself a Catholic, issued the following statement:

> I think the Missionaries as a whole should be placed under some sort of regulation. I know as a fact that religion is one of the greatest forces in the world. I cannot conceive of a world that can exist with out [sic] religion. There is a practice among the Missionaries in this part of the country which is not quite desirable. By that I mean that the practice of Missionaries going forth upon the Reservation trying to sign children for their particular Faith is not quite desirable. Certainly that should be left entirely to each Navajo family. The Navajos themselves should have the right to choose the Faith that they want to profess.[6]

These statements indicate that missionary proselytization was being executed to a degree significant enough to be considered threatening by leading council members. The Phelps-Stokes Report (1939), while praising missionaries for their service and avowed desire "to help the people whom they serve," agreed that mistakes had been made. The authors cautioned against generalization, declaring it "unjust to regard missionary service as a process of ruthless imposition of convictions and modes of life on other people." However, they followed this up with criticism of evangelistic attitudes: "Unfortunately, some of the evangelistic types are inclined to exclude the human needs from their concerns and to limit their efforts to emotional appeals for conversion to belief in a religious creed. Such a conception of Christian service often becomes intolerant of racial heritage and tends to adopt the method of thoughtless imposition of creedal regulations upon others." When describing the Christian Reformed Board of Missionaries, Phelps-Stokes lamented that "the missionaries have not adequately realized the importance of working *with* the Navajos rather than *for* them. This means, of course, an earnest effort to understand and appreciate all that is worthwhile in the ceremonies and traditions of Indian life."[7] And the Meriam Report, hardly an unequivocal champion of cultural pluralism, had concluded that missionaries "have often failed to study, understand, and take a sympathetic attitude toward Indian ways, Indian ethics, and Indian religion."[8] The issuance of Circular 2970, with its promotion of religious tolerance, was therefore likely to meet resistance from those who believed conversion was an all-or-nothing enterprise.

Some missionaries did indeed interpret the regulations as a deliberate attempt to resurrect "outmoded" practices and to promote non-Christian religions. Vocal criticisms were directed at both the school regulations and Circular 2970 itself, and these tended to feature one or more of four key concerns: the primacy of Christianity as a global panacea; the alleged harmful nature of Native American traditional religious ceremonies and medical practices; possible fiscal exploitation and commercialization of traditional practices by unscrupulous entrepreneurs; and the fear that a policy which "emphasizes the native arts, crafts, religion, and life ... would make of the Indian a glass case specimen in the midst of a white man's civilization."[9] Some criticisms were indirect rather than explicit denunciations of traditional religions: the "Annual Report on Our Negro and Indian Missions" sent to all US Catholic clergy in 1935 declared that "Indian welfare and progress, corporate as well as individual, will be wrought only by Christian truths, values, and manner of living"—a statement that implicitly cast non-Christian faiths as inimical to "progress" and wellbeing.[10] The National Fellowship of Indian Workers (NFIW), an organization formed by field missionaries in 1935 specifically to protest Circular 2970, also promoted Christianity as the bringer of progress, proclaiming, "We recognize the constitutional rights of the Indian people to worship according to the dictates of their own conscience. As missionaries we are convinced, however, that in offering Christ we are offering what is best in culture and present well-being and also what is infinitely more worth-while,—the Christian hope of life everlasting."[11]

Both these statements posited welfare, rather than doctrine alone, as the key concern of missionary organizations. Individual missionaries couched their opposition in more lurid language, offering grim, allegedly eyewitness accounts of ritual self-scarification, extreme fasting, nudity, and apparent sexual debauchery. The message from contemporary and former field missionaries such as G. Lee Phelps and Elaine Eastman was that traditional Native ceremonies were not merely spiritually unedifying but severely hazardous to physical and moral health.[12] As one reservation superintendent noted, "One of the objections that has been raised to the present administration is the feeling of some of the missionaries that the

Office should continue a policy of suppression of Indian ceremonials."[13] Reverend J. H. Golden of Eagle Butte, South Dakota, put it more strongly to Collier: "It certainly does not require much brain to see clearly, that your high-sounded slogans 'Toleration' and 'Religious Liberty' not only make the Christian work of the missionary hard, in some cases impossible, but that your policies are detrimental to the spiritual and bodely [sic] welfare of the Indians." Indeed, he accused Collier of "ignorance or malice ... that you can't see or that you do not want to see and to admit the dangerous consequences for our poor Indians."[14] On the Navajo Reservation, George Boyce recalled some missionaries denouncing Diné religious beliefs as "pagan": "Any condoning of Medicine Men as having religious rights, or even attendance at Indian religious occasions, was viewed as support to the tenets of atheism."[15] Missionary and future tribal chairman Jacob Morgan used doctors' concerns to aid his denunciation of Circular 2970 which, he charged, strove "to encourage the Indians to keep their own paganistic practices" rather than following the twin emancipators, Christianity and American medicine.[16]

Even the more moderate missionary critics in the 1930s and 1940s opposed cultural tolerance on the grounds that it promoted artificial resurrection of "primitive" cultures and would, they feared, obstruct Native Americans' progress into the modern world. Nevill Joyner, Episcopalian priest-in-charge at Oglala Boarding School, feared that the new policy, coming after fifty years of state-sponsored Christianization programs, would only instill confusion in the younger generation. In his view, "These young people have not received and cannot receive from their parents whatever was good in the Indian religion of centuries ago; and no doubt there was much good in it as some old type of Indian lead us to believe." Joyner, who had spent decades promoting Christianity through churches and schools on Pine Ridge Reservation, viewed Native traditional religions not as active threats but as extinct—and Native parents as incapable of providing spiritual guidance for their children, a role that could only be fulfilled by Christian ministers.[17] Likewise, J. S. Bocher and Reverend Vander Stoep, who worked as missionaries on the Navajo Reservation in the 1930s, interpreted the new approach as a bid "to work back towards the native cultures, away from education, away from white man's practices," in effect a reversion to "the culture of Pre-Columbian days, whatever that could mean."[18]

Field missionaries thus cast themselves as protectors of Native communities against the apparent confusion, anti-modernism, and health risks that they feared a culturally tolerant education program would unleash.

The extent of the missionary backlash against both Circular 2970 and the school order suggests the policy was stringently implemented. However, historian David Daily has demonstrated that Christian missionaries continued to exercise considerable influence at some boarding schools throughout the New Deal. Missionaries lived on-site (and rent free) at Chemawa Indian School (Oregon) in 1944, and in 1942 Chilocco Indian School (Oklahoma) offered its students a credit-bearing course on religion and biblical studies, taught by a missionary. The NFIW, under the direction of avowed assimilationist G. E. E. Lindquist, urged missionaries to maintain a presence at the BIA schools through the performance of secular services designed to support overworked school personnel: for example, organizing weekend social activities and covering sick teachers' classes.[19] Such support was invaluable to bureau schools, especially in the period 1942–45 when many personnel were seconded to military service or war work. According to Daily, this proved "an effective strategy for preserving the missionary establishment in Indian education."[20] However, continued missionary *presence* at the schools does not in itself indicate widespread proselytization of children without parental consent—nor does secular activity alone contravene the 1934 order. Collier himself had stated that "nothing contained above [in the order] shall be interpreted as a prohibition or advice against the fullest participation by missionaries, ministers, or outside members of denominations, in the *secular* activities of the school," notably Scout and Campfire Girls activities and adult education programs.[21] The question therefore remains of whether the restriction on missionary *proselytization* was enforced or not.

Some flouting of the regulations undeniably occurred. In 1943 a matron at Oraibi government school admitted she encouraged Hopi pupils to attend weekly Christian services at the local Mennonite mission, irrespective of whether they had parental permission. Her justification of this "breach of federal regulation" was that the services were harmless and apparently had a pacifying effect on the children: "It doesn't do them any harm to be exposed to a little of the Gospel. Besides, we are glad to have something for the children to do one evening a week. It keeps them quiet."[22] This was no isolated occurrence. In 1935 the superintendent of Salem Indian School maintained pupil attendance at church services through a canny misreading of the regulation as an opt-out rather than opt-in system—excusing from church only those students whose parents expressly requested that their children *not* receive Christian teaching.[23] And in March 1935, Collier wrote the acting administrator of the Eastern Navajo Agency, William Zeh, to complain, "I am receiving indirect reports from the field that these instructions [regulations for religious worship and instruction], in some instances, are not being followed strictly in both the letter and the spirit." He reminded Zeh that they "must be followed."[24]

Individual school records show that the restrictions on missionary teaching were applied, at least in part, on the UPA and the Navajo Reservation. In 1936, Almira Franchville, associate supervisor of education (UPA), cautioned the teacher-in-charge at San Juan Day School that "it would be very unwise for you or your teachers to hold any of your students after school for religious instruction without first securing the written request of the children's parents." Franchville's opening statement was particularly telling: "I feel very strongly that the day schools and the day school personnel cannot afford to enter into any controversies over religious instruction, and I am very anxious that you be protected to as great an extent as possible."[25] Clearly Franchville feared that a flouting of the regulations would incur serious consequences.

The situation at Isleta Day School in 1938 was perhaps less fraught. The UPA general superintendent wrote Governor Pasqual Abeita to ask if he approved one hour's teaching per week by the Catholic Sisters for children with written parental consent. Abeita agreed.[26] This arrangement seems to have been widespread across the UPA: in 1940, Franchville issued a circular to day school teachers noting, "It has been customary in the Pueblos area to allow one hour a week for religious instruction at the day school, provided that parents request such instruction for their children and provided that certain missionaries or priests have been requested by parents to give instruction."[27] It therefore appears that parental consent for missionary teaching at UPA day schools was taken seriously.

Correspondence between General Superintendent E. R. Fryer and a missionary identified as Mrs. G. Bloomfield gives an indication of how the regulations were enforced on the Navajo Reservation. In 1942 Fryer informed Bloomfield that she had permission to give religious instruction to children at school provided she possessed signed written parental consent *and* the children had expressed a desire to attend. Fryer assured her, "You will be accorded the same courtesies shown other religious teachers who are authorized to use the school if such use does not conflict with the school schedules, and previously arranged religious instruction." This suggests a formal system was already in place to ensure the missionary regulations were adhered to. Yet Fryer also noted that no "regular" forms were used to obtain parental consent; rather, "The simplest possible statement showing that parental consent is given is all that is needed."[28] Church services were also held at Burnhams Day School by Mr. and Mrs. Jacob Morgan and Mr. Burd of Farmington Mission, and they were attended by thirty to forty adults, as recorded by Assistant Supervisor of Education Norma Runyan in her memorandum "Observations of Burnhams Day School" (January 1943). Runyan's matter-of-fact tone suggests such services were hardly extraordinary and indicates a cordial relationship between the school and missionaries—two teachers were even invited to attend.[29]

Tension between school personnel and missionaries did sometimes occur, however. In December 1941, Jacob Morgan wrote Leola Kessler, the girls' adviser at Shiprock Agricultural High School, to complain of mismanagement of religious activities by school employees. Morgan noted that since the beginning of the school year, six girls who were signed up for extracurricular bible class at the Camp School had failed to attend. Upon investigation, he learned they were detailed to the school dining room by the matron until six o'clock and then mistakenly sent to another missionary. Arguing that the matron "should help to carry out the program," Morgan informed Kessler that "I shall appreciate it if you would give notice that these girls, and any other girls who with their own free will want to attend our Bible classes to come. We do not draw any line to bar out any body."[30] In her reply Kessler noted that one girl was not recorded as belonging to Morgan's church and that "the matron can only follow the enrollment slip unless the parents wish to change it." She reminded him that "church attendance is no longer compulsory in our schools"—thereby indicating the enforcement of the regulations. But Kessler then acknowledged the "greater part" of the Shiprock student body did attend church services, and she assured Morgan that the school's Tuesday meal schedule had been rearranged in a manner that "will work out better for the churches."[31] Kessler therefore operated a system which simultaneously obeyed the regulations yet made concessions to local missionaries. Interestingly, the strong pupil interest in church services at the Shiprock School was perhaps not characteristic of the reservation schools as a whole: Phelps-Stokes claimed that many older pupils tended "to follow their own desires" concerning religion and that since 1934 many had eschewed contact with the missionaries altogether.[32]

A further controversy between Jacob Morgan and the Shiprock School concerned the timing of Christmas entertainments. In December 1940, due to "considerable misunderstanding" between church and school, the Navajo Church's Christmas program was held on the same night as the school's holiday event. Morgan charged that the church had selected Tuesday on the grounds that "Tuesday is recognized as the night set aside for religious instructions" and that the eleventh-hour notification of the school's competing event ensured "our program was ruin [sic] by such action at the last moment." Writing in December 1941, Morgan requested advance notice of the school's program so as to avoid "any friction." However, he expressed hope that Tuesday night would be reserved for religious instruction.[33] A prompt reply from Principal Arthur Snyder assured Morgan that the church could keep its program on Tuesday, December 23rd, and the school would hold its program the following day. Snyder concluded his letter on a conciliatory note: "I appreciate your calling my attention to this problem and I wish you a most successful service."[34] Again, the problem appears to have been miscommunication rather than any infringement of, or ill will over, the regulations—although it is significant that Morgan had to bring the matter to Snyder's attention and not the other way around.

More entrenched tension between missionaries and Navajo Service personnel was recalled by Morris Burge, a field representative for the American Association of Indian Affairs in the late 1930s. In a 1970 interview with Donald Parman, Burge claimed Collier's aim was "to see that Navajo children had the right to practice Navajo religion," and in his view the policy had generated "a good deal of fear and opposition on the part of the missionaries." Indeed, Burge felt "the missionaries had good reason to be opposed to Collier and the program, and the general influence of the government," indicating that, in his opinion, the school regulations were being implemented.[35] The Phelps-Stokes Report also described friction between missionaries and Indian Service personnel, noting that some missionaries felt unwelcome at the government schools, and some bureau employees believed it "expedient" to avoid any interest in missionary services. This suggests two things: firstly, that some missionaries felt threatened and undermined by the policy of religious tolerance; and secondly, that some bureau personnel believed the administration was actively hostile to missionary involvement in education. The impact was considerable: according to Phelps-Stokes, the 1934 regulations had created a change in long-established relationships between the Navajo Service and missionaries.[36]

The bid to curtail missionary influence at the government schools, based upon the New Deal administration's desire to preserve freedom of conscience, therefore generated significant criticism both from missionaries and proponents of a total assimilation policy towards Native Americans. As such, it hardly constituted a "safe" policy approach for the BIA. By seeking to bar Native children from unsolicited Christian indoctrination, Collier's order suggests the New Deal BIA viewed Indigenous religious beliefs as something which should be protected, not merely tolerated. Yet the defense of religious freedom also had implications for the successful execution of the BIA school program, namely the requirement for children to be permitted leave from school for the attendance of ceremonies. As will be shown, this challenges the "safety zone" concept. From the perspective of 1930s school staff, religious freedom scarcely fitted the "harmless" cultural category.

School Absences for Religio-Cultural Purposes

The extent to which pupils' religio-cultural leave was actually implemented in the New Deal has been questioned: Lomawaima and McCarty rightly note the exaggerated depiction conveyed by the bureau-commissioned bilingual reader *Sun Journey*, in which a Zuni boy is permitted a year's leave from boarding school to experience religious training at Zuni Pueblo.[37] However, some UPA day schools did permit leave for limited periods for the purpose of religious instruction. Taos Day School (UPA) reports indicate that in 1937, five boys, aged nine to sixteen, left school for an unspecified amount of time to enter religious training in the pueblo. The report for 1938 states that five boys aged ten and eleven were permitted leave for the same reason.[38] The reports do not indicate how long the boys expected to be away for, nor whether they returned to school. A letter from Superintendent Seth Wilson (Hopi Agency) to UPA General Superintendent Sophie Aberle, dated March 1940, offers more detail. Wilson refers to two students who were granted permission by Aberle to return home for initiation ceremonies at Chimopavy in November 1939; he notes that the boys were now ready to return to school.[39] This may have been an isolated incident, but it does suggest that some pupils were permitted to leave school for several months in order to receive religious training in their home community.

Day and boarding school records indicate that Diné and Pueblo schools in the 1930s and 1940s allowed pupils to attend ceremonials and festivals during term time. This contrasts sharply with the policy implemented at Santa Fe Indian School (SFIS) in much of the Assimilation Era, when students often had to run away in order to attend Pueblo ceremonies.[40] Some Albuquerque (AIS) and SFIS superintendents from the 1890s through the 1920s railed against what they perceived to be the malign influence of Pueblo festivals and dances which pupils could usually only attend when home for the summer or after graduation.[41] In contrast, Zuni children in 1935 were granted formal leave to return home from SFIS to attend the Shalako ceremony.[42] At the request of the Acoma governor, children were allowed time off from McCarty's Day School to attend the annual fiesta at the Pueblo.[43] A footnote to the 1940 primer *Little Boy with Three Names: A Story of Taos Pueblo* proclaimed that "all" children at SFIS "are permitted to return home during their summer vacation, and many of them also return home for the various religious festivals which are an important part of pueblo life."[44] Even Lucy Adams, in her "Program for Navajo Schools" (1937), indicated an appreciation of the importance of ceremonial dances: she floated the idea that school terms be made flexible and the timing of school holidays be set to reflect Diné ceremonies.[45]

These were not isolated incidents. Whereas earlier, sporadic instances of permitted cultural absence had depended upon the personal attitudes of individual authority figures such as John DeHuff (SFIS superintendent, 1916–27), pupil attendance at ceremonies and fiestas in the New Deal era was on a scale that produced a noticeable impact upon school programs.[46] Some UPA day schools, including Nutria, closed for the day of the Zuni Shalako ceremony.[47] Mesita Day School reported that no pupils attended school for four days in February 1939 as they were attending the governor's feast at Laguna.[48] In fall 1942, the Cochiti Day School teacher complained of "unusually poor" attendance due to a high number of ceremonial dances.[49] Adams acknowledged that attendance at the Navajo day schools fluctuated due to a series of factors including "dances and ceremonials"—an admission reiterated by her successor, George Boyce, in 1945.[50] Indeed, an official commenting on enrollment at Navajo day schools in October 1943 noted, "Our enrollment even in normal times fluctuates greatly due to migration caused by seasonal occupation and ceremonials." He then expressed hope that enrollment would increase once a particular dance season had ended, as "children are often not enrolled until . . . dances are over."[51] Similar sentiments were expressed at Seba Dalkai Day School the same year.[52] Adams's suggestion that the school term be organized so as to reflect key ceremonial periods had apparently not been implemented.

As the New Deal program progressed, an exasperated tone emerged in some teachers' correspondence concerning absences. The author of Taos Day School's quarterly report, dated March 1938, exclaimed that attendance would be significantly higher if "there were not so many religious ceremonies in the pueblo."[53] In November 1943, Crystal Day School reported that attendance at Diné dances had resulted in a small enrollment and an average daily attendance that was "only fair."[54] And, while such absences were permitted, the tone became increasingly grudging.

Consider UPA Education Superintendent Virgil Whitaker's response to a Zuni parent's request for her daughter's return from SFIS for a week to help with Shalako preparations. Whitaker permitted the absence but remarked, "All this fall we have been making a special effort to cut down absences from school, since our teachers all agree that irregular attendance is the greatest handicap our Indian schools have to face. It keeps us from doing as good work with the children as we should like to."[55] Whitaker may have been exaggerating the position of irregular attendance as education enemy number one; school records from this period are replete with complaints (both staff and parental) concerning dangerous and damaged school buildings, a paucity of personnel due to wartime enrollment, and water shortages at day schools—all of which constituted serious, practical obstacles to the successful delivery of classroom education. Still, this incident does attest to a belief amongst BIA education staff that the scale of student attendance at ceremonies during the term actively damaged the school program.

By 1945 some school principals were refusing permission for attendance at events whose religio-cultural significance they deemed tenuous, notably Thanksgiving and Halloween.[56] When SFIS principal Lucia Page refused to allow fifty pupils time off school to attend Halloween celebrations, she stated, "I must take some measure to stop the exodus"—thus indicating the frequency of such absences.[57] And attempts to formalize religio-cultural absences were not restricted to BIA personnel: in 1941 the governor of San Ildefonso, Julian Martinez, informed UPA general superintendent Aberle that "in the future no children will be allowed to leave school unless the person or persons has or have a written statement from the Governor."[58] Yet, despite teachers' complaints, the principle of allowing school leave for the attendance of religious ceremonies/festivals remained in place.

The issue of pupil absences for religio-cultural purposes does raise potential questions for the safety zone model. Freedom to practice religious worship was regarded by Collier and Beatty as an important citizenship right, an essential component of Indigenous societies, and an intrinsic aspect of community well-being; hence, they upheld the principle of granting students leave to attend religio-cultural events. Whether this can be termed "safe" with regards to BIA policy, however, is contentious. The safety zone theory defines safe as "safe for the agendas and interests of dominant power structures."[59] Some teachers, while implementing the policy, clearly felt that the volume and extent of the absences was actively harmful to the school program. The absences were not permitted for monetary value, nor were they viewed as harmless or infantile by those who sanctioned them. Therefore, they differ from earlier cultural tolerance based on assumption of innocuity or assimilation into the US wage economy. The defense of religio-cultural school absences stemmed from a positive standpoint: the belief that attendance at ceremonies was an inherent right and was actively beneficial both to the individual pupil and the wider community. In effect, attendance at the ceremonies was not merely *safe*, it was *vital*, trumping any disruption to the school program.

Traditional Religions and Cultures Inside the School Environment

Religio-cultural absences, while a significant break with past policy, represented a removal rather than an addition to the school curricula: absences didn't introduce Native cultures to the classroom but instead sought to ensure that religio-cultural practice could continue *outside* of the classroom. The question remains as to how Native religions and cultures were treated *within* the schools, for example in textbooks and lesson plans.

Given the bureau's promotion of progressive education, it is hardly surprising that song had a role on the Navajo school curriculum, particularly for younger children. Some song selections were Euro-American in origin and were used to introduce younger pupils to the English language. In her account of beginners' activities at Hunter's Point Day School, teacher Rhoda Hughes highlighted the children's enthusiasm for the sung nursery rhymes "Jack Be Nimble" and "Little Boy Blue." Hughes claimed the rhymes helped the pupils adopt English words, which pleased their parents: "An unexpected development from this work was that the parents were greatly pleased when their children could go home from school and recite several of these verses in English for them."[60]

In a more innovative pedagogical approach, however, Hughes included Diné songs in her classes. In her words:

> Another thing we have enjoyed doing this year—was the singing of a group of Navajo songs which the children have brought in from their homes. We have been very careful not to sing songs concerning the work of healing and religious rites. Our Navajo assistants have been called in to listen to each song and approve it before it was included in our repertoire. . . . We took our children to Fort Defiance and made a few phonograph recordings of their Navajo songs. The children were greatly thrilled when they heard the recordings of their own voices.[61]

The role played by the Diné assistants was vital in ensuring that teachers did not inadvertently breach religious and cultural protocols by appropriating sacred material. Perhaps teachers had learnt from earlier cultural blunders, such as the unfortunate introduction of taboo animals at Tuba City Vocational High School.[62] Hughes, in 1941, was clearly aware that some elements of Diné culture and religion were off-limits to her. Significantly, this also demonstrates the balance of power between non-Diné teacher and Diné assistant—the latter held some authority when it came to including Diné culture on the curriculum, although not in the actual devising of lesson plans. As with Howard Gorman's role regarding the Pageant of Navajo History script, the Diné assistants were valued as checkers, not creators of lessons—there to remove any sensitive material rather than to install actual content.

What role did the Diné songs play in the class-based learning process? Their inclusion indicates an attempt to diverge from a purely Euro-American-centered knowledge base, and the fact that the children brought the songs from their homes (from parents and grandparents) suggests that the demonizing of Native cultures and communities promoted by earlier bureau educators had diminished. For an Indian Service teacher to encourage children to use knowledge gained from the home as a resource for school-based classes marks a strong break with previous practice. However, Hughes's report does not show *how* the songs were used in the school environment, beyond the fact they were recorded and therefore preserved. Whereas Esther Horne incorporated Native songs into her lessons to teach pupils "the importance of remembering their past," Hughes does not appear to have used the songs for a specifically didactic purpose.[63]

Using the home as a potential learning resource, even in a very limited sense, was one break with earlier education policy. Another was the production of textbooks on the customs and history of certain communities "prepared primarily for use in Federal Indian schools."[64] The Indian Life and Customs series consisted of detailed presentations by anthropologists of the history, customs, and societal structures of communities including the Tohono O'odham, all Pueblos, the Diné, and the Paiutes. As discussed in a previous chapter, the focus of these texts was largely the recording of historical customs and ways of life, with a final chapter that summarized the present day. Apart from the Diné text, the histories were presented from a contemporary, Western academic perspective (chronological progression; focus on post-Contact events; and reliance upon archaeological and tree-ring data rather than tribal histories and oral sources), and many customs and traditions were described using the past tense.[65] However, the primary author, anthropologist Ruth Underhill, did attempt to avoid religio-cultural offence. Ceremonies which she viewed as living were described in positive terms—for example, the "magnificent ceremonial relay race" held at Isleta or "beautiful and comforting" Diné sings.[66] Presumably for the benefit of her non-Pueblo readers, including teachers, she noted that "white people who wish to show courtesy in an Indian pueblo, note where a kiva is and walk in some other direction." To emphasize the sacred nature of kivas still further, she urged any visitor permitted entry to "refrain from touching and prying" and to behave as they would "when being shown around some famous church."[67] For the greater part, she did not describe contemporary ceremonies and religious beliefs at all. In *Workaday Life of the Pueblos*, Underhill stated, "We shall not describe this ceremonial part of pueblo life.... Pueblo people prefer to do their own describing—or not to do it. To them much of the power of a ceremony comes from its being secret and for them alone. They ask outsiders to leave it to them."[68] Her later text *Here Come The Navaho!* didn't mention ceremonies, other than a brief reference to the beauty of sings.[69] This marked a welcome recognition that sacred knowledge was not for non-Native teachers or academics to teach. Despite good intentions, the series still perpetuated Eurocentric perceptions and framing of Indigenous lives. Underhill was at pains to emphasize that her *Pueblos* book "deals with the daily life of the pueblos, not their religion."[70] But, as she noted elsewhere in the text, religion permeates traditional Pueblo cultures, extending to work, play, and health—it cannot easily be separated from what are viewed as largely secular phenomena in Eurocentric cultures.[71]

Culturally sensitive Life and Customs textbooks were a change from previous policy, yet none were published until well into the 1940s. Teachers, for the greater part, had to implement cultural tolerance in the absence of printed materials, with little initial guidance from the Indian Office. Predictably, the results were patchy and depended in part upon individual personalities. Some sensitivity and awareness was demonstrated. Gertrude Giesen, beginners' teacher at Fort Defiance Boarding School, wrote of the "exceptional teaching possibilities" inherent in her Christmas unit, suggesting the promotion of Christian values. However, she then reminded her readers that not only is "Christmas and its implications . . . new to the Navajo beginner," but "Native customs and taboos must be respected."[72] This contrasts sharply with the festive debacle at the government Supai School in the early 1900s, as recalled by teacher Flora Greg Iliff. The staff had excitedly prepared a Christmas pageant for Havasupai students and parents, culminating in a surprise visit from Santa Claus. Unfortunately, they failed to appreciate that the large, bewhiskered, red-robed figure bursting through the door bore an alarming resemblance to a malevolent spirit in Havasupai belief, which caused considerable distress to children and parents alike.[73] Giesen's report, while continuing to promote and use Christmas for didactic purposes, did acknowledge that Diné beliefs should be considered in the devising and execution of lessons.

The Ojibwe civil rights activist Adam Fortunate Eagle's account of his school years at Pipestone Indian Boarding School (Minnesota) also suggests that school staff in the period 1935–45 were at least *aware* of the new policy of religio-cultural tolerance. Although Native histories and cultures were not included on the Pipestone curriculum ("I had to learn that on my own"), he recalls that the boys' adviser, Mr. Burns (Southern Cheyenne), "told the other employees to stay away from the parching place because it's the boys' sacred area. That's why we never see any grownups around there. I'm really proud that grownups respect our traditional ways."[74] The housemother, Mrs. Bea Burns (Peoria), when asked whether the school sought to remove Native cultures, drew a distinction between earlier policy and the New Deal and assured the students that "we're all proud to be Indians here at the school." And the students interpreted the 9th grade graduation ceremony in 1945, which involved the graduating class presenting the school pipe to the incoming 9th grade cohort, as "a strong message for us Indian students to carry on the traditions, culture, and spirituality of our people, so we can pass it on to future generations."[75] This suggests that Native traditional beliefs and identities were neither actively denigrated nor discouraged at Pipestone during the New Deal, even if they weren't actually taught there. In an afterword to his memoirs, Fortunate Eagle described the "sweeping changes" introduced at the boarding schools in the 1930s, which forbade interference with Native religious expression and languages, and he contrasts this with the monocultural approach of on-reservation mission schools. He concludes by stating, "Our arrival at the boarding school in 1935 could not have occurred at a better time; it was just as Collier's new, more liberal policies were being implemented."[76] Like Esther Horne, Polingaysi Qoyawayma, and Marguerite Stoltz, Adam Fortunate Eagle recalled that religio-cultural tolerance was at least being attempted at the government schools in the New Deal era.

"Old Guard" and Insensitive Personnel

Not all staff, however, were on the same page when it came to interpretation of Circular 2970. The case of Mrs. William J. McGranahan, wife of the principal of the Hé Dog Consolidated Day School on Rosebud Reservation, is interesting for what it reveals of leading BIA officials' views on cultural respect. In 1937 McGranahan wrote an eyewitness account of a ceremony dedicated to the "Thunder Spirits," which she hoped would be published in the bureau journal *Indians at Work*.[77] The associate director of education, Paul Fickinger, was less than impressed by her tone: "Mrs. McGranahan has spoiled a very excellent story by the style she has used."[78] Head of the BIA's Applied Anthropology Unit, Scudder Mekeel, offered a more detailed critique: in his view McGranahan's stance was "at once amused, supercilious, patronizing, and condescending, toward the ceremony and the Indians in it."[79] Indeed, he informed Collier that she possessed "an abominable attitude toward Indians in her article—an attitude which is borne out by those who know her."[80] Collier himself advised McGranahan that her article had been rejected on the grounds that all "who have read it say that it suggests a patronizing and somewhat condescending attitude."[81]

The McGranahan furor leaves much unanswered. At no point in the correspondence do Mekeel, Fickinger, or Collier refer to Lakota reactions to McGranahan's essay, nor is there any comment on her work at the school. There is no indication of whether she was popular or despised by the communities served by the Hé Dog school. All we can gather from the correspondence is that Mekeel and Fickinger found her description of the ceremony to be condescending and hardly in keeping with Circular 2970. It is possible that McGranahan was one of the "old guard" BIA personnel who struggled with the transition from monoculturalism to cultural tolerance—a difficulty evidently experienced by Samuel Stacher, superintendent of the Eastern Navajo Agency in 1933. Stacher had run the Crownpoint Boarding School in the 1910s and 1920s and had attracted criticism from then-commissioner, and avowed assimilationist, Charles Burke for chaining runaway female students by their ankles for days on end. In 1933, Secretary of the Interior Harold Ickes sent a memorandum to all reservation superintendents and agents requesting information on dance and ceremony prohibition. Ickes demanded each jurisdiction supply a list of dance and ceremony requests, along with information as to which had been permitted and which were refused and why.[82] Stacher did not reply, and he received a terse reminder.[83] The eventual report suggests he had conspicuously failed to transition from earlier policy. Stacher argued that three-day "squaw dances" posed a serious obstacle to crop tending and economic self-sufficiency, hence his duty to restrict and discourage them. He denounced Diné sings and dances as opportunities for inebriation, claiming that "the result is more or less trouble." Stacher did acknowledge that "we [superintendents] have no right to issue any mandatory order prohibiting any dance or ceremonial"—perhaps for this reason he sought to blame his restrictive actions on others, claiming that "the better class of Indians" had asked him to curtail the dances.[84]

Ickes was unconvinced by Stacher's arguments. Describing the letter as "just a little disingenuous," he drew upon alternative sources of "information" that indicated Stacher "is too easily persuaded by some of the missionaries in the matter of the Indians dancing." Indeed, Ickes took issue with the superintendent's use of the word "encourage" in his defense of limiting dances, believing the term covered "a multitude of sins"—in other words, active oppression. Ickes contrasted Stacher's report with his own interpretation of bureau policy, that Native Americans had the right "to be let alone when it comes to observing their own customs"—something he felt Stacher was clearly not doing. Ickes's missive also suggests his own failure to recognize the religious nature of some dances. Note his defense of the right to hold dances:

> It is shocking to some white people to see Indians waste time dancing but the Indians don't take off much time for movies or baseball games, or football games or automobile trips, and the annual vac[a]tion of from two weeks to a month is, I believe, an unknown custom. I doubt if they "waste" any more time with their dances and ceremonies than we whites take off for our vacations.

By equating ceremonial dances and sings with sports and cinema trips, Ickes relegates the ceremonial to the recreational, despite defending the dances against active oppression.[85]

Stacher was not alone in finding the transition to cultural tolerance a difficult one. Marguerite Stoltz recalled that staff at the Carson Indian Boarding School found the new approach "confusing" and that the matrons had particularly struggled to adjust. According to Stoltz:

> It was confusing for the matrons. Formerly all children dressed and went on schedule [to Sunday services and Sunday school]. Now the youngsters had discussions. Who wanted to go? Who did not? Some would start out and then change their minds. Who could say what went on spiritually in a child's mind from the time he left the dormitory until he arrived at the mission! The poor missionaries could appeal only to those employees who volunteered to help them. They must have had many discouraging times.[86]

Interestingly, the Carson School principal, in his zeal to enforce the missionary regulations, appears to have given freedom of choice directly to the students rather than their parents, resulting in a noticeably reduced Christian congregation.

Incidents of cultural insensitivity and prejudice also occurred on the Navajo Reservation during the New Deal. In an interview conducted in 1970, former superintendent E. R. Fryer ascribed this not to "old guard" employees but to new hires, particularly Soil Conservation Service (SCS) personnel. According to Fryer, SCS staff were "newer people to government. Most of them were professionals, and none of them had any long traditions in service with the Indians. Many of them were inclined to make judgements without reference to Indian value systems or Navajo customs."[87] This view is supported by an unfortunate episode documented by anthropologists Clyde Kluckhohn and Dorothea Leighton, who lamented policymakers' failure to appreciate the interconnectedness of Diné culture, economics, and religion. They cited an SCS employee's attempt to show a documentary film on range management at a Diné ceremonial, which sparked considerable opposition and distress. The head "medicine man" suggested the film be held at a school "instead of coming around our ceremonial, which is no place for it," and participants denounced the film's inclusion of coyote and snake images "which is a very bad thing to have around a religious ceremonial." Rather than rescheduling for a more appropriate time, the employee blithely went ahead with the screening, demonstrating not merely cultural ignorance but willful disregard for Diné values and opinions.[88]

While Fryer may have been correct in attributing cultural ignorance to new staff who had little experience or knowledge of Diné beliefs, he was wrong to paint this as an SCS-only phenomenon. Condescension and ignorance towards rural communities' needs and values had been an early feature of some rural social case work organized by the Federal Emergency Relief Administration (FERA) across the US. According to one contemporary commentator, "The imposing of state and district case work supervisors upon states by the FERA has not always met with the most friendly response.... Few even of the better trained workers have any appreciation of rural community mores."[89] And the BIA's vaunted Southwest Field Training Program (SFTP) appears to have shared this wider New Deal flaw. The initial report produced by Walter Olson, an SFTP participant in 1940, is notable for its cultural condescension. The program, established in 1937, was a joint BIA–National Institute of Public Affairs venture that trained around twelve university graduates a year for a career in federal administration.

Each was assigned to a Southwest-based Native jurisdiction (Zuni, Navajo, UPA) and spent twelve months engaged in administrative tasks, such as researching local trade problems, aiding range management, and conducting land, water, and boundary surveys. Described by Collier as "an experiment," the program had some success: graduates went on to serve as reservation superintendents and as General Land Service officials, and one became assistant secretary of the Department of the Interior.[90]

The SFTP was undoubtedly an ambitious venture that sought to enhance the quality of Indian Service administrators through practical training: it appeared in the Indian Affairs section of the 1940 *Annual Report of the Secretary of the Interior* under the heading "Effort toward Better Personnel."[91] Yet Olson's report following his first month of fieldwork on the Navajo Reservation suggests cultural sensitivity was not a prerequisite for the course. Olson, freshly graduated from university, spent his first weeks helping range riders and veterinarians to inspect sheep, assess dams and water tanks, and mend fences. During this time he visited Diné homes and attended local gatherings. He found the Indian Service personnel friendly and pronounced himself "satisfied with the experience I have had." He was less enthusiastic about Diné food, sanitation, social customs, religio-cultural beliefs, and general attitudes to range management. When describing the hospitality of a Diné family who shared their mutton and home with him following a lecture on branding, Olson dwelt mainly on the flies and sand inside the hogan: "When you see what the Indian has to eat and how he lives it makes one get a bit weak at the stomach." The condescension was also extended to his appraisal of medicine men and sings. He was pessimistic concerning efforts to train and employ Diné range riders, since "as little as I know of the Indians it seems that Medicine Men might influence unduely [sic] the way a fellow Indian administered a sub-district." His follow-up remark was telling: "Whenever it is possible to educate an Indian to the point where he does not believe in a 'sing' then will he be ready to take over the recommending of permits for live stock [sic], etc." Olson went on to criticize Diné marriage customs and to accuse Diné men of laziness and neglect. Yet he then launched into a diatribe against racism, arguing,

> If a man thinks that another man belongs to a race inferior to his own he is of very little value in a Service such as this. Instead he must realize

that his opportunity has been much greater than others and that given the same opportunity there is nothing to prove that one race is inferior to another. Such beliefs may be fostered from the policy making members of an organization to those who carry that policy out.

Olson reported that most Indian Service personnel he had met lacked "violent race prejudice"—though "some do."[92]

Olson's report is troubling on several levels, not least the suggestion that some Navajo Service personnel held "violent" prejudiced views. It is striking that Olson himself didn't recognize that his dismissal of Diné religious beliefs and ceremonies, his belittling of familial and marital relations, and his use of pejorative language also constituted prejudice. He may have rejected racial formalist views of human potential, yet at this stage of his career he clearly perceived Euro-American cultural and societal structures to be superior to their Diné counterparts. It is tempting to dismiss his views as those of an inexperienced trainee rather than as evidence of wider cultural condescension within the Navajo Service; this was, after all, his first report, written after one month's training. Yet the unnamed appraiser who ticked the aforementioned antiracism statement remained silent on the dismissal of sings and the use of derogatory language. There is no recorded Navajo Service or bureau response to either Olson's failure to understand the connection between the increased frequency of sings and the rising desertification nor his dismissal of Diné opposition to range management as mere stubbornness and ignorance.[93] Presumably, Olson developed a much greater understanding of Indigenous religions and cultures during the remainder of his training—upon completion he embarked upon a long career in the Indian Service in the Southwest.

Olson did not detail Diné school experiences in his training report. However, the Phelps-Stokes Report did note the persistence of intolerant or ignorant attitudes amongst some day-school personnel on the Navajo Reservation in the late 1930s. It concluded that "practically all the day school teachers are from traditionally minded teachers' colleges," and "few if any can speak the Navajo language." Consequently some demonstrated "a certain bewilderment" at the new policy.[94] Evelyn Crady Adams shared this concern in her otherwise enthusiastic analysis of the New Deal education program: in a chapter tellingly entitled "Problems and Outlook," she lamented the speed at which reforms had been introduced, noting, "Insufficient time has elapsed for the current program to obliterate old rigidities and take root with sufficient fluidity to achieve lasting results."[95] Such "old rigidities" likely referred to traditionally assimilationist personnel. Even more worrying was Phelps-Stokes's observation that some teachers "have apparently entered the Navajo Service, not out of any real interest or belief in the Navajos, but as a relatively well-paid job"—or even just because "jobs are there." This careerism, the report charged, resulted in cultural insensitivity, for such persons held purely "a professional rather than a combined human and professional interest in their work." Indeed, Phelps-Stokes recommended the introduction of new job criteria for prospective Navajo Service teachers: the possession of genuine interest and belief in the Diné; a working knowledge of the Navajo language; and, significantly, "an appreciation and a respect for Navajo culture."[96] This suggests that the grassroots implementation of a culturally tolerant curriculum and teaching program still had some way to go by 1939.

The criticisms may account for the "Changed Requirements for Teachers" presented in the 1940 *Report of the Secretary of the Interior*. Collier referenced recent changes to Civil Service teaching examinations, including such criteria as "rural living, training for rural life, teaching in schools which actively participate in community activities, and experience in adapting curricula to local needs." These qualifications, together with "initiative, ingenuity," represent practical attributes and experience rather than specific requirements for cultural tolerance and understanding. True, teachers were told to "make friends with the older Indians of the community" and demonstrate "sympathy with the problems to be faced"—yet even these instructions fell short of the cultural appreciation advised by Phelps-Stokes.[97] And the problem of assimilationist and discriminatory attitudes persisted well into the 1940s. Anthropologist Laura Thompson observed in 1942–43 that some Indian Service personnel held negative views on Hopi religion, traditional home life, and even intellectual capability; she described such prejudices as "prevalent" in Hopiland "chiefly among the newer Indian Service personnel, especially those from the southern states, among many wives of employees."[98] Clearly the New Deal administration had failed to eradicate both racial and cultural prejudice from the Indian Service ranks.

And conscious discrimination wasn't the only problem: sometimes inclusion could have damaging impact. In December 1939, visiting Diné students from Wingate performed the *Yéii' bicheii* in front of pupils and staff at Crownpoint Boarding School. While the circumstances surrounding the incident are unclear—who authorized the performance, what did the Diné teaching assistants advise—the ceremony is sacred and meant to be performed by adults, not schoolchildren. As Farina King notes, the school assembly, including non-Diné teaching staff, was hardly an appropriate context for a consecrated Diné ceremony.[99] In this unfortunate instance, attempted cultural inclusion signified desecration.

The treatment of Native religions and cultures, both inside and outside the classroom, raises important questions for the Indian New Deal. The enforcement of the missionary regulations and the sanctioning of school absences for religious purposes on the Navajo Reservation and the UPA indicate a sincere belief in religious freedom. Both policies proved problematic for the Indian Service—the missionary backlash generated damaging criticism of BIA policy, and the absences disrupted the existing school program. That Beatty and other policymakers continued to insist upon them suggests that religious freedom (as BIA officials perceived it) was a key New Deal aim. Furthermore, teacher and pupil memoirs indicate that *active* denigration of Native American cultures and religions in the classroom largely ceased during the 1930s, suggesting cultural tolerance was attempted at the government schools, even if some employees resisted.

Yet what is striking about the missionary regulations, school absences, and the ending of deliberate cultural denigration is that they are subtractive as opposed to additive policies. They were designed to *remove* obstacles to the continuation of traditional religious and cultural practices, not to teach those beliefs in the classroom environment. In part this reflects the bureau's recognition that Diné and Pueblo communities did not want sacred knowledge to be taught by non-Native teachers and in non-traditional contexts. As Lucy Adams stated in her "Program for Navajo Schools," "The school should recognize and accept the importance of the learning that takes place in the home and the community, and not attempt to take over or duplicate it in the school."[100] UPA superintendent Sophie Aberle offered a stronger statement: "My work with them [Pueblo communities] does not permit my asking questions about their customs, and they are hesitant about discussing their religious . . . life with white people."[101] However, the Indian Service did not seek to invite Pueblo and Diné custodians of religio-cultural knowledge to the schools to either provide religious instruction or to devise culturally acceptable lessons—an omission that was recognized by contemporary commentators.[102] This had serious implications for boarding school students who, despite the more sympathetic class environment of the 1930s, remained detached from home culture. Religion-related absences didn't reach everyone; a Diné student interviewed by government-sponsored researchers in the early 1940s noted poignantly, "I do not know any sings because I am in school studying things. I [have] never seen yeibichai [sic] yet." Some communities also expressed concern that boarding school students were ignorant of ceremonial knowledge, and even worse, had picked up incorrect information amongst themselves, performing their own (unauthorized) versions of dances at the wrong time. As a Diné adult interviewed by Leighton and Kluckhohn exclaimed:

> Well, it's no wonder that it doesn't rain anymore like it used to. The reason that isn't a grass meadow any more but just a bunch of washes isn't because we have too many sheep like the white people say. It's because these young boys aren't learning what they should and aren't doing what they should. They even sing Night Way songs in the summer and do those dances. We were taught that this would pack the ground so hard that the grass would stop growing. [103]

Traditional religion and cultural practice clearly remained outside the formal school environment in the 1930s.

The failure to amend the school terms to reflect Diné and Pueblo religious and cultural requirements also points to a deeper New Deal flaw. Kluckhohn and Leighton, in their 1946 study of the Navajo Reservation, wryly observed that "the system (for all its 'progressiveness') is still amusingly culture bound."[104] Despite New Dealers' apparent willingness to permit Diné religious expression and facilitate participation in ceremonies, they stopped short of changing the Euro-American framework through which education was delivered—again leaving religion and culture *outside* the classroom rather than letting it shape the term schedule. And they repeated this approach vis-à-vis the curriculum. While championing religio-cultural freedom, policymakers remained incapable of moving beyond their own concepts of post-Enlightenment, Judeo-Christian religious structures and systems. They understood religion to involve ceremonies, festivals, and sacred physical locations, and they saw no meaningful links between the spiritual and scientific or otherwise "temporal" spheres—with the possible exception of traditional healing.[105] As Superintendent T. B. Hall informed the Tohono O'odham community at Sells Agency in 1936:

> You can have all the old ceremonies because they have nothing to do with this Government, and nobody is trying to stop them. So, you need not fear that the Government wants to stop the old ways because it is the Government that is trying to keep them. There are some new ways which you like to have too. You like to have your children go to school to learn English and to learn counting so that they can get jobs and so they can sell their cattle.... You can send your children to school and you can keep the old ceremonies too. You can have the two ways go together and the Government is glad to have you do that.[106]

The religious freedom the New Dealers implemented at the Navajo and Pueblo schools, while a significant break from previous policy, therefore did not reflect the realities of non-Christian Indigenous religions. Cultural tolerance applied largely to a realm that existed outside the classroom—a realm that, in bureau eyes, should continue and flourish but whose practitioners were excluded from curriculum development. This resulted in a curriculum that was vaguely pluralist in intent, yet in practice, it fell far short of meaningful pluralism by failing to actively *teach* cultural and religious knowledge or to approach the curriculum (scheduling, ecology, health care, history) from a Diné or Pueblo perspective. As Isleta teacher Miguel Trujillo noted in his assessment of Indian Service education policy over the decades, "There has appeared a sympathetic attitude of the Government in the appreciation and acceptance of the Indians' cultural contribution and non-interference in the religious life and expression of the Indians."[107] Noninterference—while a significant break from previous policy—translated into noninclusion of Indigenous knowledge, values, and perspectives at the schools in the New Deal era.

BILINGUAL EDUCATION AND DUAL-LANGUAGE PRIMERS

5

The 1930s witnessed significant involvement by the BIA in the development of a written version of the Navajo language (Diné bizaad) and in the production of bilingual texts ("Indian Life Readers") for use in Diné, Pueblo, Hopi, and Lakota schools. Promotion of bilingual instruction marked a clear break with earlier bureau education policy, reflecting the New Deal belief that Indigenous languages should have an active future. As Willard Beatty declared in 1935, "It is desired that the Indians be bilingual, fluent, and literate in the English language and fluent in their vital, beautiful, and efficient native languages."[1] The bilingual primers commissioned by the BIA for the government schools also affirmed a partial preservationist purpose. The afterword to the Lakota texts advised they would "contribute most effectively to the development of *active* bilingualism upon the part of both children and their elders," envisaging English in the classroom and "reading the native tongue" at home. In this way, it was hoped, the children would help their parents learn English and "the new readers [will] assist the adults in preserving the use of the native language among their children."[2] While acknowledging the historic role played by missionaries in developing written forms of Native languages, Beatty affirmed that the government had "reversed its policy" of monolingualism and "is endeavoring through the Indian schools to increase familiarity with the written form of the languages spoken by large numbers of Indians."[3] The promotion and utilization of written forms of Diné bizaad, Hopi, and Lakota suggests that policymakers envisaged a future for them as active languages practiced by the next generation—a clear break with previous government policy. There is little, however, to suggest the New Dealers considered language beyond its practical uses—for example, the profound religious and cultural role of Diné bizaad.[4] This chapter explores attitudes towards language at the government schools; the tensions surrounding the development of a written Navajo orthography; and the plot content of the dual-language primers in order to assess the motivations behind the bilingual teaching, government attitudes to the survival of Indigenous languages and cultures, and the power dynamics at work. Once again, the Indian Service proved unable to detach itself from a hierarchical assumption of knowledge/authenticity, even as it challenged assimilationist denigration of Indigenous languages, ceremonies, and traditions.

Prioritization of English

While the Assimilation Era English-only policy was officially overturned in the 1930s, the teaching of spoken and written English remained a priority at New Deal schools. Beatty's statement on "The Direction of Education" emphasized the importance of English fluency: "Because good education and 'the good life' depend largely upon increased ability to communicate freely, language use will have a vital place in the curriculum. This will involve the ability to speak, and later to read and write the English language with fluency and exactness."[5] George Boyce, in his account of his tenure as director of Navajo education, recalled that a key Navajo school goal was to ensure children could "understand English, with particular emphasis upon words and concepts as applied to animal husbandry, farming, Navajo law and other aspects of reservation life."[6] In other words, English language lessons were intended to facilitate the transmission of wider aspects of the BIA program, notably soil conservation and range management. Phelps-Stokes corroborated this, noting that the teaching of English was "the principal task in the [day] school room" and that English was the medium for all subject areas.[7] Indeed, the promotion of English was highlighted in Lucy Wilcox Adams's "Program for Navajo Schools" in December 1937.[8]

School records suggest that teachers did prioritize English language learning in their classes. Diné teacher Florence Little, who taught beginners through 3rd grade at Huerfano Point Day School, listed "English-learning" as a key feature of the school program. According to Little: "To my opinion the core of daily activities in the classroom should revolve around the ultimate use of the spoken English and I think that most of the Navajo Schools work toward that end. I emphasize the practice no matter how elementary it is in form."[9] Gertrude Giesen, beginners' teacher at Fort Defiance, also stressed English language teaching for younger students. She listed the acquisition of English (and the development of "initiative in using it") as her number one class objective, above health education and safety.[10] Sixth-grade instructor Ora Medley prioritized health, homemaking, and character-building lessons for her students aged thirteen to eighteen. But she also emphasized the need to speak, read, and write English so her students could "be able to help the Navajos who were not fortunate enough to have an opportunity to attend school."[11] And the 1942 Tuba City Vocational High School catalog stated on page one: "We cannot stress too much the need for our pupils' becoming intimately acquainted with the English language. We feel that our students must not only be able to speak, read, and write the English language, but they must be able also to think in English." Significantly, English was placed first, with general science, agriculture, and home economics relegated to the second page.[12] English language education was therefore key for all grades at the Navajo Service schools—including adult beginners who were to achieve "a practical working English vocabulary as rapidly as it can be acquired."[13]

Indian Service teachers were not alone in prioritizing English at school. For many Diné and Tohono O'odham parents, the main reason for sending their children to school (and therefore removing them from essential herding, farming, or household tasks) was to learn to speak, read, and write in English.[14] As a Diné father of two informed the principal of Shiprock Boarding School, "The main thing I brought them here for is to learn English."[15] According to Navajo Tribal Council vice-chairman Howard Gorman, "They do not want their children to study Navajo—they are only interested in having their children learn English."[16] The practical value of English fluency was affirmed by a schoolgirl interviewed by BIA-commissioned researchers: "When my father wants to talk to an English man, he always wants us to talk for him, and then tell him what the white man says. Or when the white man comes to our home, we talk for my father and mother."[17] Diné parents thus expected evidence of their children's learning; however, judging by the complaints voiced at council meetings and to researchers, many were disappointed in what they heard and observed. The highly critical NMAIA Report (1940), based on interviews with around 150 households, noted a near-universal Diné criticism of the day school program: that pupils simply didn't learn enough English because they returned home in the evening and spoke Diné bizaad with friends and family.[18] This was echoed by Diné participants in the Wingate adult short course in 1939, who felt that "the most detrimental point was that the Navajo Child [sic] starts talking Navajo as soon as he arrives home and forgets what he learned during the few hours at the Day School."[19]

School records suggest this wasn't the sole concern: some parents, observers, and teachers felt that too much Diné bizaad was spoken *within* the school environment. Mike Ashihi, a participant in the Wingate short course, observed, "Too much Navajo language [is] spoken on the campus. Too much Navajo singing."[20] Some day-school teachers shared his concern. Florence Little (Huerfano Point) blamed progressive education techniques. As she noted, "From my observations in Navajo Schoolrooms [sic], I find, contrary to the belief that the varied manuel [sic] activities carried on in the room bring on self-expression in English, that it does not. There is no doubt that there is presence of enjoyment but the conversations are in Navajo and the topic divert[s] from the particular activity carried on."[21]

In November 1941, a few months after Little's observations, Education Supervisor Norma Runyan visited Huerfano Point to evaluate the teachers and the school program. She praised the appearance of the school plant ("by far the best kept up day school plant in the Shiprock Area") and the teaching in general, but she had one major criticism: "The children also speak Navajo almost constantly, though they do understand and can speak English. The teacher and assistants say they work on this problem but that the people of the community speak disparagingly to the children when they use English, which of course prevents their doing so." Runyan didn't mention Little's concerns about the damaging impact of progressive education techniques but instead blamed the teachers and the community: "Either there is a decided weakness on the part of the teachers and assistants in the community work ... or the community is a peculiar one and needs the help of other people." She doesn't appear to have consulted community leaders or parents as to why the English language was so unpopular amongst both students and family members. Given that the school's community days had apparently "not been very successful," distress caused by stock reduction may well have played a role in turning the community against BIA institutions—yet Runyan doesn't seem to have considered this.[22]

In contrast to the day schools and the observers' impressions of Wingate Vocational High School, some boarding schools appear to have proscribed Indigenous languages in the 1930s. As Davina Ruth Two Bears has shown, former students of Old Leupp Boarding School in the period 1939–42 recalled having their mouths washed out with bitter soap for the crime of speaking their own language[23]—one of the "stupid, humiliating punishments" that had been officially banned by Harold Ickes in 1934.[24] Significantly, pupils described one oasis of Diné cultural freedom at Old Leupp: the girls' home economics class, where traditional weaving and Diné cookery were taught by Diné teacher Marie Martin and Diné bizaad went unpunished.[25] The situation at Old Leupp in the late 1930s suggests the competing existence of "old guard" personnel who clearly adhered to coercive assimilation tenets, alongside the agency of Martin, who sought to ensure that Diné language and culture had a life at Old Leupp beyond the loom.

Parents also criticized UPA day schools for failing to teach fluency in English. The complaint made by Governor Antonio Vigil of Nambe Pueblo to UPA education supervisor Almira Franchville is particularly telling. According to Franchville:

> The Governor and his men stated, emphatically, that they were not satisfied with the teaching that was being done in the Day Schools.... They thought the children should be taught to use English fluently and easily so they could talk face to face with white men and that they should be given more opportunities to learn and use Arithmetic; that the teacher should be more concerned with the teaching of their children than with the teaching of their women; that she should not fool around with wool and beads so much.... The men apologized for making complaints about the school and expressed a desire to have the new teacher told before she entered on duty, that she was to teach their children how to talk English and use Arithmetic.[26]

The Nambe community clearly valued the learning of English and were deeply concerned that it was apparently not prioritized at the day school.

Concern at poor English language skills in the 1930s went beyond the classroom. Health and soil conservation officials expressed frustration that policy presentations were sometimes misunderstood by Diné communities. W. W. Peter, the Navajo area medical director, was exasperated by what he perceived to be the Navajo Tribal Council's inability to understand Superintendent Fryer's two-hour speech on range management. In his correspondence with Fryer, Peter laid the blame for the incomprehension squarely on the council: "Yet from the questions asked from the floor it appears that many present did not understand you in spite of your using short sentences, slow rate of speech, clear enunciation, and simple language. Certainly after several years of discussion of this question [range management program], the 61 members of the Tribal Council present should not have presented such apparent hurdles blocking the arrival of your ideas into their heads." Peter appears to have been suggesting willful incomprehension by council members rather than purely language limitations. He then contradicted his own accusation by proposing the future use of visual material to facilitate understanding.[27]

Skilled interpreters, fluent in Diné bizaad and English, were evidently vital to the success of the range management program and were relied upon by council members, community leaders, and BIA staff to communicate policy and questions between the people and government personnel. Interpreting was highly valued within Diné society and constituted a recognized leadership quality.[28] However, by the late 1930s, reports abounded of mistakes in the interpreting process. Clyde Blair, then superintendent of Navajo Schools, believed that miscommunication was severely hampering the stock reduction program, for "the language is limited in its capacity to furnish a basis for ample understanding of government policy and much lack of cooperation has been received from certain members of the tribe as a result of this fact and faulty interpretation."[29] Once again bureau personnel ascribed the hostility to stock reduction to *Diné* linguistic shortcomings and failure to understand the program rather than acknowledging policy errors and the need for improved communication.

Respected interpreter Howard Gorman also accepted that translation errors were occurring, but he offered a more nuanced explanation—and a practical solution. The problem, he argued, was a lack of standardization of technical terms. For example, the Diné word for "jurisdiction" and the English word "district" were being used interchangeably in communications, which had created "the impression of the reservation being divided into eighteen separate reservations rather than eighteen units of the larger reservation." Gorman recommended "some standardization of meaning... for the more important concepts of the Land Management Program."[30] Unfortunately, little immediate action was taken. Over a year later, Soil Conservation Service (SCS) statistician J. Nixon Hadley complained that misinterpretations were "all too frequent" and advised "it would be well to have in readiness a fairly exhaustive list of terms frequently used in speaking of land management problems"—in other words, Gorman's proposed standardization. In contrast to Blair and Peter, Hadley recognized that SCS/BIA staff were at least partly responsible for the errors. He recommended that SCS staff work *with* the Diné to "determine the common faults of our English-speaking personnel in talking through interpreters." These faults included "speaking at great length before stopping for interpretation, or using vocabulary unfamiliar to the interpreter." Such basic, practical blunders create problems for interpreters in any language/situation, rather than reflecting deficiencies in Diné comprehension or inherent "limitations" of the Navajo language.[31] Indeed, shortly after this memo, Hadley asked Gorman to help him "get good translations, into Navajo, of many English words that Navajo interpreters were having trouble translating."[32]

Both the Phelps-Stokes and NMAIA reports also emphasized federal employees' responsibility for communication problems. The NMAIA Report lamented the day schools' widespread failure to communicate government policy effectively, while Phelps-Stokes acknowledged that "the almost exclusive use of the Navajo language has always had and still has a unique function in every place of Navajo life."[33] The remedy, according to both investigations, was for day-school teachers to possess at least a working knowledge of Diné bizaad; Phelps-Stokes recommended this be made an essential criterion for new hires, and the NMAIA advocated compulsory staff summer schools in Navajo language and culture.[34] Interestingly, staff summer schools had been operating (albeit with optional attendance) on the Navajo Reservation since summer 1936: according to the *Navajo Service News*, the two 1936 classes were filled to capacity, suggesting considerable enthusiasm for learning Diné bizaad both "as a cultural asset and a practical tool in carrying on the Navajo program."[35] However, the NMAIA Report indicates these classes, while welcomed by many personnel, did not reach everyone. The NMAIA cited an "elderly Navajo" who noted: "It would be a good thing if the white people understand our language so we can all understand these things. It seems like it all on one side; the Navajo children learn the English language; it would be a good thing if some white people would learn this Navajo language." Some notable individual efforts aside, bilingualism in the New Deal era was, in BIA thought, a largely one-sided expectation.[36]

Despite the *Navajo Service News*' reference to Diné bizaad as a "cultural asset," bilingual education was often officially promoted by the BIA as a means to an end: facilitating an understanding of government policy and promoting English language skills. Although the Lakota primers referred to the preservation of Native languages through bilingual education, the afterword to the Diné primers referred only to "difficulties of translation" that impeded communities' understanding of government policy, especially soil conservation.[37] The NMAIA and Phelps-Stokes reports clearly advocated the learning of Diné bizaad for the pragmatic purpose of transmitting government policy more successfully, not for any intrinsic value of the language itself. In similar vein, Evelyn Crady Adams asserted in her overview of the New Deal education program, "The use of the native language in schools . . . is not at all concerned with its perpetuation, but is for the primary purpose of making contact with non-English speaking students in order to make them literate."[38] This reflects Boyce's recollections of a 1948 hearing between Beatty and conservative congresspersons, at which Beatty defended the use of Diné language instruction against staunch proponents of English-only teaching. Beatty reassured his congressional audience that "the basic purpose of Indian education for Navajo children is to teach them to speak, think, and read and write the English language." Diné language instruction and literacy was pursued with this aim, for "the initial academic approach through the Navajo language, while the student is learning English, speeds up the total education process by approximately two years."[39] Beatty was evidently at pains to convince congress that bilingual education did not signify equality of status between Native languages and English—and given the assimilationist stance of influential representatives such as Arthur Watkins and William Lemke, he doubtless feared the severing of vital congressional appropriations.[40] Whatever the underlying reasons for Beatty's approach, Boyce's appraisal of the hearings is sobering: "No one entertained the idea, nor defended the proposition, that the Navajo tongue was a living language entirely worthy of preserving."[41]

Indeed, Watkins demonstrated his ignorance by asserting that "the Navajos do not have a written language"—eight years after the publication of the first Diné-English bilingual primer and five years after the production of a bilingual dictionary used by Diné military personnel during World War II.[42]

Congressional representatives from Utah, North Dakota, and Montana may not have seen any value or future in the Navajo language in the 1940s, but others certainly did. Boyce recalled that many Diné who took adult education classes "wanted more instruction in reading and writing Navajo."[43] Clyde Beyale, who attended the Wingate Adult short course in 1939, expressed his approval of "boys and girls learning the English and Navajo language alike."[44] And dedicated Diné linguists such as William Morgan, Adolph Dodge Bittany Jr., Howard Gorman, and Albert "Chic" Sandoval, in conjunction with non-Diné linguists and ethnologists, devoted extensive time and labor to the creation of a standardized Diné written orthography. The BIA sponsored three separate Diné language projects in the 1930s, the scale of which, even if the stated aim was to facilitate literacy in English, represented the bureau's acknowledgement that the language had a viable future as a living language, despite the impression given at the 1948 congressional hearings. True, the main project, involving Smithsonian academic John Harrington, linguist Robert Young, and Fort Wingate graduate William Morgan, sought to devise an alphabet using mainly English letters and "comparable sound values." However, this appears to have been adopted more for pragmatic than ideological (assimilationist) reasons. In both Gorman and Beatty's view, using English letters was the most practical option, given that it was the only written alphabet that most bilingual Diné had experience of at that time, whether at school or via signs, publications, and media on the reservation. A further indication that the English alphabet was prioritized for practical reasons is suggested by Beatty's afterword to the *Little Herder* primer series, in which he noted that the language "may be reproduced on any typewriter or linotype."[45] The discussions and debates over the Harrington language project offer a striking insight into the dynamics of power and authority between the BIA, Diné representatives, and the academic community. The debates also show the profound disconnect between 1930s BIA/academic and Diné conceptions of the meaning and significance of language, which fundamentally limited the realization of meaningful cultural pluralism in the New Deal era.

Harrington vs. Gorman/Laves: Control of Navajo Orthography

In 1937, the BIA sponsored the renowned Smithsonian ethnolinguist John P. Harrington to compile a standardized Navajo orthography to replace competing versions compiled over the years by missionaries and anthropologists. Harrington worked on the language from his offices in Washington, DC, while receiving information from his associate Robert Young who was employed at the Wingate sheep lab. Harrington presented his orthography to an Indian Service workshop at Wingate in July 1939—to considerable dismay from Diné interpreters and an Indian Service teacher, Gerhardt Laves. Harrington's orthography followed the Smithsonian's phonetic system (notably the use of *p*, *t*, and *k* instead of *b*, *d*, and *g*), which was rejected both by Laves and Howard Gorman. Laves produced a rival orthography favored by the majority of Diné representatives at the workshop, including renowned interpreter and linguist Chic Sandoval, who was personal interpreter to linguist Father Berard Haile.[46] The stage was set for a vociferous linguistic battle, or, in Beatty's words, "a serious jamb."[47]

Harrington did little to endear himself to the Diné linguists and translators assembled for the workshop. Demonstrating, in Beatty's words, "inexcusable tardiness," Harrington missed the start of the workshop on July 6th—he didn't materialize until the 21st, two days after it was originally scheduled to end.[48] Beatty, perhaps rather sententiously, ascribed the resultant tension and impasse to his own absence: having intended to "award decisions on the successive rounds, much as a referee at a prize fight has to do," he regretfully "left the men to fight it out by themselves."[49] This analogy indicates the extent of tension already generated over Harrington's proposed amendments to the orthography, which had dismayed Howard Gorman. Gorman described how "the talented group of educated Navajos" worked well with Hadley and Laves, and he pointedly noted, "We did a lot of hard work before Mr. Harrington came." When Harrington finally graced the workshop with his presence, he offered, in Gorman's estimation, a "very tiresome" lecture on the scientific phonetic system.[50] Things went downhill from there.

Harrington based his authority squarely (and rigidly) on the primacy of the scientific linguistic system in contemporary Euro-American academic thought. In his view, "The scientific system can never be disproved and will prevail in the long run as no makeshift can do." He believed the Gorman/

Laves system was doomed to failure "because ... [it] is not founded on the basic fundamentals of the scientific alphabet."[51] Anthropologist Richard Van Valkenburgh concurred, arguing, "The scientific system is one which will stand up through years ... therefore why not use the one system that is standard and universal."[52] Both academics subscribed to a source of authority external to the Navajo Reservation, which they believed was irrefutable, timeless, and omnipresent: to them, "The system which is used by scientists will continue no matter what anyone may do.... It is something beyond the Indian Office, the Smithsonian Institution and all of us."[53] In short, they cast the debate as scientific "truth" pitched against transient local sentiment and makeshift compromise.

Harrington's claim to scientific authority was challenged from two directions. Gerhardt Laves, a former linguistics PhD student taught by the linguist and anthropologist Edward Sapir, was himself a product of the Western academic system championed by Harrington. Yet Laves cast doubt on whether the Smithsonian system was as "scientific" or as accepted as Harrington claimed. Laves noted that the International Phonetic Alphabet (IPA) used *b*, *d*, and *g* for "unaspirated, unvoiced sounds" and that Sapir, Haile, and Hadley all applied this to their fledgling Navajo orthographies. Laves charged that leading academic journals such as *American Anthropologist* used "various systems according to author," and he concluded that "the number of scientists using p t k is only small." He also queried whether the Smithsonian system had actually been set as the standard for the Indian Service in 1939, given that the "Sioux" bilingual project was at an earlier stage of development to the Diné project and that consequently no standard had been established.[54]

Diné objections to the Smithsonian authority were based on practical and accuracy concerns. John Charles argued that most Diné were not "scientific minded" and thus found the Smithsonian system incomprehensible.[55] He had previously noted that many Diné teaching assistants disagreed with Harrington's earlier (1938) version, which ignored several key sounds of letters (including *b* and *d*). For this reason, "The majority of our assistant[s] have not taken the opportunity of interesting themselves in the study of the Navajo written language which was brought before them last summer."[56] Howard Gorman also challenged the accuracy of the Smithsonian system. After listening to Harrington outline his scholarly methodology, Gorman referred to "actual sounds in Navajo words" to show that the sounds *b*, *d*, and *g* were more accurate than the *p*, *t*, and *k* advocated by the Smithsonian.[57] According to Gorman, "There are many sounds in the Navajo language that are not covered by the scientific system."[58] In similar vein, Chic Sandoval's "main objection is leaving out b[,] d and g." Indeed, he claimed, "I have never heard anyone use the letter p in writing a Navajo word."[59] Significantly, Sandoval had been training teachers in Diné bizaad at Fort Wingate since 1936. Unlike Harrington, he was well-versed in the mechanics and practicalities of the language as a living, spoken medium. To all three Diné linguists, the Smithsonian system simply didn't represent the Diné language accurately, particularly in terms of its relationship to spoken language. The one Diné representative at the Wingate conference who supported the Smithsonian system, printer and teacher Willetto Antonio, argued that a standardized system for all Native languages was desirable from a *printer's* standpoint—he did not comment on its accuracy.[60]

Gorman offered a multilayered challenge to the Smithsonian system. In a letter to Superintendent Fryer after the workshop, he outlined his opposition to Harrington's approach. In his own words:

> I would like to give the Navajo viewpoint on how to write our Navajo language.... For many years I have studied with many older Navajos who know their language according to the perfect manner of speaking the language—not as the present day, and the younger Navajo children use Navajo. I also had the opportunity of working with many older Navajos who know the writing system of the late Rev. F. G. Mitchell, who translated many chapters of the Bible and Gospel Hymns in the Navajo language. My experiences as an informant and as an interpreter were derived from the hard way of translation, persistently basing all translation of Navajo on the English language foundation which I acquired earlier in life. Whenever you would ask me to translate your important speeches for radio broadcasts, I used to prepare the Navajo translation according to the Mitchell System, which I can read and write very easily. ... It is not based on the scientific way of writing; it is a plain and practical way of writing Navajo.[61]

Gorman thus emphasized both his knowledge of Diné bizaad, as taught him by Diné elders, and his practical experience as a translator. He opposed Harrington's system for two reasons: it did not accurately represent the

Navajo language, and it was cumbersome and unintelligible: "It was full of letters stuck together and we could not hardly read it at all."[62] While acknowledging that the Laves system wasn't perfect, Gorman felt it was practical and offered a more accurate reflection of Diné linguistic sounds. He had commented earlier on Laves's experience, as recorded in the workshop notes: "Mr. Gorman said Laves had quite a bit of knowledge of Navajos and had been among the Navajos while Mr. Harrington had not the Navajo background that Laves has.... He said if Mr. Harrington had been on the Navajo Reservation for two years instead of at his desk in Washington, he would present the same argument for the Navajo Service—he would come to a more practical standpoint."[63] In other words, Laves, by virtue of his work amongst the Diné, had more authority to construct an orthography than Harrington. Gorman then levelled a damning accusation against the Smithsonian linguistics expert: "It appeared he was afraid to speak our language." This reflected Harrington's tendency to write a word on the board and ask Sandoval to pronounce it, rather than attempting it himself.[64]

Beatty did not share Gorman's faith in Laves's knowledge. He confided to Fryer that "Harrington actually knows more Navajo than Laves and Hadley combined, and we can depend upon him for translations which actually say what we want them to say." In contrast, he dismissed the Laves-Hadley version as a mere "concoction."[65] While Beatty then went on to promote practicality and compromise, it was clear he personally favored the Smithsonian system as the more accurate approach, despite Diné objections.

Accuracy was not the only area of dispute surrounding the proposed orthography. The Wingate workshop revealed conflicting interpretations over *who* the standardized orthography was meant to serve—whose interests were being represented and valued? Both Charles and Laves feared Diné school children would struggle with the Smithsonian system. Charles, representing "the present students [sic] standpoint," noted that those who had already learned some English would be disadvantaged by the unfamiliar constructs Harrington was introducing.[66] Gorman argued the orthography was needed for "practical use" by field personnel (range riders, district supervisors, Indian assistants) and school children, "who are not interested in scientific methods."[67] Harrington, in contrast, appealed to an external audience—the global community of scholars interested in Native American languages. According to the workshop report, "Mr. Harrington felt that it is owed to the world in general to have languages written on a uniform basic scientific system, in order that basic principles will be the same."⁶⁸ Van Valkenburgh agreed, noting that his work—including place names and locations on maps—had to be spelled according to a "universally accepted" system to satisfy the Geological Board and the US Geological Survey.⁶⁹ Homer Howard, representing the BIA, also advocated for the Smithsonian system, as it would be instantly recognizable by all students of Indigenous languages. He raised the specter of Diné linguistic isolation, asserting, "You would not want a fence to be built around the Navajo so as to limit or shut it off, because we have chosen a way of writing it that makes it impossible for other people who are interested."⁷⁰ Gorman replied, "If you bring into the argument outside white people who are interested, let them learn the Navajo way."⁷¹

The debate was also marred by an unfortunate incident of cultural insensitivity. In a bid to convince his opponents of the Smithsonian system's merits, Harrington blithely noted that contemporary Zuni and Hopi orthographic projects also used it.⁷² He appeared oblivious of the historical and cultural implications of this comparison, seeing nothing wrong in grouping all regional Indigenous languages together and denying the cultural sovereignty of Native nations. Gorman was particularly incensed at the seeming equation of the distinct languages, arguing that many of the sounds were not the same and that "we do not care about what the Zunis or Hopis do."⁷³ Indeed, the offence generated by Harrington's generalized comparison outlasted the workshop, and to some extent it appears to have cemented some Diné opposition to the Smithsonian system: Gorman later reiterated to Fryer that Diné bizaad was not at all similar to Zuni or Hopi but "is a language of its own."⁷⁴ Harrington and his BIA sponsors clearly failed to appreciate the religio-cultural significance of Diné bizaad, which forms an essential role in the ceremonial connection between the Diné and the *Diyin Din'é* (the Holy People). As Lloyd Lee explains, "Diné bizaad was used to create the world. It is sacred and has power."⁷⁵ Gorman and Sandoval were not just defending the practical mechanics of a language (its written appearance and relationship to speech) but its cultural integrity, identity, and power.

In addition to academics, another group of "outsiders" was cited as grounds for adopting the Smithsonian standard. Homer Howard feared that if the Navajo Service rejected the academic system in favor of the Laves/Gorman "isolated" one, Congress would be less inclined to authorize appropriations for Diné literacy and scholastic projects, also subjecting Beatty to lengthy interrogation over the decision. In an eerie premonition of the 1948 congressional hearings, Howard warned that "there are always people who are trying to find something wrong with what the Indian Office is doing—as soon as these self-appointed critics get hold of a point like this, they try to make trouble," to which Gorman countered, "Let the money part go and accept the right thing for the Navajo."[76]

The debate over the orthography therefore represented a conflict between those who spoke Diné bizaad as their first language and those who viewed it as an area of academic study. The bureau was more inclined to favor the latter, both in terms of expertise/authority and in terms of external considerations such as congressional and scholarly reaction. Interestingly, rigid academic authority did not prevail unchecked: the orthography which survives to this day bears closer resemblance to some of the preferences of Gorman, Sandoval, and Charles, indicating Harrington had to adapt.

In his 1940 afterword to the *Little Herder* bilingual primer series, Beatty summarized the Navajo literacy project:

> In careful use over several years by Dr. Harrington and his associate, Mr. Robert W. Young, this alphabet has been proved adequate for the purpose, and relatively simple to use. The Navaho [sic] manuscripts for this and other volumes in the *Little Herder* series has been carefully prepared by Harrington and Young, and checked for colloquial correctness by a number of Navahos, chief among whom were Willetto Antonio, Adolph Bittany, Hoke Denetsosie, George Hood, Chic Sandoval and Howard Gorman.[77]

Bizarrely, William Morgan's contribution is not mentioned, despite the pivotal role he played in partnership with Young. Also striking is the lack of title accorded to any of the Diné contributors; in contrast to Young, none are described as "Mr." or given any form of address.[78] The pattern was repeated across the range of Indian Service primers: while non-Native academic experts and content contributors were referred to as "Dr.," "Professor," "Mrs.," and "Mr.," the Indigenous translators and artists received no such formality. While this was a step up from Carrie Lyford's "Indian Handcrafts" booklets, which didn't even name Native contributors, the apparent hierarchy presented in the primers is troubling. Perhaps the hierarchy presented by Beatty was one of perceived expertise, with translation and artistry placed below authorship and academic knowledge, or perhaps it was racialized, with non-Native contributors placed above their Native colleagues. Either way, what was hailed as a joint enterprise bringing Native languages and English together on the same page appears, in practice, to have been tarnished by unequal treatment of contributors.

Indian Life Readers: Seeking Assimilation or Pluralism?

Although the dual-language "Indian Life Readers" were commissioned primarily as language-learning aides (with English on one page and a Diné/Hopi/Spanish/Lakota translation on the next), they also feature references to cultural and religious activities and impart moral lessons; these can tell us much about how Indigenous cultures and social structures were presented in the New Deal classroom. Straightforward works of fiction, with no overt pretensions to scholarly significance or wider intellectual purpose (in contrast to both the Indian Life and Customs and Indian Handicrafts series), the Indian Life Readers were commissioned as "simple readers" that described settings, characters, and situations familiar to the pupils who read them.[79] As Peter Iverson has noted of the Diné texts, they enabled school children to "read about a known and valued world."[80] This marked a sharp departure from earlier textbooks, where students were confronted with arcane European fairy tales of golden chairs and castle moats or Dick and Jane–style escapades that bore little relation to many Indigenous lives in the early twentieth century. Such stories likely deepened the sense of alienation felt by some pupils toward the school environment.[81] Indian Service adviser Scudder Mekeel argued that the use of Euro-American fairy tales and popular American picture symbols obstructed Native children's learning, because "a [cultural] background is assumed which the Indian child lacks."[82] In contrast, the Indian Life Readers featured Native characters and used familiar settings—Diné, Pueblo, and Lakota. This marked a radical change of *policy*, but it wasn't entirely new: some Native teachers had used Native stories and characters to facilitate learning during the Assimilation Era. Hopi teacher Polingaysi Qoyawayma had translated Hopi songs and stories into English to encourage children's interest at Hotevilla Day School in the mid-1920s, when the Hopi language was banned on campus.[83] To emphasize the shift from individual, often clandestine, teacher practice to formal New Deal policy, Qoyawayma, like Esther Horne, was invited to demonstrate her teaching methods at an Indian Service summer teaching institute.[84]

The settings of the New Deal stories may have been "Indian," but the authors were not. Beatty was keen to promote the expertise and knowledge of the main author, Ann Nolan Clark, who had worked as a day-school teacher at Tesuque Pueblo. An end note to the *Little Herder* English-Diné primer series introduced Clark as "an Indian Service teacher who has lived among the Navaho, and tells her story with a sure feeling for Navajo life."[85] Similarly, the afterword to *Young Hunter of Picuris* outlines Clark's years of teaching experience in Pueblo communities, which apparently granted her stories "a high degree of authenticity."[86] Also lauded was the involvement of George Sanchez, professor of Latin American education at University of Texas, "for many years a resident of New Mexico and student of Spanish American and Indian culture in that state."[87] Anthropologist Edward Kennard, who lived for a time at Zuni, wrote the Hopi reader *Field-Mouse Goes to War* and edited Clark's Lakota stories. Native American involvement in the texts was limited to translation from English (not vice versa) and to illustrations. Reflecting the non-Native control of the narrative, the Diné and Lakota translators experienced considerable difficulty constructing meaningful translations from the English text, which contained alien words, idioms, and constructs.[88] As Lomawaima and McCarty have noted, the texts follow Euro-American narratives supplemented with "bits and pieces of Native cultural practices, settings, and values"—they are certainly not genuine representations of Diné, Pueblo, or Lakota literature. Lomawaima and McCarty also interpret the texts as largely assimilationist in intent and argue they aimed to promote "obedience to federal authority."[89] Some of the Lakota-aimed texts contained unsubtle messages promoting the joy of hard work, the keeping of root cellars, and the need to be a productive citizen—all straight from the old-time assimilation rulebook. The Diné primers, however, followed a slightly different path: while unabashedly promoting the range management program, they featured human protagonists rather than animals and seemed at pains to promote Diné home life and religious beliefs as worthy and meritorious, themes repeated in the Pueblo books. Indeed, across the board, the tenets contained in the primers are more complicated (and contradictory) than scholars have accepted, with even the Just for Fun Lakota stories sending decidedly mixed messages on assimilation.

The four Just for Fun stories were produced in English and Lakota and published from 1940 to 1943. They each feature a misguided animal protagonist; humans are background characters and generally presented as examples of good behavior, neighborliness, and skill. In each case, the animal protagonists run into difficulties when they attempt to replicate (and exaggerate) aspects of human behavior. For example, the irascible Pine Ridge Porcupine creates problems for himself when he tries to use his quills for pecuniary gain rather than as a defense mechanism as nature intended. Realizing that Lakota women had been collecting his fallen quills and using them in marketable quillwork, the porcupine decides to flex his artistic muscles, spending many laborious hours making traditional Lakota dyes and sewing the quills into a belt. Alas, what he achieves in effort he lacks in skill; the enterprise fails commercially, forcing him to return to his old habit of striking his quills against walls. The women benefit by using the discarded quills in their beautiful, and profitable, craftwork. The moral of the story seems clear: do not go against your nature, or you, and others, will suffer. At the same time, the story goes against the old assimilationist narrative that labor is innately worthy and profitable—the porcupine's hard graft goes wholly unrewarded. In essence, the message appears to be that hard work is good *provided it is profitable* and that skilled craftwork was profitable provided the artisan had the *skill*. In other words, craftwork was a serious enterprise that had to be *learned*.[90] This reflects the message imparted by Ruth Underhill's Diné history primer, that "learning a craft takes years of practice. One must go to school to learn it or have someone at home who can teach it day by day."[91]

The *Pine Ridge Porcupine* may have championed skilled, traditional Lakota craftwork, but it avoided reference to traditional ceremonies or dances. *About the Slim Butte Raccoon* went further. Like the porcupine before him, the eponymous raccoon makes the mistake of trying to be different. He shuns the company of his family and instead becomes entranced by a Lakota community tending a communal garden. In an early example of "wannabe" culture, the raccoon becomes desperate to be an "Indian"—he walks on two legs and tries to join human society. The traditional Lakota community he idolizes is portrayed as generous and tolerant. They allow the raccoon to attend Omaha dances and a giveaway, even bestowing a gift upon him. Unfortunately for them, the raccoon fails to understand the meaning of the ceremonies. When his family visits, he decides to impress them by holding a giveaway of his own, but not only does he seek to honor himself, he chooses to give away items that don't belong to him—the community's melon crop. Disowned by the disappointed humans, he realizes he belongs with his own family. Once again, the tale cautions against being something you are not. The raccoon had also failed to work and produce; he therefore had nothing of his own to give away. So far, so old-style assimilationist. What remains interesting is the story's treatment of the Lakota giveaway. While not described in any detail, it is portrayed as an honorable gathering, and the holder is characterized as generous. The Omaha dance is also not described in the narrative (though it is featured in a drawing by the Lakota artist Andrew Standing Soldier), but it is presented as a normal community occurrence; there is no implicit condemnation as was usual in Assimilation Era BIA statements. The tale censures the raccoon's theft, indolence, and ignorance—*not* the Lakota customs. It is made clear that he has completely misunderstood the giveaway ceremony.[92] He is not "brought low by his give-away" per se but by his attempt to abandon his community and misappropriate another culture.[93] However, the printed page and illustrations, while conveying the views of author and artist, cannot tell us how the story was interpreted by teachers and pupils in the classroom.

Hard work again gets promoted in *About the Grass Mountain Mouse*—although asceticism and overwork are also implicitly criticized. Echoing the European fable of the hedonistic grasshopper and industrious ant, the *Mouse* plotline ultimately cautions against living in the moment and neglecting the future. A compulsive overworker, the "wonderful" mouse is described as "so busy . . . she almost never stops working." The narrator approvingly details her well-stocked larder—her home amply equipped for whatever challenges the seasons may bring. Until, that is, her relatives make a surprise visit and persuade her to accompany them to a rodeo. Initially traumatized at the mere suggestion of recreation, the mouse reluctantly agrees to go. She then transfers her obsessiveness to the rodeo; rather than just admiring the horsemanship on display, she emulates the male cowboys via her language, clothes, and whistling (though, perhaps significantly, not their practical skills), which horrifies her relatives. While they return home at the event's end, she compulsively attends every rodeo event and fritters the summer away, returning in winter to bare cupboards and a freezing home. Happily, she is saved from starvation by her kindly Lakota neighbor, Old Mrs. Two Bears, and realizes the hard lesson that:

> It is a terrible thing
> to have to say, "I played
> when I should have worked."

The story concludes with the mouse's admission that she has learned her lesson and is "through with rodeos. Unless they should have them in winter."⁹⁴

At first glance, *Grass Mountain Mouse* seems a simple rehash of early twentieth-century BIA arguments against ceremonies and gatherings which supposedly distracted people from crop-tending. Clark clearly sought to remind readers to make provision for the future, echoing the uncomfortable paternalism of Stella Young's words in the *Navajo Native Dyes* bulletin introduction: "As the Navajo of today is trained to accumulate supplies for a year in advance, planned rugs may now be woven."⁹⁵ Yet the treatment of the rodeo itself suggests a more nuanced message. Firstly, whereas earlier bureau officials and missionaries had targeted dances and ceremonies, Clark steered clear of the religious sphere and focused on a purely recreational event, thereby satisfying the demands of Circular 2970. Secondly, the rodeo *itself* is not criticized—indeed, Clark praises the horsemanship and wrangling skills of the human participants and affirms the spectators' right to appreciate the event: the mouse's relatives were able to enjoy the rodeo and then return to their routines. In fact, moderation appears to be the tale's underlying message. By depriving herself of any form of recreation—even visiting kin—the mouse had rendered herself vulnerable to a breakdown of self-control, resulting in an addiction to entertainment and an inability to resume daily self-maintenance. The rodeo itself, as a community gathering, is not presented as the problem: *multiple* rodeo attendance and, by implication, behavioral extremes are.⁹⁶ In some ways this message reflects the concerns voiced by Vine Deloria Jr., that protracted participation in summertime gatherings at the behest of ill-informed anthropologists was economically damaging to Lakota and Dakota families in the 1950s and 1960s.⁹⁷

Even the most obviously assimilationist tale, *The Hen of Wahpeton*, sends out mixed messages. Like the other Just for Fun stories, it is both humorous and cautionary, but unlike them, it ends on a grim note. The story features an industrious Lakota family, the War-Bonnets, who are keen to expand their small farm by raising chickens. They are helped by the local teacher who provides a bright yellow incubator chick from the school. The incubator chick stands out from the standard black and white chicks and is immediately pampered by the excited family. She unfortunately develops a superiority complex: "She became too proud of being different. She thought being different meant being better," and she shuns her brethren's barnyard activities in favor of literacy skills. The story then takes an unexpected turn for a schoolbook: book learning facilitates the hen's downfall. She not only pursues an activity that separates her from her community ("What does a chicken need with books?"), but she chooses an unsuitable text as her life guide: "How to Be an Opera Singer in Five Easy Lessons." Rather than earning her keep by laying eggs, she aims to become an opera and movie star. A familiar theme emerges: the pullet is far from lazy, devoting hours to practicing tones and scales, yet the work is wasted as she has no singing ability. Frustrated by the lack of eggs, the War-Bonnets decide to cook her for dinner; her doomed response is to search frantically for a book entitled "How to Lay an Egg in Five Easy Lessons."[98]

The unhappy (albeit off-page) fate of the fame-chasing hen sends a clear message to readers: unrealistic hopes and dreams end in tears. Once again, work by itself is not a guarantee of success; skill and production are presented as vital ingredients for happiness. Snobbery is punished, as is foolishness, as the hen refuses to listen to the commonsense advice of her pullet peers. The War-Bonnets are praised by the narrator for their root cellar and smallholding—suggesting their acceptance of BIA economic counsel. Yet amidst these familiar assimilationist tropes, the tale contains elements of subversion, countering the argument that Clark sought purely to promote "obedience to federal authority."[99] For an administration that emphasized the apparent superiority of Western science and which promoted day schools as valuable providers of community services, the selection of the school incubator chick as the source of strife seems curious. The hen gains a false sense of superiority from her scientific origins, proudly proclaiming, "I'm an incubator songster and I'm different."[100] Yet by the tale's end, the incubator becomes the object of disdain, with the disappointed War-Bonnets exclaiming, "That incubator hen, what good is she anyway! She doesn't earn her chicken feed!"[101] The schoolteacher, and scientific innovation, fails on this occasion—the family would presumably have been better off without the incubator chick. This perhaps reflects widespread frustration amongst rural communities at the United Farm

Program's promotion of brooder-raised "government chickens," which hadn't learned how to "scratch" from their mothers and so followed farm workers around, waiting to be fed.[102] In similar vein, the hen's fondness for literature is presented as part and parcel of her foolishness: instead of heeding the warnings, she struts off "with her book under her wing and her head full of ideas."[103] What message were children, sat in school, learning from a textbook, supposed to take from this? Apparently, book learning alone did not guarantee success. Learning itself, however, was emphasized—and in a rather inaccurate way. The pullets are depicted learning to lay eggs from the mother hen, hardly the "scientific" explanation for the egg-laying process. So what *The Hen of Wahpeton* teaches us is to learn from your elders, not just books; to listen to your community, not books; to do what is expected of you, not what you dream of doing (perhaps an insidious dig against higher education?); to work hard, but only at a productive task; to avoid arrogance and, if you want a large clutch of hens' eggs and no drama, avoid school incubators.

The emphasis on community advice, support, and participation rather than reckless individualism is perhaps the dominant theme of the Just for Fun tales. The porcupine is an isolated individual because he chooses to be rude and bad-tempered, yet his presence at the agency proves beneficial to the skilled Lakota artisans who utilize his quills. The raccoon's problems stem from his attempt to shun his own community and attach himself to another; he returns home to his kin and all is well. The obsessive mouse is saved by the public-spiritedness of her Lakota neighbor, with whom she has an established relationship of mutual benefit. While all the tales deify productive labor (whether by the protagonist or the featured Lakota community) and all present a "right" way of behavior, they do not promote individualism or ambition that separates the individual from their own community in the way sought by earlier administrations. In the tales, strength is gained from being true to those whom you know (family, community, neighbors), not from adopting the behavior or seeking the company of alien others. The Just for Fun stories in this sense do promote an assimilation of sorts—though assimilation to one's own community (and, by extension, New Deal ideals of cooperative behavior and tribal cohesion) rather than an alien society.

In contrast to the Just for Fun stories, the Diné-English *Little Herder* primers feature a human protagonist and her family. The eponymous

"Little Herder" is a Diné girl whose parents earn a living through what the bureau interpreted as traditional Navajo occupations: pastoralism, weaving, silverwork, and pinon gathering. The family practices seasonal migration, travels by wagon, attends sings, and barters with the local trader. Little Herder doesn't seem to attend school but instead plays a vital family role herding sheep and goats. As noted in a previous chapter, the Little Herder series included long passages extolling the virtues of sheep dipping and the need to adopt range management techniques, and thus the books clearly sought to promote the government's soil conservation policy. This was acknowledged by Beatty in his afterword to *Little Herder in Autumn*, in which he laid out the rationale behind the Navajo language program: "To facilitate the spread of information which will help the Navaho [sic] in the control of overgrazing and soil depletion, and show him how to improve the livestock on which his livelihood depends, the federal government has been working with experts in Indian languages to develop a popular alphabet which will encourage the writing of Navaho."[104]

However, as with the Lakota primers, there is more to *Little Herder* than a straightforward assimilationist message. Despite it being a schoolbook, at no point is school even mentioned in *Little Herder*, let alone advocated. Indeed, the same could be said for the Just for Fun tales, with the exception of *The Hen of Wahpeton*'s ill-advised incubator. Knowledge and comfort in *Little Herder* are amply provided by family, community, and environment. Little Herder is taught how to weave by her mother; as with the craftswomen in the *Pine Ridge Porcupine*, Clark emphasizes the traditional skill of Native artisans as well as the message that Diné children have much to learn from their parents and home environment.[105] The treatment of the sing in *Little Herder in Winter* is also significant. The book notes both its curative intent—it is held for a person who is ill—and its religious nature: as Little Herder explains,

> On the trail of the Holy Songs
> we go
> to hear the voices of the Gods.

Clark stresses the religious significance several times while avoiding any description of the ceremony itself, beyond references to "the Holy Trail of Song" and "the Gods are walking, dancing, singing," which is couched in terms of a paraphrased, sung refrain rather than a narrative account. She therefore understood the need to avoid public dissemination of sacred material. Why, then, was the sing included in the textbook? A clue lies in Little Herder's descriptions of the moments before the sing and of its aftermath. The event was well attended, indicating the vibrant, active, and unifying nature of Diné religion. Recreational horse racing after the sing is described at length, too, with a clear emphasis on fun, acumen, and reward. Clark does not condemn the betting and suggests it produced useful gains for Little Herder's family. This is a decisive break from earlier bureau depictions of gambling as a ruinous vice. True, there is no mention of the patient's fate—perhaps reflecting bureau concern over tensions with Health Service personnel—so the book stops short of affirming the sing's curative efficacy. Yet note Little Herder's concluding reflection on the sing as she journeys home:

> We have listened
> to the Holy Songs.
> We have walked
> on the Holy Trail.
> It is finished.
> Our hearts are good.
> All around us is good.[106]

The story—*Little Herder in Winter*—thus ends on a positive note: the sing has created happiness and goodness for all. While the account in no way accurately represents the spirituality and religious significance of these ceremonies for the Diné, the book strongly conveys the theme that Diné religion is a beautiful and positive phenomenon; this went beyond merely including aspects of daily life that would make the primer more relatable for its young audience. The Little Herder series therefore sent its young readers (and schoolteachers) several messages: strictly follow bureau policy on range management, but also continue to practice traditional religion, maintain existing community and family relationships, and learn craft skills from your elders. Spirituality, social organization, and the arts were not only accepted in the bureau's eyes but deemed wholesome and necessary.

The Pueblo Life Readers differed from the Little Herder series and Just for Fun tales in that some expressly featured or referenced BIA schools. The aforementioned *Sun Journey* follows a year in the life of Ze Do, a Zuni boy who is allowed a year off school in order to receive religious training at Zuni Pueblo. The boarding school features in Ze Do's memories, usually for comparative purposes.[107] The device is replicated in *Little Boy with Three Names: A Story of Taos Pueblo*, which takes place during the protagonist's summer break from Santa Fe Indian School (SFIS).[108] Both stories depict the boys' initial longing for the comforts of school life, in particular the warmth of the dormitories and abundant supply of food—hardly an image supported by real-life memoirs of uncomfortable boarding school conditions. However, school isn't the focus of either tale; rather, the narratives involve the children learning about social and cultural life in their respective communities and coming to appreciate both their home learning and their school learning. The stories depict the Pueblo children living in two worlds—the boarding school and their home community—with the school terms bookending the plot. Each sphere is seen to impart its own useful knowledge and skills to be learned and valued. Lomawaima and McCarty note that *Sun Journey* presents Zuni culture as "unchanging and static—categorically of the past, not the present or future."[109] There is certainly repeated emphasis in the Pueblo readers on the ancient origins of Pueblo songs, dances, prayers, and on elders' roles in maintaining religious and cultural knowledge. Yet the dances and prayers are presented as part of living cultures and are attended by the whole community, young and old. The elderly in the stories *actively* engage in transmitting cultural and religious education to the young: "Old men teach the boys. These boys must learn perfectly for some day their work will be to teach the new boys in the pueblo."[110] So while the religious and cultural practices may not be shown as innovative or evolving, they are depicted as phenomena that have great importance in both the present and future life of the Zuni and Taos communities. Indeed, Clark informed the readers of *Little Boy with Three Names* that "many" SFIS students "return home for the various religious festivals which are an important part of pueblo life."[111]

What is curious, however, is Clark's apparent determination to ignore day schools, which by 1940 would have been a typical scholastic experience of many younger Pueblo and Diné children. She even includes a footnote to *Little Boy with Three Names* explaining that by now most Taos children attended the day school from grades one through nine.[112] Presumably the day school did not fit with the "separate spheres" narrative that highlighted the differences between "Indian" (traditional Zuni/Picuris/Taos) and "non-Indian" (Euro-American) cultures. Clark's emphasis on the cultural chasm between school and community also leaves no room for any inclusion of Native cultures on the UPA schools' curriculum—the impression given is of a (largely unexplored) school-based education that is purely Euro-American and a community-based education (spirituality; hunting; herding; communal feasting and recreation) that is of Zuni, Picuris or Taos. The reader gains little sense from these stories of the actual uses of a school education.

The Indian Life Readers remain problematic for readers seeking to analyze their messages and stance on Indigenous cultures. On the one hand, they promote long-standing elements of federal Indian policy: the need to be productive and self-supporting, the importance of soil conservation and vegetable gardens. However, in contrast to earlier policy, they also champion community support and cohesion, presenting both religious ceremonies and recreational dances as important and worthy practices that played a vital role in the present and future. Perhaps the most significant departure is the value accorded to family and community knowledge. Whereas schools had previously denigrated the Native home and family, and indeed health lessons *continued* to depict traditional homes as potential health hazards, the primers suggest that children have much to learn from their parents and elders. The children in the Diné and Pueblo texts learn crafts, cooking, herding, and hunting skills from their families, as well as spiritual values and moral lessons. The Native home and community are depicted as places of warmth, cooperation, and knowledge, which the child needs as much as the education provided by the school. Yet the limitation of the primers is obvious. The books relied not on Indigenous knowledge for their plots and narrative content but on a Euro-American author. The separation between home and school therefore went beyond the physical separation depicted in the stories—it applied also to spheres of knowledge. Indigenous knowledge was portrayed as valuable in the home, community, and spiritual zones, yet it was not used in the creation of school lessons and didactic material.

Contemporary Indigenous Concerns

The Indian Service in the 1930s did invest effort and funds in "Indianizing" some elements of the curriculum, notably textbooks and bilingual education. The question remains as to whether this was welcomed by Indigenous communities. As seen with the McGranahan incident, bureau personnel demonstrated little appetite for asking communities what they felt about the new approach. Where Diné opinions were sought, the findings were sometimes less than enthusiastic—as illustrated by the 1939 Wingate adult short course. The Diné participants were there to learn, but they also contributed to the school's regular classes. According to the acting principal S. Prock, the adults "were often able to offer valuable source of material and criticism" in the Navajo history lessons—an experience that contrasts sharply with Raines's dismissal of Diné historical knowledge for the Pageant of Navajo History a year later.[113] At the course's conclusion, participants discussed their impressions of the school. Alongside numerous requests for better academic standards and improved higher education opportunities for the students, criticism was directed towards the cultural dimension of the curriculum. As the course report's unnamed author summarized,

> Some objections of the school and its teachings were that the girls were cooking the Indian way, teachers telling tales and legends of the Navajos. They seem to have the impression that some were not rightly told. Also that the students were talking too much in the native tongue. They say that all this Indian cooking, telling of tales and legends, could easily and correctly be taught to them during the summer months while the students are at home.[114]

Far from praise for the supposedly inclusive curriculum, there was serious concern that BIA teachers were simply not up to the job of teaching Diné culture. Moreover, the criticisms suggest a deeper disconnect between community and policymaker conceptions of the schools' purpose. The short course participants believed the day schools were failing to produce bilingual students: "They consider the Day School as a place where the young boys and girls should learn to speak the English language but it seemed in some cases they were not doing much about it and in some places nothing at all."[115] Speaking at a council meeting in 1942, District

13 delegate Yellowman reiterated concerns that the government schools were not teaching what many Diné expected them to teach. He condemned the use of textbooks containing Diné pictures and designs; he urged the teacher to "wrap those books up and use the books the white people use. That is what we want." The statement was met with applause, indicating widespread approval.[116] In 1952 council delegate Hoskie Cronemeyer decried the teaching of Diné customs and the holding of tribal dances at the schools—arguing that schools should teach "educational problems" rather than "customs we already know." Indeed, Cronemeyer accused the schools of prioritizing the teaching of Diné customs *over* the teaching of English.[117] Delegate Lily Neil (District 19), the first woman appointed to the Navajo Tribal Council, shared this concern: in 1947 she informed Beatty that the teaching of the Navajo language at the schools was confusing to the children. She charged that not only were the children learning less English and so would be unable to compete with Euro-Americans but that they were being taught "to speak Navajo the broken White Mans [sic] way."[118] And Etsitty Begay of Chinle, a guest speaker and participant in the 1939 Wingate short course, lamented, "Too many young students interested in doings outside such as: squaw dances, etc on the reservation." He claimed that the students "leave school to attend these dances and consequently lose interest in school."[119]

Dakota anthropologist and linguistics scholar Ella Deloria, in her 1944 book *Speaking of Indians*, noted a similar criticism voiced by Native parents she had consulted: "They have been saying they want their children to learn what the other children in the state are required to learn. They can teach them all the Indian lore and language they themselves choose, they say, and do a better job of it. They want the schools to concentrate on things the children cannot learn at home. I think they have something there." Deloria feared that the schools were not preparing Native pupils for life in postwar America, either on or off the reservation.[120] This echoes Polingaysi Qoyawayma's experience at Hotevilla Day School, where parents were unimpressed by her deployment of traditional Hopi songs and stories in class. According to the parents, "We send them to school to learn the white man's way, not Hopi. They can learn the Hopi way at home. Why should they go to school to learn about little squirrel picking pinyons? All Hopi children know about him."[121] The view that "the family should transmit the culture," not the government schools, also came through in interviews conducted with Jemez and Tesuque parents in the late 1960s.[122]

These criticisms of the New Deal curriculum suggest two things. Firstly, that the cultural and language lessons were at times poorly constructed and inaccurate. Secondly, that they were viewed as a distraction from the teaching of English and other "school" subjects. Those who denounced the teaching of Diné language, customs, and dance performances at the schools were not necessarily rejecting traditional Diné culture; Cronemeyer demanded that at school children should "learn what we are sending them over there for" rather than "customs we already know."[123] This doesn't indicate such customs were considered outmoded in the 1930s and 1940s—rather, they belonged to the home/community sphere where they could be expertly taught, in contrast to English language skills which were at that time the specialty of the schoolteachers. In similar vein, Etsitty Begay's view that traditional dances distracted the students from their studies does not, on its own, indicate he opposed them. For him, school was the place to learn "American" skills, home was the place for traditional Diné practices, and when taught together, one could distract from the other. Interestingly, Begay was listed as a contributor to Ruth Underhill's BIA-commissioned history text *Here Come the Navaho!*, indicating he had considerable interest in Diné history and believed it should be taught to the next generation; it was aspects of religion and culture, though, that should be instructed outside of school.[124]

The contemporary criticisms illustrate a key flaw in the New Deal program: the bureau's failure to involve Native communities as active partners in curriculum construction. This unsurprisingly resulted in a curriculum that did not match the expectations of parents, council members, and community leaders. The dichotomy between home and school remained entrenched, despite the emphasis on community day schools. While textbooks championed traditional skills and knowledge, these seemed to be confined to the home environment—few teachers invited community elders and experts to address their classes or comment on the lessons. The books themselves were written wholly by non-Native authors; Native artists were invited to illustrate the texts *after* the narrative content had been composed. In the case of the Diné orthography, Diné speakers had to fight hard to make their voices heard against academic experts whose first language was English, not Diné bizaad. School-based education remained out of community control, even as it incorporated the community's language and professed respect for the community's faith and culture.

The authorship of the school primers and the struggle over the Diné orthography both indicate the New Dealers' tendency to view Native Americans as junior partners in the education process. While the primer narratives depicted Diné and Pueblo elders as authorities on their respective traditional cultures and ceremonies, the Indian Service could not bring itself to utilize their expert knowledge in the composition of the schoolbooks. The primers and the Harrington debate reveal a clear power struggle over who had the authentic and expert knowledge of specific cultures and languages. The undeniable shortcomings of the bilingual primers have led Lomawaima and McCarty to argue that the New Deal "did not envision a 'maintenance' bilingualism and biculturalism that would actively preserve, vitalize, and renew Native cultures into the future."[125] Certainly the primers offered little information on how Native cultures could or should develop, and their depictions were not based on accurate knowledge or any meaningful cultural understanding. However, what is perhaps surprising about many of the primers, given their context and authorial limitations, is their portrayal of Diné and Pueblo cultures as vibrant, community-focused cultures that are integral to present-day life and are being actively passed on to the next generation. Even the Lakota Just for Fun texts, by their positive inclusion of giveaways and Omaha dances, may have helped reinforce the notion of these ceremonies as ongoing and valued practices to their young readers. Indeed, the Lakota anthropologist Beatrice Medicine wrote positively of the bilingual readers that had "astonished" her as a student, describing Clark's texts as "welcome additions to the Christian hymnals and Bibles that were often the main sources of our abilities to read our Native languages." While acknowledging that the primers reached "but a segment" of the Indigenous population in the 1940s, Medicine interpreted them as "a part of cultural revitalization" and argued they "may be evaluated in the historical record as the initial impact of bilingual and bicultural education."[126] This suggests a maintenance *intention* on the part of the primer authors, despite the lack of inclusivity in their creation process.

The Indian Life Readers promoted bureau ideals about community gardens, sheep dips, and soil conservation techniques. But they simultaneously transmitted depictions of traditional Diné, Pueblo, and Lakota ceremonies, customs, and community structures as an *accepted* part of the present and future, conveyed through the medium of Indigenous languages. While this fell far short of biculturalism, and the depictions were both inaccurate and paternalistic, it does suggest the bureau envisaged the maintenance *and* continuation of Indigenous languages, traditional ceremonies, and selected aspects of traditional cultures, albeit all within a Eurocentric framework of federal control, academic authority, and productive citizenship ideals. The federal bilingualism projects and dual-language primers therefore reflect the messy, culturally amorphous nature of the New Deal education program.

EVALUATING THE NEW DEAL EDUCATION REFORMS

6

The New Deal education reforms did not last long. By 1943 Collier was facing considerable congressional opposition to specific programs, notably the Indian Arts and Crafts Board, and a wider consensus within government that the Indian New Deal was an anti-assimilationist policy that sought to suspend Native Americans in a romanticized, pre-Columbian time warp. As one congressional investigation angrily charged, "We are striving mightily to help him [the Indian] recapture his ancient worn-out cultures which are now hardly a vague memory to him and are absolutely unable to function in this present world."[1] Beatty faced regular battles with congress to secure ever-diminishing education appropriations, which had always been inadequate but, by the early 1940s, plumbed new depths of parsimony.[2] World War II made a difficult situation worse, squeezing funding still further and diverting school personnel to the war effort. The Navajo Reservation schools were hit particularly hard: war-induced cutbacks forced nineteen day schools to close by 1944. In addition to staff shortages and decreased funding, the schools suffered from the near-total collapse of the bus system, which, although never fit for purpose, had at least ensured some children could get to the more remote schools. In a sharp rebuke to BIA officials who had, throughout the New Deal, accused them of not supporting the education program, Diné parents and communities strove to keep some schools open by turning them into weekday boarding schools, serving as unofficial dormitory mothers, and providing meals.

Despite heroic local efforts, the program buckled badly under continued financial strain and the secondment of teaching staff to war service.[3]

Strikingly, neither the financial deprivation nor the efforts of Diné communities to keep schools open featured in the 1944 report of the House Select Committee to Investigate Indian Affairs and Conditions. The report effectively denounced the New Deal education reforms as an embarrassing ideological failure that had perpetuated the economic poverty found on many reservations. The Select Committee singled out day schools as a backward step in Indian education—and they bolstered their argument with a familiar trope: the condemnation of Native American home environments. Through being educated in or close to their home communities, Native children apparently faced the "handicap of having to spend their out of school hours in teepees, in shacks with dirt floors and no windows, in tents, in wickiups, in hogans where English is never spoken ... and where there is sometimes an active antagonism or an abysmal indifference to the virtues of education."[4] The parallel with early-twentieth-century reports promoting off-reservation boarding schools is striking: yet again Native homes were denounced as unclean, and Native parents were blamed for failing to appreciate the need for formal schooling. The message was clear: lawmakers wanted a return to residential education for young Native Americans—an education that eschewed "Indian dancing, Indian music, Indian languages, and Indian arts and crafts";[5] that would physically distance children from the "limitations" of their communities; and that would inculcate "American" rather than "Indian" values.[6] As Senators Elmer Thomas, Denis Chavez, Burton Wheeler, and Henrik Shipstead summarized, the government should "eliminate the rehabilitation of Indians as Indians."[7] With the war's end, cost cutting intensified, and the Indian Service moved towards the anti-reservation, pro-assimilation ethos of termination and relocation policies: the future of the New Deal education reforms looked bleak. Although Beatty remained in post until 1952, the attempted "Indianization" of the curriculum—however limited it had been in practice—fell by the wayside.

On the Navajo Reservation, the end of World War II heralded major physical and ideological changes to the government school program. Bureau personnel credited war service and participation in the wartime industries with inspiring a sudden, widespread Diné enthusiasm for formal schooling. In this they blithely ignored the efforts of council members who had continuously lobbied for improved education and the parents who had kept day schools going as makeshift boarding schools.[8] In spring 1946 a Diné delegation headed to Washington to request the fulfilment of the 1868 treaty, which had promised a schoolhouse and a "competent" teacher for every thirty Diné children of school age (six to sixteen).[9] The situation facing the Navajo nation at the war's end was dire: less than half the school-age population—estimated to be twenty to twenty-two thousand—were enrolled in school, and many overage students had received no schooling at all. The congressional appropriation was so meager that only half of the closed day schools were authorized to reopen in fall 1946. As George Boyce recalled, "There was a necessity of discontinuing purchases even of such essentials as pencils, repairs however urgent, toilet paper, and so on."[10] To make matters worse, condemned buildings forced the closure of four on-reservation boarding schools by 1946, leaving dangerous levels of overcrowding in the rest.[11] As an emergency measure to offer schooling to those who had missed out, Beatty, Boyce, and Hildegard Thompson devised the Special Navajo Education Program, which offered pupils aged twelve and above a five-year residential course at Sherman Institute, California.

The Special Navajo Program was, in many ways, the antithesis of the New Deal reforms. It promoted off-reservation residential education for Diné students, firstly at Sherman and then, due to high demand, at Chilocco, Phoenix, Carson, Albuquerque, Chemawa, and Concho boarding schools. The curriculum focused on a single aim: to provide "enough skill in one vocation to enable the graduate to earn at least a modest level of self-support."[12] To achieve this, the program went beyond vocational training and embraced the teaching of English, the conventional 3 Rs, and American etiquette and social mores—dubbed "social adjustment for off-reservation living."[13] Diné culture was off the curriculum: graduates were to gain skills and knowledge for employment away from the reservation. The Special Navajo Program was hailed as a success by its architects; it lasted from 1946 to the early 1960s, was often over-subscribed, and reported encouraging results in terms of graduates' employability and fluency in English. According to Boyce, "A sizable number of Navajo boys and girls who entered the special Navajo program caught up academically, to complete high school, go on to college, and become successful professional workers in various fields."[14]

While the aims and emphases of the Special Navajo Program mirrored the pre–New Deal, Assimilation Era education policy, there was a subtle difference. The Special Navajo Program did not attempt to teach traditional Diné culture in the classroom—yet, unlike earlier assimilation policy, it didn't condemn or belittle it either. As Boyce noted, "Even though students were having to face off-reservation life for self-support, intentional destruction of Navajo culture was avoided as being unwise, unnecessary, and improper."[15] The Navajo language was not forbidden; indeed, much of the instruction for the earlier part of the course was bilingual, with a Diné teacher-interpreter mandated for every class. In a further departure from early-twentieth-century policy, "Only teachers already familiar with Navajo culture through firsthand experience were selected on the faculty." This was to ensure staff "understood the differences in codes of reservation behavior and off-reservation expectations."[16] Bilingual instruction and cultural empathy were deployed as strategies to facilitate the uptake of American social and economic values, not as components of a bicultural curriculum. The Special Navajo Program was not predicated on assumptions that Diné culture and community were dying. Nor were negative forces to be expunged from the pupils' psyches. Diné culture was absent from the classroom, but it was accepted by staff as a valid part of the students' home life. In this sense, something had changed since the 1920s; an assimilationist program could be taught without simultaneously demanding the denigration of Native cultures or assuming their imminent extinction. As Beatty summarized in 1951,

> To avoid the creation of tensions and emotional conflicts, it is essential to preserve respect for the mores of Indian life, while teaching the ways of the white man. Neither is necessarily "better"—familiarity with both is essential to today's Indian youth. Older Indian schools which ridiculed and repressed all expressions of Indian life tended to warp and distort the personalities of their students, and bred resistance to and suspicion of the white man's school in the minds of Indian parents.[17]

By the early 1950s, then, the Indian Service had shifted from seeking "real Navajo schools," which would include Diné history, culture, and art on the curriculum, to "education for cultural change," which would ensure students' "easy transition from life among reservation Indians, to life among urban non-Indians."[18] Although Beatty was at pains to stress that maintenance of Native identity and "racial pride" was not incompatible with the new emphasis on Euro-American cultural and social values and language, and that Native cultures would not be attacked in the school environment, the Indian Service had effectively turned its back on any attempt at a pluralist or bicultural education program.[19] Monoculturalism, albeit with a less destructive face, returned to the government schools. And the power to shape and devise the curriculum remained wholly in government hands until the advent of tribally controlled schools in the late 1960s.

Interpreting the New Deal Education Reforms

So how should we evaluate the New Deal education reforms? They certainly fell short of a true bicultural program, which involves an equal partnership between policymakers and community; the active involvement of the community in curriculum development; and the creation of a curriculum that seeks to maintain traditional cultures and belief systems, not replace certain values with those of the dominant society. Instead, the New Dealers added bits and pieces of Native cultures to school curricula, with scant thought given to Native interpretations or of potential clashes between differing epistemologies. There was no attempt to approach education through a bicultural lens; BIA policymakers continued to develop curricula based on their own concepts of history, science, ecology, and geography, treating them as subjects devoid of any cultural and religious significance. Diné and Pueblo communities were not consulted in the devising of lesson plans, and despite Collier, Ryan, and Beatty's professed aims, few Diné and Pueblo teachers were hired at the reservation schools. The result was a supposedly "Indian" curriculum that was based primarily on Euro-American knowledge and was taught, for the most part, by non-Native instructors. The school program proved largely unpopular amongst the communities it was supposed to serve, in part due to poor academic standards, devaluation of academic instruction, alien teaching methods, and the active decision to use the Diné schools to promote the hated stock reduction policy. It was also unpopular with congressional critics of the Indian New Deal, who viewed it as an attempt to preserve "outmoded" Native cultures and undermine assimilation. In short, the New Deal education reforms on the Navajo Reservation and the UPA could hardly be judged a glowing success.

Contemporary reactions to the New Deal policy of "cultural tolerance" are particularly striking, as they demonstrate that—despite its limitations—it was interpreted *at the time* as a marked departure from the previous assimilationist policy. The education program was roundly criticized by some Native and non-Native contemporaries for what they perceived to be the attempted inclusion of Native cultures. The reforms attracted disapproval both from assimilationists, who feared a "back to the blanket" approach, and from traditionalists, who decried attempts to transplant sacred and community knowledge to the classroom environment and to alien instructors.[20] Clearly neither group viewed the program as Assimilation Mark II. Yet if it wasn't biculturalism, and it wasn't something recognized by contemporaries as assimilation, what was it?

It is tempting to view the New Deal education reforms as a soft-edged approach to assimilation, a gradualist tactic to sugar the pill of eventual cultural change with limited, strictly controlled cultural tolerance. In his research on Māori education reforms in Aotearoa/New Zealand, education scholar Keith Sullivan has identified the "Integration stage" of government policy, signifying "the start of the acknowledgement of cultural diversity." Such acknowledgement is limited, largely cosmetic, and reflects the perceptions of the dominant society. Tellingly, anything that feels threatening or overtly alien to the dominant culture is rejected.[21] Education and diversity studies scholar James Banks has termed this stage the "Ethnic additive paradigm," in which select bits of Indigenous content and themes are bolted onto the curriculum, but no attempt is made to recontextualize them or to restructure the curriculum to reflect non-European perspectives.[22] These arguments have much in common with the safety zone model of Native American education policy. Both models cite government acceptance of the presumed picturesque aspects of Indigenous cultures, notably arts and crafts. Beatty's focus on Native histories and traditional arts suggests that New Deal policymakers felt more comfortable with Native American cultural pasts than with their evolving, dynamic futures, while Native healthcare and political ideologies were largely ignored. As Lomawaima and McCarty convincingly conclude, assimilation to Euro-American democratic (political) and healthcare ideals remained a major component of the government education program through the 1930s—in some respects continuing earlier pathologization of Native homes as insanitary and unhealthy environments that needed to change.[23] Arts and histories were simply added on to a largely Eurocentric curricular framework.

Yet some elements of the New Deal approach challenge the perimeters of the safety zone/Integration stage/ethnic additive model. The acceptance of religious freedom, even at the expense of delivering the school program, suggests some reforms were based on more than just concepts of safety or compliance with government policy. Religious ceremonies were not viewed by Collier, Ryan, and Beatty as harmless or quaint pursuits unaffecting bureau policy but as crucial aspects of Diné and Pueblo cultures integral to community vitality and wellbeing. The presentation of Diné and Pueblo religions and cultures in the primers, while neither detailed nor accurate, also challenges the view that the New Dealers sought to neutralize Native religions by fixing them to the distant past. True, the religions were described as ancient and unchanging—the timeless, static portrayals noted in the safety zone thesis. Yet it was the knowledge and rituals that were described as old, not the ongoing practice and community impact, which were located in the present. The sing in *Little Herder* was presented as vital for the Diné community who attended; it was depicted as important *in the present*, and there is no suggestion in the text that it would be any less important in the future.[24] The hoop dances taught by the Taos elders to the younger men and boys in *Little Boy with Three Names* are also depicted as of the present and future: "These boys must learn perfectly for some day their work will be to teach the new boys in the pueblo."[25] This description does not suggest the dances and beliefs were "categorically of the past, not the present or future."[26] Rather, the author suggests they *will* continue into the future and that they have a dynamic impact on the community who practices them. New Dealers did emphasize the "ancient" or "age-old" origins of the sacred knowledge and ritual performance, thereby ignoring the living, evolving nature of Indigenous religions and cultures. Yet Clark and Beatty declined to confine the *practice* and *impact* of Diné and Pueblo religions to the past—they believed they were necessary for the communities' survival. Again, the concept of safety or harmlessness doesn't neatly fit here; the 1930s policymakers didn't grudgingly permit religious freedom because they thought Indigenous traditional religions were innocuous and therefore inconsequential, but because they believed them to be essential to the cohesion and wellbeing of those communities. This resembles an attempted pluralistic approach towards religions rather than a superficial tokenistic tolerance. Indeed, active bilingual instruction and the acceptance of religious belief and worship suggest a movement towards what Banks terms the "cultural difference paradigm," whereby educators acknowledge the value of a community's culture and view its language, values, and cultural traditions as functional, or essential, for that community. In this model, bilingualism is seen as a strength, not a weakness, and cultural diversity is accepted as an enriching characteristic, not as divisive or damaging; cultural identification is both acknowledged and developed by the school.[27] The New Dealers appear to have adopted this in terms of accepting religious freedom (albeit based on *their* cultural perception of religious worship) and teaching bilingualism, while flagrantly ignoring it regarding science.

Untangling the Contradictions: The Indian New Deal and Colonial Education Paradigms

Despite the championing of freedom for ceremonies, Native languages, and community structures, however, the New Deal education reforms continued to promote federal control over Native lives. Curriculum development remained largely the preserve of non-Native bureau personnel, who also dominated the teaching cohort. Control of education, both at the developmental (curricular) and practical (teaching) stages, remained Euro-American, hence the perpetuation of a curriculum that reflected Eurocentric ideals such as Western science. This dominance of the curriculum suggests links to wider colonial education paradigms, such as cultural invasion and epistemicide, which can help explain the contradictions inherent in the New Deal reforms.

Cultural invasion, identified in 1968 by the Brazilian education scholar Paulo Freire, is the process through which an invasive group (colonizers, political elites) seeks to consolidate its dominance over another group by imposing its own cultural values and narratives. In this model, "The invaders penetrate the cultural context of another group, in disrespect of the latter's potentialities; they impose their own view of the world upon those they invade and inhibit the creativity of the invaded by curbing their expression." Control is therefore at the heart of cultural invasion: "The invaders are the authors of, and actors in, the process; those they invade are the objects. The invaders mold; those they invade are molded. The invaders choose; those they invade follow that choice—or are expected to follow it." According to Freire, the aim of cultural invasion is to deprive the invaded of their decision-making powers and to convince them of their own cultural inferiority so that they will embrace the invaders' culture and, by extension, authority. And the invasion need not be a military one—so-called camouflaged invasion, in which the invader appears as "a helping friend," can also result in cultural domination of the invaded. Significantly, Freire argues that cultural invasion can be carried out for both self-interested (imperial) and benevolent (imposed "development") motives: irrespective of the invaders' intent, both forms are damaging to the invaded.[28]

Freire based his research upon the experiences of economically impoverished or marginalized rural communities in Brazil in the middle decades of the twentieth century. However, his model has resonance for BIA education policy. Indian Service educators in the early twentieth century—the coercive Assimilation Era—certainly tried to impose their cultural and economic values upon Native children and to convince pupils of their cultural inferiority. This invasion was aggressive, coercive, and was based upon assumptions of total Euro-American cultural superiority. In contrast, the New Deal, with its piecemeal forays into cultural pluralism, appears less of a match for this schema. Yet a closer look reveals some links. The New Dealers believed Western science and medicine to be superior to Diné ecological and medical knowledge, and they expected the Diné to accept this. They assumed key decision-making roles—whether as education directors, teachers, textbook authors, or soil conservation experts—and largely relegated Native Americans to subordinate positions in the education experience. And they did so in the belief they were helping Native communities—in other words, Freire's camouflaged invasion. But the model falls short of an exact fit. Freire described cultural invasion as the intended *total* replacement of one culture with another; he did not allow for exceptions. Once again, the New Deal emphasis on religious freedom proves problematic. The New Dealers practiced cultural invasion in some aspects of Native cultural lives but not in others.

Epistemicide, as defined by anthropologist Francis Nyamnjoh, is another colonial education paradigm that bears some similarity to historic BIA education policy.[29] Describing the education programs imposed by European colonial powers in African localities, Nyamnjoh argues that colonial authorities sought to annihilate Indigenous knowledge systems and replace them with European-based theories. He defines epistemicide as "the decimation or near complete killing and replacement of endogenous epistemologies with the epistemological paradigm of the conqueror"—a process that promotes "mimicry over creativity."[30] According to Nyamnjoh, the purpose of epistemicide was completely selfish: "to provide colonialism with the local support staff it needed to achieve its hegemonic imperialist purpose."[31] Like cultural invasion, the impact could be catastrophic, resulting in internalized feelings of inadequacy and devalued Indigenous creativity and decision-making powers.[32] Again, this bears closer resemblance to BIA education policy in the Assimilation Era—attempted destruction and denigration of Native epistemologies with the aim of effecting total assimilation and unquestioning compliance with federal government initiatives. The use of martial or violent language (decimation, destruction, epistemicide) even mirrors the militaristic "Kill the Indian to save the Man" rhetoric favored by noted "Friends of the Indian" such as Merill Gates and Richard Henry Pratt.[33]

Were the New Dealers seeking the epistemicide of Native knowledge systems? In some ways, no: they didn't want total cultural assimilation; they promoted Native languages; and Ryan and Beatty would have balked at any suggestion of "killing" Native cultures. Yet Nyamnjoh's deconstruction of the colonial (Eurocentric) education rationale offers pause for thought. In his words, colonial epistemology "tends to limit reality to appearances (the observable, the here and now, the ethnographic present, the quantifiable), which it then seeks to justify (without explaining) with meta-narratives claiming objectivity and a more epistemologically-secure truth status."[34] This echoes the New Dealers' promotion of Western science and Eurocentric academic research over Diné, Pueblo, and Tohono O'odham knowledge, ecological theories, and metaphysics. Soil conservationists attempted to reduce Diné Bikéyah to a series of measurements, drainage assessments, and water sources—all quantifiable and observable data, but they ignored the human knowledge and experience that could aid the interpretation of the findings and thus help shape policy development in a way that was representative of both US and Diné thought and understanding. Children at the schools were taught Western scientific explanations of weather and other natural phenomena, again prioritizing the quantifiable over the metaphysical. Such teaching of scientific epistemology actively challenged Diné traditional epistemology and sought to replace it. Klamath sociologist Clayton Dumont Jr. has described such refusal to recognize Native knowledge systems as "an epistemological violence," which continues to damage

Native American sovereignty today, particularly concerning the repatriation of human remains.[35]

Dumont Jr. and Nyamnjoh each raise the fraught issue of scientific "truth," and this has considerable relevance to the New Deal education program. While Nyamnjoh charges that the colonizing epistemology "takes the form of science as ideology and hegemony," Dumont Jr. points to widespread promotion of Western science as "a universally valid and morally neutral form of knowing" —becoming to many "the *only* legitimate form of authority."[36] The link between truth and power is therefore significant and has both political and cultural implications; as Dumont Jr. states, "The power to narrate truth is critical to the pursuit of native sovereignty."[37] French philosopher Michel Foucault also considered the truth-power relationship and its relation to science and academic research. He proposed that in Western (Eurocentric) societies truth is grounded in scientific discourse, and it is circulated through schools, the media, and published writings, which are valued as transmitters of truth. In this system, truth becomes a regime, linked to and propagated by the dominant system of power/governance: "'Truth' is to be understood as a system of ordered procedures for the production, regulation, distribution, circulation and operation of statements." And it remains "linked in a circular relation with systems of power which produce and sustain it, and to effects of power which it induces and which extend it." In other words, "truth," and by extension "scientific truth," is neither an automatically neutral nor objective entity. Foucault also acknowledged that "truth" can be culturally relative; each society possesses its own "regime of truth." This regime encompasses the following: "The types of discourse which it [society] accepts and makes function as true; the mechanisms and instances which enable one to distinguish true and false statements, the means by which each is sanctioned; the techniques and procedures accorded value in the acquisition of truth; the status of those who are charged with saying what counts as true." In this model, truth becomes a commodity which must be verified through recognized *tests* conducted by designated *experts*. The designation of experts and the criteria for the tests are a part of the established power system.[38]

This interpretation of the relationship between "truth" and "power" may go some way toward explaining the inconsistencies and failings of the New Deal cultural tolerance experiment. A key contradiction presented in this book is the BIA's professed championing of religious freedom and admiration for Native cultures, alongside the simultaneous prioritization of Western science. The sanctioning of school absences for ceremonial reasons, the willingness to alienate the bureau's missionary partners by prohibiting unsolicited proselytization in schools, and the lifting of the dance bans all suggest that the professed religio-cultural tolerance was sincere, at least from the uppermost policymaking tiers. How then could Ryan, Beatty, and Collier aggressively promote scientific soil conservation measures which actively contradicted Diné traditional religion? The answer perhaps lays in their faith in Western science as an objective truth. Range management, as prescribed by the Soil Conservation Service (SCS), was based on the latest scientific knowledge of soil drainage, grazing capacity, and plant growth and decline, and it was supported by observable tests, measurements, pictorial evidence, and mathematical equations. Such data was held in high regard by US government authorities in the 1930s: *The Farmer's Irrigation Guide* issued by the Bureau of Reclamation in 1939 directed US farmers to create their own "experiment station" on each farm, to use moisture probes, and discover their land's subsoil conditions. It cautioned against reliance on "traditional methods" of farming which had apparently caused washing and leaching and consequently reduced productivity.[39] In similar vein, the Arizona State Board of Health in 1938 proposed a public health intervention for the state's rural communities, whereby a "corps" of "well-trained, intelligent sanitarians" would educate the rural population "in proper methods of sewerage construction," "proper" fly control measures, and in the maintenance of new privies in a bid to improve living conditions and reduce death rates.[40] The parallel with the language used by the SCS towards the Diné is striking.

Scientific theory and academic-directed research formed the basis for wider New Deal rural policy in the 1930s. Soil erosion was, in the words of Morris Cooke of the Rural Electrification Administration, the nation's "insidious enemy"—and necessitated significant government intervention into the lives of American farmers.[41] The Mississippi Valley Committee, reporting on deforestation and soil erosion, advised that "the people cannot reach the highest standard of well-being unless there is the *wisest* use of the land and water."[42] As early as 1936, sociologist Paul Landis observed the significant reach of range management initiatives across the United States: "The great expansion of the Soil Conservation Service and the placing of erosion projects in the various states, along with propaganda staffs, has been calling the attention of the public to the need for erosion control.... This department is teaching farmers the means of soil conservation." The Resettlement Administration had, he summarized, "stressed the retiring of poor land from destructive use, and the learning of proper ways of using all lands."[43] And this attempt to *reeducate* American farmers in their craft was implemented by an unprecedented coalition of academics and policymakers. As Landis enthused, "This situation has provided the first great opportunity for the politically-minded and research-minded to meet on a common ground and face from a common vantage point the needs of 'the people' and try to adjust the nation's heritage in natural resources to those needs. It is a golden age for rural research."[44]

Significantly, this "benevolent paternalism on the part of the national government" did not stop at soil conservation education but extended to "organized recreation" and to homemaking and dietary instruction; indeed, the Department of Agriculture urged American farm women to adopt the "corrective diets," food preparation, and housecleaning techniques taught by the federal home extension service.[45] The implication was that American rural communities, despite having worked on the land for generations, were ignorant of modern healthcare principles and of responsible agrarian practices. Rural sociologists and soil conservation experts would educate them to manage their natural resources and to elevate their standard of living to a modern (and, by implication, urban) American level through technological advances in agriculture, healthcare, and home management. And with mixed results. Landis, while applauding the government's aims, lamented the haste with which some interventionist projects were executed: "Even the hurried New Deal research did not always produce information until the new social experiments had been launched.... Rehabilitation projects were begun before any research was available even through the fast working research staffs. Because of this there has been considerable backing up and starting over after the facts have been analyzed."[46] Haste and rushed experimentation clearly weren't confined to the Indian Service in the 1930s; they characterized rural policy more widely. Certain shared themes—rushed policy, paternalism, government prioritization of soil conservation and academic experts, extensive government-sponsored intervention in community life—suggest that the Indian New Deal should also be regarded as an essential part of wider New Deal history.

Science-based environmental and healthcare theories were therefore a key part of the 1930s "regime of truth" in the United States. Scientific explanations had become the discourse which was accepted by government as true; scientific testing was the mechanism which enabled society to distinguish between true and false; scientific and sociological research was the procedure valued in the acquisition of truth; and professional scientists were charged with saying what counts as truth. The same veneration was accorded to medical science, another zone of knowledge accepted by policymakers as objective truth, devoid of cultural context and impact. The statements made by leading New Dealers on the necessity of stock reduction and the importance of Western medicine reflected their unquestioning acceptance that science provided the best (and sole) solutions to ecological and medical problems. It is here that Nyamnjoh's description of science in colonial education as "hegemony" becomes significant: BIA policymakers, educators, and SCS ecologists treated scientific conclusions as incontrovertible truth.[47] They spoke of soil conservation theory and Western medicine as undisputed facts that everyone understood and had to accept—failing to realize that, as Jack Forbes noted, science is itself culturally informed and therefore a subjective truth.[48] Even Collier and Beatty, with their repeated spoken and written admiration for Native religions, could not conceive of challenging the SCS recommendations or accepting Diné healthcare as an equal partner to Western medicine in the fight against illness. Rather, they themselves had been so thoroughly indoctrinated with Western scientific truth that they could not recognize the possibility of viable alternative truths and so imposed their own understanding of truth upon Native nations. And it is this superimposition of narratives that forms a link to settler colonialism, despite the New Deal's emphasis on land reclamation, religious freedom, and tribal sovereignty. As Veracini notes in his overview of settler colonial narratives, "Settlers do not discover: they carry their sovereignty and lifestyles with them.... They move towards what amounts to *a representation of their world.... They transform the land into their image.*"[49] The New Dealers may not have sought the alienation of Native lands via allotment or the erasure of Native nations to make way for settlers, but they did attempt the erasure of non-Western medical and ecological knowledge systems through their inability to move beyond the confines of their own experience and worldview.

Freire also warned of "well-intentioned professionals" who "use [cultural] invasion not as deliberate ideology but as the expression of their own upbringing"—in other words, invaders who don't seek to destroy the culture of the invaded but whose immersion in the hegemonic ideology of their own society is so complete as to blind them to the notion of differing cultural concepts and realities.[50] This also relates to the BIA's unquestioning elevation of academic expertise over local Indigenous knowledge in the 1930s. Reflecting the Roosevelt administration's promotion of experts as policy advisors, notably the "Brains Trust," Collier, Ryan, and Beatty put their faith in language professors, anthropologists, professional historians, scientists, and engineers, whose authority and credentials reflected contemporary US concepts of truth and knowledge.[51] In so doing, they posed a new threat to Indigenous cultural sovereignty, not through deliberate cultural destruction but through the often unthinking attempted replacement of Indigenous knowledge systems and narratives. As Rebecca Tsosie reminds us, cultural sovereignty for Native nations involves "the power to constitute their own histories and identities and counter what they perceive as the false images that have been presented as 'truth' by non-Natives."[52]

The all-pervading hegemony of scientific and academic truth does not, however, tell the whole story of the Indian New Deal's limitations. The New Dealers also failed to implement a fully pluralistic education program because they imposed their own *concepts* of culture and religion onto Native communities. As Donald Fixico has argued, "Modern academia excludes the indigenous mind and neglects to infuse it as a part of the American experience in textbooks, films, and in classrooms."[53] The New Dealers committed a similar error: they excluded Indigenous interpretations of culture, history, medicine, and ecology from their policymaking, instead persisting in viewing Diné and Pueblo lives through a Eurocentric conceptual framework. Like the 1960s rural extension workers lambasted by Freire, they ignored the cultural totality of traditional Native communities and failed to understand the interconnectedness of what he identifies as a "cultural structure."[54] Scudder Mekeel raised the alarm in 1936, cautioning, "It is not yet appreciated by administrators of peripheral peoples that culture is a delicately balanced mechanism, a part of which cannot be tinkered with, without in some degree affecting the whole."[55] His warning was ignored. The Indian Service in the New Deal effectively compartmentalized the life processes of Native communities into self-contained, nonpermeable spheres, with "history" distinct from "culture" and "ecology" distinct from "religion" or metaphysical understanding.[56] This categorization and isolation of community beliefs and outlooks was attempted both inside and outside the schoolhouse. Individual staff may have warned of the cultural and creedal clashes, but ultimately no one at the upper echelons of bureau decision-making listened. Compartmentalization along Eurocentric lines rendered any meaningful attempt at a culturally pluralistic curriculum defunct.

The BIA was not the only compartmentalizer in action at that time. Indigenous parents and communities in the 1930s may have been left out of the curriculum-building process, but they had their own expectations of school curricula and of the cultural limits of formal education programs. Many Diné, Pueblo, and Hopi parents did not want traditional cultural knowledge taught at the BIA schools in the 1930s and 1940s; they viewed the home and community as the rightful location for cultural and religious instruction. School, in contrast, was for the learning of "American" subjects, notably the English language and the vocational skills necessary for the US job market. As Colleen O'Neill has shown in her examination of Diné labor history in the twentieth century, Diné workers applied a similar strategy to their involvement in the US wage economy that allowed them to both earn money and maintain their cultural traditions. A worker might leave the reservation for up to four months at a time in order to participate in the US economy, but they would return home to attend ceremonials and fulfill family obligations—often to the frustration of employers who had to adjust to their workers' cultural demands.[57] The Diné and Pueblo communities in the early twentieth century had not stood passively by as economic and political conditions changed. They had devised their own strategies for navigating the separate spheres of both their own cultures and the US economy, holding their own views as to how best to maintain the balance between them. The New Dealers' patchy pluralism, devised without Diné or Pueblo involvement, risked transgressing these epistemic boundaries, infringing cultural authority, and threatening to dilute the education that these communities expected schools to provide. As Katharine Jensen has argued, "Collier wanted to correct the common belief that in Indian education a choice must be made between traditional and contemporary lifestyles."[58] However, the reality was that Native communities had already made choices of their own as to what should be taught, where, and by whom. This perhaps explains why the Special Navajo Program of the late 1940s and 1950s gained significant Diné support, including the approval of the Navajo Tribal Council: by providing an education geared towards participation in the US economy that did not attack Diné culture in the classroom nor include it on the curriculum, the program did not threaten existing epistemic and cultural boundaries, boundaries which the Diné had carefully erected to protect their cultural sovereignty and defend their economic interests in the first half of the twentieth century.

The education reforms implemented by the Indian Service in the 1930s did mark a policy change from the total assimilation pursued by previous administrations. The New Deal approach was not bicultural in theory or practice: Native communities were not involved in curriculum design, and non-Native policymakers and teachers ensured the curriculum retained a Euro-American perspective. In part, the New Dealers' "cultural tolerance" resembled the safety zone or ethnic additive model, with its selective inclusion of Indigenous cultural elements. Yet some of the 1930s and early 1940s reforms went beyond just what policymakers viewed as the "quaint" and cosmetic aspects of culture. By attempting to include active bilingualism and accepting religious freedom, the New Deal education program arguably sought to maintain those components of Native cultures (languages and religions) and so came close to an *intended* pluralist approach in these areas. However, the continued reliance on Euro-American interpretations of subjects, and the failure to adapt the curriculum to include Indigenous perspectives and philosophies, places the New Deal education program *in practice* in the ethnic additive education paradigm. This was a tentative first step on the path to biculturalism but far short of a curriculum that could educate Native children to live in "two worlds" without alienating them from their traditional cultures. Despite professed admiration for Native cultures and a sincere commitment to religious freedom, Collier, Ryan, and Beatty remained bound and blinkered by the constraints of their own cultural values and regime of truth—founded on Western science and deference to academic and technical authority—which blinded them to the contradictions and limitations of their education program.

And that is the underlying failure of the Indian New Deal education policy: pluralist acceptance, indeed celebration, of Native religions, languages, and community identity was shackled to Eurocentric scientific and scholastic interpretations and conceptions of authority, while remaining divorced from community input. What emerged was an ethnic additive curriculum that tentatively and sporadically crossed into a pluralist model, ironically via a subtractive element (the sanctioning of pupils' leave to attend religious ceremonies) which demonstrated pluralist intent. Part pluralism and part Eurocentrism, set within a Euro-American curricular framework—the New Deal adopted an approach that confused many and satisfied few. As an early example of government-directed pluralist education, it offers a cautionary lesson to future educators and policymakers seeking to develop cross-cultural curricula.

EPILOGUE: MONOCULTURAL RESURGENCE AND BICULTURAL EDUCATION IN PRACTICE

Tribal control [of education] is necessary not only to achieve tribal and individual self-sufficiency but to reclaim and strengthen the use of Native languages and cultures in schools and communities, thus ensuring a strong future for all Indian people.
—John W. Tippeconnic III

This book began with Jack Forbes's warning of a resurgence of monocultural, assimilationist education in the US public school system.[1] Studies conducted by education scholars in the 1990s and early 2000s not only supported his fears but extended them to BIA-controlled schools. A two-year survey of Native American parents conducted by Carol Robinson-Zanartu and Juanita Majel-Dixon between 1993–95 revealed significant parental concern that public and BIA schools devalued Native cultures and held lower expectations of Native children. The authors' summary of parental responses is sobering: "On the whole, they perceived a great deal of ignorance about and disrespect for themselves, their children, their communities and their cultures from the public and bureau or boarding schools. In fact, the sentiment against the BIA boarding schools was so strong, that narrative comments went beyond commentary about schools not knowing or caring about Indian people, but cautioned that BIA schools actually hurt the children." The 234 parents and community members, representing fifty-five tribes, had a "fairly strong" knowledge of the curriculum—but many felt ignored by BIA and public schools. They believed the schools were ignorant of Native cultures, didn't include them on the curriculum, and were doing little to prevent cultural alienation. These findings indicate that, by the end of the twentieth century, much formal schooling for Native American children remained nonpluralist. As Robinson-Zanartu and Majel-Dixon note, "In mainstream education, culture has often been relegated to a position of 'background data,' and viewed as something separate from learning, from relationships in classrooms, and from parent support of educational processes."[2]

Significantly, the majority of the parents surveyed wanted their cultures to feature on the curriculum and their histories to be taught accurately, while also seeking improvements in math and science teaching. As the study concludes, parents "have spoken loudly of the need to preserve and value their cultures as integral to [their children's] learning" and have also expressed "the need to be able to walk successfully in two worlds."[3] The Indian Nations at Risk Task Force, an investigation commissioned by the secretary of education which surveyed Native parents and educators in 1990–91, also found that parents wanted their communities' histories and cultures included on school curricula. The Task Force recommended that schools catering for Indigenous students should "maintain native languages and cultures."[4] A school-based education program that featured both traditional Native beliefs and Euro-American beliefs was therefore being demanded and debated, if not actually implemented, by the closing years of the twentieth century—some fifty years after the New Deal.

Compartmentalization, and the token inclusion of some cultural elements, was also rejected by Native teachers who participated in a 2007 survey by Diné education scholar Timothy Begaye.[5] The teachers, all of whom identified as Native American, had completed a four-year college teacher education program and were in the first two years of teaching in Native communities; they strongly supported the inclusion of Native languages and cultures on school curricula. Most participants agreed that the "younger generation must understand their history, stories, traditions, and beliefs" and that placing traditional languages and cultures on the curriculum would aid cultural survival.[6] Yet the majority also cautioned against the instruction of "religious concepts" in the school environment, which would be best taught by elders and traditional medicine practitioners.[7] This reflected the concerns expressed by Hopi parents in a University of Kansas sociological survey sponsored by the National Institute of Education between 1970–72.[8] As one Hotevilla parent noted, "We do not want our beliefs and dances taught in the school. That is for the village—it is not for school."[9] These echo the sentiments voiced by some communities in the 1930s and reflect the potential for religious desecration and cultural blunders, such as taboo animals in the classroom and ceremonial dances performed out of context. Like the teachers interviewed by Begaye, the Hopi parents in the early 1970s did not want religion to be taught in an alien context or by unauthorized instructors. The issue of authority in education offers a sharp counterpoint to the stance of New Deal policymakers: for the Native teachers and parents interviewed, authority lay in specially tasked individuals from the community, not academic "experts" from the outside. These concerns indicate that mere inclusion of Native cultures on school curricula is not enough; rather, communities must be consulted as to what aspects of cultures and beliefs can be taught in a school environment and who has the authority to teach them. As Judy Iseke and Leisa Desmoulins conclude from interviews with Métis elders involved in teaching Indigenous science, "Only those who have a relationship to the medicines should perform sacred teaching and oversee learning so the knowledge is respected and used appropriately. Misuse and misunderstandings could be dangerous."[10]

The tensions between monoculturalism and pluralism, and between cultural inclusion and cultural authority, continue to affect Native American students at BIA and public schools to this day.[11] Yet significant developments have occurred at the higher education level. Since the late 1960s, tribally run colleges have sought to combine traditional and nontraditional learning. As the author of a 1989 report sponsored by the Carnegie Foundation testified, "Tribal colleges offer culture-based curriculum where traditional Indian culture is celebrated.... But this emphasis on Native American culture should not be seen as an attempt to withdraw from contemporary society."[12] The report argued that tribal colleges taught traditional culture as an important component of the *present* rather than a distant past and that they viewed traditional culture "as their social and intellectual frame of reference."[13] This differs significantly from the New Deal's isolation and detachment of cultural components (history, geography, nature, arts and crafts) into separate lessons. Tribal colleges and community-controlled schools were created by Native communities in the later decades of the twentieth century in direct response to continued monocultural and insensitive teaching at BIA and public schools.

Bicultural Education in Action: Navajo Community College, 1970

The Diné were among the first Native nations to take control of the formal schooling process in this period. By 1970, Diné pupils and parents were voicing concern at both the pervading monoculturalism and the poor caliber of education offered at the public and BIA schools. In the summer of 1970, Diné students at Shiprock Public High School, which had a 90 percent Diné cohort, produced a damning report on the curriculum. As Diné teacher Gloria Emerson summarized before a congressional hearing two years later, "Their report showed that the school curriculum did not reflect the uniqueness of their cultural heritage. In fact, educators there are extremely condescending of, and negative to requests by Navajo students, their well-informed parents and other Navajo educators that they begin to work to offer quality and not mediocre education to their students."[14] Emerson cited the school board's dismissal of parents' requests for the removal of a textbook deemed disrespectful of Indigenous history. At the same hearings, Diné educator Ned Hatathli offered a scathing assessment of government failure to consult or involve Native communities in education policy. He also poured scorn on policymakers' recent bicultural rhetoric, which he felt was unhelpful and insincere: "As to the word 'bicultural.' Here again is this word, which does not properly reflect the intense pride Indian people have in being Indian and their earnest desire that schools deliberately and conscientiously develop meaningful and extensive programs dealing with the history and culture of individual tribes and of the Indian people in general. I view the inadequate recognition of this need as a major weakness."[15]

Hatathli was the inaugural president of Navajo Community College (NCC), chartered in 1968. The first tribal college established by Native Americans, it built upon the success of Rough Rock Demonstration School, a community-operated school founded by the Diné in 1966. The then Navajo Tribal chairman, Raymond Nakai, believed that parents should be "a vital force in Navajo education" and that schools should "make the Navajo children proud of who they are and knowledgeable about their community, tribe, and history."[16] With a mission to preserve and transmit Diné language and culture, NCC under Hatathli offered a curriculum which centered Diné cultural studies and prioritized Diné faculty. The initial aims were conveyed by Howard Gorman, a member of NCC's first board of regents: "Now we have a college on the reservation so our students can go to college here at home. We have our own language and culture in the curriculum. We will be able to provide another chance for the many that never before had a chance. The college is guided and controlled by an eight-member board of regents. We provide the direction. It is our college."[17] The board of regents and school staff, with the aid of an Office of Education grant, embarked upon a major project to devise a Navajo Studies curriculum "which would reflect the thinking of the Navajo themselves."[18] This was a significant undertaking—in 1970 less than one school in twenty on the Navajo Reservation taught Diné culture, citing a dearth of teaching materials and specialist staff.[19] With the board of regents serving as a curricular advisory committee, the NCC staff, in conjunction with Rough Rock colleagues, produced modules on Diné history, arts and crafts, current affairs, and language, which were implemented in the 1970 fall semester. The differences between the NCC history program and the New Deal Navajo history lessons are significant and highlight the limitations of 1930s pluralism.

The first key area of difference lays in NCC's prioritization of Diné perspectives on Diné history and culture. This was especially true for the module on Diné Origin narratives (Navajo History and Culture I), which examined "the origin of the Navajo people as seen through the eyes of the Navajos" and was based largely upon "stories told by Navajo for Navajo."[20] The curriculum advisory board, composed of "Navajo Statesmen and elders" including Howard Gorman, Chic Sandoval, and Denet Tsosie, was instrumental in shaping the module's structure and content so as to avoid temporal divisions that "did not make sense in terms of Navajo thoughts and desires." Notably, the board removed any dates for the origin era, stating that no date is acceptable for this period.[21]

The follow-up module, Navajo History and Culture II, examined the period from roughly 1860 to 1960 and presented the past "from the Navajo point of view and as seen by Navajo themselves."[22] The module covered topics such as the Long Walk, the 1868 treaty, and the New Deal and stock reduction, with a focus on Diné perspectives and historical actors. In stark contrast to the 1940 Pageant of Navajo History, Kit Carson was presented as an unprincipled and cowardly commander, who "fought no pitched battles but harassed the Navajo, burned his cornfields and hogans." The students were left in no doubt as to the naked cruelty of Carson's tactics.[23] While the pageant presented James Henry Carleton as an authoritative and rational leader, the NCC course cited local media and academic accounts that showed him to have been incompetent and despised by his American contemporaries.[24] Particularly striking is the module's emphasis on

US violation of existing treaties and on the federal government's folly in making treaties with individual groups of Diné and then expecting all Diné to abide by them.[25] Unlike the pageant, which rebuked the Diné for making promises *they* didn't keep, the NCC module ascribed the 1860 attack on Fort Defiance to "the utter despair of the Navajo at understanding the whites who failed to keep their promises and the determination of the Navajo to keep their land and their way of life."[26] Indeed, the course materials emphasized, "There is nothing in the historical records to show that the Navajo who signed the treaty failed to honor its provisions." It explained that any Diné treaty violation stemmed from the government's failure to understand the contemporary Diné political system, described as "one of the purest forms of democracy which did not recognize the control of one person over the lives and future of others."[27]

The NCC history and culture curriculum prioritized Diné sources. The Origin module was based primarily on the testimony of medicine men collated by Gorman, Sandoval, and Scott Preston.[28] Recordings of interviews with elderly Diné formed part of the basis for the History and Culture II module. Students embarked on field trips to the geographic locations cited in both the origin and post-1860 courses.[29] The Origin narratives themselves provided source material for the module section "Reconstruction of Early Navajo Life and Culture." As the curriculum synopsis notes, "Through a careful study of the various origin myths and chantway legends, it is possible to reconstruction [sic] early Navajo life and culture. It is possible to determine the kind of social organization, economy and other facets of early Navajo culture from such a study."[30] This practice contrasts sharply with the New Deal–era history module in which the teacher used archaeological material and "imagination" to construct the distant past. The NCC course did not eschew non-Diné material entirely—anthropological and archaeological research were used as supplementary material to Diné sources. As the Origin module's course overview stated:

> The material used in this course is based on stories told by Navajo for Navajo. In addition to the original sources, written materials collected by anthropologists and archaeologists will be examined. The similarities and differences between these sources will be studied. Nevertheless, it should be clearly and emphatically stated that this course has as its

prime source and major thrust the stories by the Navajo about their origin and only in a limited and secondary manner does the course include the anthropological version of that origin.[31]

The New Dealer emphasis on academic (and non-Diné) authenticity had been turned on its head, with Diné sources of authority trumping Western scholarly research. Federal government sources such as the 1868 treaty were utilized for the post-1860 course, but greater emphasis was placed on transcripts of 1860s council proceedings involving Diné and US military leaders, with notable prominence given to Barboncito's words.[32] Diné voices, as well as Diné perspectives, were clearly a mainstay of the 1970 NCC history and culture lessons. Decolonization of the curriculum had begun.

Despite these key differences concerning perspectives and sources, however, the 1970 NCC curriculum did perhaps share some—albeit slight—similarities with the New Deal education program. Like Ryan and Beatty, the Navajo Studies course emphasized class discussion, coursework, and practical instruction over formal exams. As the curriculum outline introduction advises, "Traditional types of written tests are not valuable but actual field experiences—helping with ceremonies, learning ceremonies, etc—are the best ways to evaluate learning."[33] Emphases on pictorial sources and learning materials, and on practical arts and crafts instruction, also echoed New Dealer initiatives, although the NCC basketry and weaving courses adopted a holistic approach that included the cultural significance and processes of both products and materials.[34] The NCC Navajo Studies objectives include, "To learn and respect Navajo history, culture and language" and "To develop pride in one's heritage and confidence in one's future"—which recalls Ryan's rhetoric from 1934.[35] Yet the two curricula are separated by a major distinction, conveyed by NCC Director of Navajo Studies Ruth Roessel's description of the scope of the Navajo Studies course.[36] According to Roessel, Navajo Studies is no mere add-on to a Euro-American curriculum, "not a series of courses which mean little" but "the heart of the College."[37] And Navajo Studies went beyond the eleven specific Diné cultural/arts/history/linguistics courses—Roessel claimed they permeated the entire curriculum. This integrated approach distinguished NCC in the early 1970s from other colleges:

It is different because all other aspects of NCC incorporate Indian studies into their individual programs and courses: for example English is concerned with Indian literature, Economics is concerned with Indian development, Science is concerned with reservation resources, etc. In other words, while we have a separate area of Navajo Studies other parts of the total program are a part of it in that they bring out the Indian and Navajo aspect.[38]

In other words, Navajo Studies at NCC was both a course *and* a school-wide ethos. Whereas the New Dealers had fashioned a program that they believed was Diné-centric because it focused on local issues (geography, reservation economy, community organization, healthcare, local ecology) and didn't consciously denigrate Diné culture, NCC devised a program that *actively* represented Diné culture, identity, and perspectives. Like the New Dealers, the NCC board believed that schools should have an impact on the community they served. But rather than transmitting federal government messages on health and range management, NCC intended that students in the Navajo Studies course would teach Diné culture at reservation high schools and elementary schools. As the advisory board concluded, "This maximizes learning and makes it possible for more Navajo young people to learn about Navajo culture."[39]

The NCC curriculum was a radical and innovative departure from existing reservation school programs. The students were reminded that they themselves were involved in its development—that their research and discussions would form textbook material for future cohorts. The education program did not historicize or isolate Diné culture from contemporary life; the module "American Indian Seminar" featured such topics as "contemporary Indian Affairs," "American Indian Economic Development," and "Indian Laws and Government," while the "Navajo and Acculturation" module offered "a study of cultural change as exemplified in the growth and development of the Navajo Nation," including the study of "the mutual impacts of the dominant and Navajo cultures upon each other."[40] This wasn't a program based purely on preservation of the past but rather one that acknowledged cultural and social change and which anticipated Diné cultural perseverance amidst future challenges. The curricular assumption was that Diné culture would survive, though it needed to be taught—such instruction and learning was no longer confined to the home environment.

What emerged in 1970 was a teaching program that rejected cultural compartmentalization of education and taught a wide range of subjects from a Diné perspective.

The curriculum endured and continues to develop. In 2018, Diné College established a Bachelor of Arts degree in Diné studies. The course overview is striking: "Graduates in Diné Studies will apply their unique Diné knowledge, thought, language and culture to all aspects of their daily lives, including family and community.... The central purpose of Diné Studies is to nurture students and graduates to possess the skills and knowledge to address professional situations by uniquely applying Diné perspectives." The college remains "focused on creating opportunities for in-depth learning of Diné culture, language, and to reaffirm Diné identity" but has moved beyond a cultural preservation and development focus to an active presentation of Diné cultural beliefs and perspectives as vital aids in the solving of professional challenges. Areas addressed by the program include tribal sovereignty, law, Diné culture, agriculture, Diné language, and public health—demonstrating the application of Diné traditional knowledge and values to economic, ecological, political, and scientific issues. The curriculum's bicultural nature is reflected in the suggested list of graduate job prospects, including teacher, linguist, historian, agriculturalist, *hataalii* (ceremonial practitioner), lawyer, Navajo medical doctor, public health representative, environmental advisor, Navajo scientific researcher, hospitality/tourism, and council delegate.[41]

Bicultural programs continue to develop at tribal colleges. At Sinte Gleska University (SGU), the Lakota Studies Department promotes a bicultural approach that reflects Lakota cultural values.[42] In such an approach, traditional cultural values form a context for teaching and instruction, including in technology. Pioneering efforts are also underway in some high schools and cultural centers to devise bicultural science pedagogies that involve stories and storytelling, core cultural values of Indigenous students, and the expertise of elders as keepers of knowledge.[43]

In 1933 the Lakota author Luther Standing Bear demanded radical reform of the government's education program for Native American pupils. Standing Bear's call for a "double" education went further than merely including Indigenous history topics and languages on the curriculum—he challenged his readers to consider education through a bicultural lens: "Why not a school of Indian thought, built on the Indian pattern and conducted by Indian instructors? Why not a school of tribal art?"⁴⁴ Where Standing Bear's BIA contemporaries Ryan and Beatty stumbled—both in their misframing of Indigenous worldviews and in their deification of culturally bound academic knowledge and Eurocentric regimes of "truth"—tribal colleges are showing how Indigenous visions of a holistic education can be realized.

NOTES

Abbreviations

AIOHC (CSWR) American Indian Oral History Collection, Center for Southwest Research, University of New Mexico Libraries, Albuquerque

ARSI (1940) *Annual Report to the Secretary of the Interior* (1940)

BIA-CCF: Series B BIA Central Classified Files, Series B: Indian Customs and Social Relations, Cambridge University Library, Cambridge

Collier Files (RIAS) Office Files of John Collier, Roosevelt Institute of American Studies, Middelburg, NL

Collier Papers (Yale) John Collier Papers, Yale University Library, New Haven, CT

IAW *Indians at Work*

IRA Papers Indian Rights Association Papers, Pennsylvania Historical Society, Philadelphia

MCMAIT Major Council Meetings of the American Indian Tribes (microfilm), Hayden Library, Arizona State University

NMAIA Report New Mexico Association on Indian Affairs, *Urgent Navajo Problems* (1940)

NSN *Navajo Service News*

Phelps-Stokes Report *The Navajo Indian Problem* (1939)

RG75-Navajo-Fldr-Box-NARA-LN Record Group 75, Central Classified Files, Navajo Area, National Archives, Laguna Niguel, CA

RG75-UPA-Fldr-Box-NARA-Denver Record Group 75, Central Classified Files, United Pueblos Agency, National Archives, Denver

Zimmerman, Jr. Papers William Zimmerman, Jr. Papers, Center for Southwest Research, University of New Mexico Libraries, Albuquerque

Introduction

1. Jack D. Forbes, "The New Assimilation Movement: Standards, Tests, and Anglo-American Supremacy," *Journal of American Indian Education* 39, no. 2 (Winter 2000): 7.

2. Forbes, "New Assimilation Movement," 7–8.

3. For insight into the cultural damage wrought by the schools, see Kevin Whalen, "Finding the Balance: Student Voices and Cultural Loss at Sherman

Institute," *American Behavioral Scientist* 58, no. 1 (2014): 124–144. Whalen cites a former Sherman employee and descendant of Sherman alumni who reminded scholars that, despite student resistance, "federal Indian boarding schools were places of cultural genocide" (128).

4. Keith James, "Identity, Cultural Values, and American Indians' Perceptions of Science and Technology," *American Indian Culture and Research Journal* 30, no. 3 (2006): 47.

5. Jon Reyhner, "American Indian Cultures and School Success," *Journal of American Indian Education* 32, no. 1 (October 1992): 33. For insight into the potentially damaging impact of monocultural education on Indigenous students, see Judy Iseke and Leisa Desmoulins, "A Two-Way Street: Indigenous Knowledge and Science Take a Ride," *Journal of American Indian Education* 54, no. 3 (Fall 2015): 31–53; and Gregory Cajete, "The Native American Learner and Bicultural Science Education," in *Next Steps: Research and Practice to Advance Indian Education*, ed. Karen Gayton Swisher and John W. Tippeconnic III (Charleston, WV: ERIC Clearinghouse, 1999), 136–137, 147.

6. See Michael Tlanusta Garrett, "'Two People': An American Indian Narrative of Bicultural Identity," *Journal of American Indian Education* 36, no. 1 (Fall 1996): 4–5.

7. Rebecca Tsosie, "Reclaiming Native Stories: An Essay on Cultural Appropriation and Cultural Rights," *Arizona State Law Journal* 34 (2002): 309.

8. Luther Standing Bear, *Land of the Spotted Eagle* (Boston: Houghton Mifflin, 1933), chapter 9.

9. Standing Bear, *Land of the Spotted Eagle*, chapter 9.

10. Kevin Whalen, *Native Students at Work: American Indian Labor and Sherman Institute's Outing Program, 1900–1945* (Seattle: University of Washington Press, 2016), 120.

11. For analyses of the political and economic dimensions of the Indian New Deal, see Graham Taylor, *The New Deal and American Indian Tribalism: The Administration of the Indian Reorganization Act, 1934–1945* (Lincoln: University of Nebraska Press, 1980); Vine Deloria Jr. and Clifford M. Lytle, *The Nations Within: The Past and Future of Native American Sovereignty* (New York: Pantheon, 1984). For insights into Collier's ideology, see Kenneth Philp, *John Collier's Crusade for Indian Reform, 1920–1954* (Tucson: University of Arizona Press, 1977); Lawrence Kelly, *The Assault on Assimilation: John Collier and the Origins of Indian Policy Reform* (Albuquerque: University of New Mexico Press, 1983); Elmer Rusco, *A Fateful Time: The Background and Legislative History of the Indian Reorganization Act* (Reno: University of Nevada Press, 2000); S. J. Kunitz, "The Social Philosophy of John Collier," *Ethnohistory* 18, no. 3 (Summer 1971): 213–229; Laurence Hauptman, "Africa View: John Collier, the British

Colonial Service and American Indian Policy, 1933–1945," *Historian* 48, no. 3 (May 1986): 359–374; E. A. Schwartz, "Red Atlantis Revisited: Community and Culture in the Writings of John Collier," *American Indian Quarterly* 18, no. 4 (September 1994): 507–531.

12. For case studies of New Deal implementation, see Donald Parman, *The Navajos and the New Deal* (New Haven, CT: Yale University Press, 1976); Laurence Hauptman, *The Iroquois and the New Deal* (Syracuse, NY: Syracuse University Press, 1981); Thomas Biolsi, *Organizing the Lakota: The Political Economy of the New Deal on the Pine Ridge and Rosebud Reservations* (Tucson: University of Arizona Press, 1992); Akim Reinhardt, *Ruling Pine Ridge: Oglala Lakota Politics from the IRA to Wounded Knee* (Lubbock: Texas Tech University Press, 2007).

13. Matthew Sakiestewa Gilbert, *Education beyond the Mesas: Hopi Students at Sherman Institute, 1902–1929* (Lincoln: University of Nebraska Press, 2010), 95.

14. See David Wallace Adams, *Education for Extinction: American Indians and the Boarding School Experience, 1875–1928* (Lawrence: University Press of Kansas, 1995); Clyde Ellis, *"To Change Them Forever": Indian Education at Rainy Mountain Boarding School, 1890–1920* (Norman: University of Oklahoma Press, 1996); Jacqueline Fear-Segal, *White Man's Club: Schools, Race, and the Struggle of Indian Acculturation* (Lincoln: University of Nebraska Press, 2007); Sakiestewa Gilbert, *Education beyond the Mesas*; Amelia Katanski, *Learning to Write "Indian": The Boarding-School Experience and American Indian Literature* (Norman: University of Oklahoma Press, 2005); Sally McBeth, *Ethnic Identity and the Boarding School Experience of West-Central Oklahoma Indians* (Washington, DC: University Press of America, 1983); Devon Mihesuah, *Cultivating the Rosebuds: The Education of Women at the Cherokee Female Seminary, 1851–1909* (Urbana: University of Illinois Press, 1993); Scott Riney, *The Rapid City Indian School: 1898–1933* (Norman: University of Oklahoma Press, 1999); Robert Trennert, *The Phoenix Indian School: Forced Assimilation in Arizona, 1891–1935* (Norman: University of Oklahoma Press, 1988).

15. Examples of studies which look beyond 1930 are K. Tsianina Lomawaima, *They Called It Prairie Light: The Story of Chilocco Indian School* (Lincoln: University of Nebraska Press, 1994), which includes examples up to 1940; Brenda Child, *Boarding School Seasons: American Indian Families, 1900–1940* (Lincoln: University of Nebraska Press, 1998); John R. Gram, *Education at the Edge of Empire: Negotiating Pueblo Identity in New Mexico's Indian Boarding Schools* (Seattle: University of Washington Press, 2015); and Whalen, *Native Students at Work*. The main focus of these works is the period up to 1933, although Whalen devotes a chapter to the New Deal curricular changes. See also Sally Hyer, *One House, One Voice, One Heart: Native American Education at the Santa Fe Indian*

School (Santa Fe: Museum of New Mexico Press, 1990): Hyer uses student oral histories to chart the school's history from 1890–1990 and devotes a chapter to 1930–45.

16. Thomas G. Andrews, "Turning the Tables on Assimilation: Oglala Lakotas and the Pine Ridge Day Schools, 1889–1920s," *Western Historical Quarterly* 33, no. 4 (Winter 2002): 407–430; Adrea Lawrence, *Lessons from an Indian Day School: Negotiating Colonization in Northern New Mexico, 1902–1907* (Lawrence: University Press of Kansas, 2011).

17. Margaret Connell Szasz, *Education and the American Indian: The Road to Self-Determination since 1928*, 3rd ed. (Albuquerque: University of New Mexico Press, 1999).

18. Szasz, *Education and the American Indian*, 80.

19. Szasz, *Education and the American Indian*, 80.

20. Szasz, *Education and the American Indian*, 80.

21. K. Tsianina Lomawaima and Teresa McCarty, *To Remain an Indian: Lessons in Democracy from a Century of American Indian Education* (New York: Teachers College Press, 2006), 76.

22. K. Tsianina Lomawaima and Teresa McCarty, "Introduction to the Special Issue: Examining and Applying Safety Zone Theory: Current Policies, Practices, and Experiences," and "Concluding Commentary: Revisiting and Clarifying the Safety Zone," *Journal of American Indian Education* 53, no. 3 (2014): 8, 65.

23. Lomawaima and McCarty, *To Remain an Indian*, 75, 96–102.

24. See Rivka Shpak Lissak, *Pluralism & Progressives: Hull House and the New Immigrants, 1890–1919* (Chicago: University of Chicago Press, 1989).

25. Reyhner, "American Indian Cultures and School Success," 34.

26. Paul Boyer, *Tribal Colleges: Shaping the Future of Native America* (Princeton, NJ: Princeton University Press, 1989), 19, 25.

27. Peter Iverson, *Diné: A History of the Navajos* (Albuquerque: University of New Mexico Press, 2002), 173.

28. Iverson, *Diné*, 176–177.

29. Beatrice Medicine, *Learning to Be an Anthropologist and Remaining "Native": Selected Writings* (Urbana: University of Illinois Press, 2001), 42, 51.

30. Whalen, *Native Students at Work*, 127, 140.

31. Farina King, *The Earth Memory Compass: Diné Landscapes and Education in the Twentieth Century* (Lawrence: University Press of Kansas, 2018). King devotes a chapter to the experiences of Diné pupils at Crownpoint Boarding School in the 1930s.

32. The Navajo education program was considered of such importance by the New Deal BIA that it had its own section in the 1934 *Annual Report of the*

Department of the Interior. See *Annual Report of the Department of the Interior* (Washington, DC: US Government Printing Office, 1934), 87–88.

33. Paulo Freire, *Pedagogy of the Oppressed* (London: Penguin, 1996), 133–134, 137; Francis Nyamnjoh, "'Potted Plants in Greenhouses': A Critical Reflection on the Resilience of Colonial Education in Africa," *Journal of Asian and African Studies* 47, no. 2 (2012): 129–154.

34. See Patrick Wolfe, "Settler Colonialism and the Elimination of the Native," *Journal of Genocide Research* 8, no. 4 (2006): 387–409.

35. See Lorenzo Veracini, *Settler Colonialism: A Theoretical Overview* (New York: Palgrave-Macmillan, 2011), 41–46.

36. *The Navajo Indian Problem: An Inquiry Sponsored by the Phelps-Stokes Fund* (New York: Phelps-Stokes Fund, 1939), hereafter cited as Phelps-Stokes Report. *Urgent Navajo Problems: Observations and Recommendations Based on a Recent Study by the New Mexico Association on Indian Affairs* (Santa Fe: New Mexico Association on Indian Affairs, 1940), hereafter cited as NMAIA Report. The Phelps-Stokes Fund (established 1911) was a philanthropic organization interested in education for Native Americans, African Americans in the southern United States, and in British colonial Africa. The Fund helped sponsor the Meriam Report research in 1926. The NMAIA was a Santa Fe–based organization interested in Native rights but with a largely non-Native membership in the 1920s and 1930s. It was critical of much Indian New Deal policy in New Mexico and Arizona.

37. Lomawaima and McCarty, *To Remain an Indian*, 11–13.

38. Anson Phelps, "Introduction," Phelps-Stokes Report, ix. The research team also included Charles Loram (Department of Race Relations, Yale) and Harold Allen (National Farm School).

39. See Szasz, *Education and the American Indian*, 50–55 (on progressive education); Katherine Jensen, "Teachers and Progressives: The Navajo Day School Experiment," *Arizona and the West* 25, no. 1 (Spring 1983): 49–62; Thomas James, "Rhetoric and Resistance: Social Science and Community Schools for Navajos in the 1930s," *History of Education Quarterly* 28, no. 4 (1988): 599–626.

Chapter 1: Federal Government Attitudes to Native American Cultures, c. 1880–1945

1. See Gary Gerstle, "Liberty, Coercion, and the Making of Americans," *Journal of American History* 84, no. 2 (September 1997): 524–558; and Rogers Smith, *Civic Ideals: Conflicting Visions of Citizenship in US History* (New Haven, CT: Yale University Press, 1997).

2. For an insight into the influence of Lewis Henry Morgan, Herbert Spencer, John Wesley Powell, and William Henry Holmes on government attitudes towards Native American cultures, see Curtis Hinsley, *The Smithsonian and the American Indian: Making a Moral Anthropology in Victorian America* (Washington, DC: Smithsonian Institution, 1981).

3. Clif Stratton, *Education for Empire: American Schools, Race, and the Paths of Good Citizenship* (Berkeley: University of California Press, 2016), 17, 27.

4. Stratton, *Education for Empire*, 17, 31–40. For an insight into US teaching initiatives in the Philippines in the early twentieth century, see Elisabeth Eittreim, *Teaching Empire: Native Americans, Filipinos, and US Imperial Education, 1879–1918* (Lawrence: University Press of Kansas, 2019).

5. For detailed analyses of the assimilation policy see Frederick Hoxie, *A Final Promise: The Campaign to Assimilate the Indians, 1880–1920* (Lincoln: University of Nebraska Press, 1984); Tom Holm, *The Great Confusion in Indian Affairs: Native Americans and Whites in the Progressive Era* (Austin: University of Texas Press, 2005).

6. For a fuller analysis of the Dawes Act, see Hoxie, *A Final Promise*, 147–189. See also Janet McDonnell, *The Dispossession of the American Indian, 1887–1934* (Bloomington: Indiana University Press, 1991); Donald J. Berthrong, "Legacies of the Dawes Act: Bureaucrats and Land Thieves at the Cheyenne-Arapaho Agencies of Oklahoma," *Arizona and the West* 21, no. 4 (Winter 1979): 335–354; K. Tsianina Lomawaima, "Estelle Reel, Superintendent of Indian Schools, 1898–1910: Politics, Curriculum, and Land," *Journal of American Indian Education* 35, no. 3 (May 1996): 5–31.

7. For a detailed examination of the dance bans and resistance, see Clyde Ellis, *A Dancing People: Powwow Culture on the Southern Plains* (Lawrence: University Press of Kansas, 2003). See also Gregory Smoak, *Ghost Dances and Identity: Prophetic Religion and American Indian Ethnogenesis in the Nineteenth Century* (Berkeley: University of California Press, 2008); and Gabriella Treglia, "Using Citizenship to Retain Identity: The Native American Dance Bans of the Later Assimilation Era, 1900–1933," *Journal of American Studies* 47, no. 3 (August 2013): 777–800.

8. Charles Burke to Superintendents, "Supplement to Circular 1665: Indian Dancing," February 14, 1923, IRA Papers, Pennsylvania Historical Society, Philadelphia, reel 38. Emphasis added.

9. See Gabriella Treglia, "The Consistency and Inconsistency of Cultural Oppression: American Indian Dance Bans, 1900–1933," *Western Historical Quarterly* 44, no. 2 (Summer 2013): 145–166.

10. Burke, "Supplement to Circular 1665."

11. See Clyde Ellis, "'We Don't Want Your Rations, We Want This Dance': The

Changing Use of Song and Dance on the Southern Plains," *Western Historical Quarterly* 30, no. 2 (Summer 1999): 133–154; and Treglia, "Using Citizenship to Retain Identity."

12. See Charles Burke to James McGregor, January 3, 1923, Records of the Bureau of Indian Affairs Central Classified Files, 1907–1939, Series B: Customs and Social Relations, microfilm, Rosebud, reel 9, Cambridge University Library. Hereafter cited as BIA-CCF: Series B.

13. Thomas Morgan, "Supplemental Report on Indian Education" (December 1, 1889), in *Americanizing the American Indians: Writings by the "Friends of the Indian," 1880–1900*, ed. Francis Paul Prucha (Cambridge, MA: Harvard University Press, 1973), 225.

14. For a fuller examination of industrial education for African Americans at Hampton Institute in the Progressive Era, see David Wallace Adams, "Education in Hues: Red and Black at Hampton Institute, 1878–1893," *South Atlantic Quarterly* 76, no. 2 (Spring 1977): 159–176. Clif Stratton, in *Education for Empire*, 118–144, presents a powerful contrast between the vocational educational agendas of Hampton and Atlanta University, with the latter offering a more meaningful path to economic equality.

15. Wayne Au, Anthony L. Brown, and Dolores Calderon, *Reclaiming the Multicultural Roots of US Curriculum: Communities of Color and Official Knowledge in Education* (New York: Teachers College Press, 2016), chapter 2.

16. For a detailed examination of the Assimilation Era boarding schools, see David Wallace Adams, *Education for Extinction*. For a useful overview see Jon Reyhner and Jeanne Eder, eds., *American Indian Education: A History* (Norman: University of Oklahoma Press, 2015), 132–167 ("Government Boarding Schools"), 168–204 ("Students and Parents"). See also Lomawaima and McCarty, *To Remain an Indian*, chapter 3.

17. In 1907 Leupp opined that nursery songs and certain arts and crafts were permissible "provided they are innocent in themselves and do not clash needlessly with the new social order." Francis Leupp quoted in Lomawaima and McCarty, *To Remain an Indian*, 54–55.

18. Miguel Trujillo, "Indian Education Throughout the Years," *Indians at Work* 4:18–19 (May 1937): 25–27. Hereafter cited as *IAW*. *Indians at Work* was a bimonthly newsletter issued by the Indian Service in the New Deal "for Indians and the Indian Service." It invariably offered a rose-tinted depiction of policy implementation. Trujillo's article promoted New Deal education reforms—yet his disgust at the earlier monocultural and punitive boarding school regime is palpable. Trujillo had firsthand experience of Assimilation Era boarding schools—he graduated from Albuquerque Indian School in 1923 and from Haskell in 1925. For an insight into Trujillo's teaching career and voting rights

activism, see Joe Sando, *Pueblo Profiles: Cultural Identity through Centuries of Change* (Santa Fe, NM: Clear Light, 1998), 57–62.

19. Esther Burnett Horne, with Sally McBeth, *Essie's Story: The Life and Legacy of a Shoshone Teacher* (Lincoln: University of Nebraska Press, 1998), xxxv. Horne attended Haskell Indian Institute, 1924–29. She embarked on a long and valued teaching career in Indian Service boarding schools from the early 1930s to 1965, receiving the Department of the Interior's Distinguished Service Citation in 1966.

20. Horne and McBeth, *Essie's Story*, 162.

21. See Horne and McBeth, *Essie's Story*, 41–42 (on Ella Deloria and Ruth Muskrat Bronson); 57–58, 67 (on her own teaching, 1929–34); and Marguerite Bigler Stoltz, *The Dove Always Cried: Narratives of Indian School Life* (Blacksburg, VA: Pocahontas, 1994), 14. Stoltz's response to being ordered to report students for speaking Diné bizaad at Southern Ute Boarding School (1927) was to "never hear anyone talking Navajo." See also Polingaysi Qoyawayma, *No Turning Back: A True Account of a Hopi Indian Girl's Struggle to Bridge the Gap Between the World of Her People and the World of the White Man* (Albuquerque: University of New Mexico Press, 1964), 127, 150. Qoyawayma spent four years at Sherman Institute. She began teaching at Tuba City Indian Boarding School in 1919 and then a series of Hopi and Navajo day and boarding schools through the 1920s. She transferred to Polacca Day School (Hopi) in 1934. Her teaching career spanned the Assimilation and New Deal eras.

22. Nyamnjoh, "'Potted Plants in Greenhouses,'" 129, 131.

23. The American Indian Citizenship Act was passed in 1924. Dance oppression was intensified through Circular 1665 (1921); the Supplement to Circular 1665 (1923); and the "Secret Dance File" which led to the Pueblo Dance Controversy c. 1923–25.

24. Lewis Meriam, et al., *The Problem of Indian Administration* (Baltimore, MD: Johns Hopkins Press, 1928), 72.

25. Meriam et al., *Problem of Indian Administration*, 3.

26. Meriam et al., *Problem of Indian Administration*, 7.

27. Not only did Indian Service agents and superintendents often fail to advise allotment holders of their rights and good land prices, but some actually colluded with opportunistic buyers to defraud them—see Berthrong, "Legacies of the Dawes Act," 335–354.

28. Meriam et al., *Problem of Indian Administration*, 376.

29. Meriam et al., *Problem of Indian Administration*, 33.

30. Meriam et al., *Problem of Indian Administration*, 88.

31. In a brief reference to the Meriam Report, Wade Davies refers to "its criticism of assimilation policy"—see Wade Davies, *Healing Ways: Navajo Healthcare*

in the Twentieth Century (Albuquerque: University of New Mexico Press, 2001), 24. Lomawaima and McCarty note that the preservation of Native cultures and the chance to "remain an Indian" were "unprecedented goals" in government policy and that the choice offered was "a radical notion." Lomawaima and McCarty, *To Remain an Indian*, 65–66.

32. Meriam et al., *Problem of Indian Administration*, 87.
33. Meriam et al., *Problem of Indian Administration*, 87.
34. Veracini, *Settler Colonialism*, 41.
35. Meriam et al., *Problem of Indian Administration*, 87–88.
36. Meriam et al., *Problem of Indian Administration*, 88.
37. Meriam et al., *Problem of Indian Administration*, 88.
38. John Haaben, "Education of the Immigrant Child," in *Education of the Immigrant: Abstracts of Papers Read at a Public Conference under the Auspices of the New York-New Jersey Committee of the North American Civic League for Immigrants, Held at New York City, May 16 and 17, 1913* (Washington, DC: US Government Printing Office, 1913), 19.
39. Winifred Gibbs, "Teaching Immigrant Mothers Proper Food," in *Education of the Immigrant*, 11.
40. Mabel Kittredge, "The Training of the Domestic Educator: Part II," in *Education of the Immigrant*, 12.
41. Meriam et al., *Problem of Indian Administration*, 45.
42. Meriam et al., *Problem of Indian Administration*, 846.
43. Meriam et al., *Problem of Indian Administration*, 412.
44. Meriam et al., *Problem of Indian Administration*, 412.
45. Meriam et al., *Problem of Indian Administration*, 412.
46. For detailed analysis of the Pueblo dance controversy and the All-Pueblo Council's defence of traditional dances as religious ceremonies, see Tisa Wenger, *We Have a Religion: The 1920s Pueblo Indian Dance Controversy and American Religious Freedom* (Chapel Hill: University of North Carolina Press, 2009).
47. For the campaign against dance oppression, see John Collier, "Indian Dances Defended," *New York Times*, December 16, 1923, 6; John Collier, "Persecuting the Pueblos: The Indian Bureau Denies Its Wards Religious Liberty," *Sunset* 53, no. 7 (July 1924): 50, 92–93; John Collier, "Do Indians Have Rights of Conscience?," *Christian Century*, March 12, 1925, 346–349. For the campaign against the Bursum Bill, see John Collier, "The Red Atlantis," *Survey* 49 (October 1922): 16; John Collier, "Politicians Pillage the Pueblos," *Searchlight* 7, no. 8 (January 31, 1923): 15–19; John Collier, "The Pueblos' Last Stand," *Sunset* 50 (February 1923): 19–22, 65–66.
48. See Schwartz, "Red Atlantis Revisited," 507–553; Kunitz, "Social

Philosophy of John Collier," 213–229; Taylor, *New Deal and American Indian Tribalism*, 12.

49. See John Collier, *From Every Zenith: A Memoir* (Denver: Sage Books, 1963).

50. Collier, *From Every Zenith*, 93.

51. John Collier, *The Indians of the Americas* (New York: New American Library, 1947), 27.

52. Oren Lyons, quoted in Kenneth R. Philp, ed., *Indian Self-Rule: First-Hand Accounts of Indian-White Relations from Roosevelt to Reagan* (Logan: Utah State University Press, 1986), 94.

53. John Collier, "Does the Government Welcome the Indian Arts?," in Mrs. Franklin D. Roosevelt, "Proceedings of the Twenty-Fifth Annual Convention of the American Federation of Arts: Washington D.C., May 14–16, 1934," *American Magazine of Art* 27, no. 12 (December 1934): 11.

54. Collier, "Does the Government Welcome the Indian Arts?," 11.

55. John Collier, untitled essay (February 21, 1939), 5, John Collier Papers, microfilm, Manuscripts and Archives, Yale University Library (New Haven), reel 32. Hereafter cited as Collier Papers (Yale).

56. Collier, "Does the Government Welcome the Indian Arts?," 11.

57. John Collier, "The Indians' Master Problem: Land," *Navajo Service News* 1 (May 1, 1936): 15. Hereafter cited as *NSN*.

58. Hauptman, "Africa View," 369.

59. Hauptman, "Africa View," 359–374. See also Akim Reinhardt, "A Crude Replacement: The Indian New Deal, Indirect Colonialism, and Pine Ridge Reservation," *Journal of Colonialism and Colonial History* 6, no. 1 (2005).

60. For analyses of the Indian Arts and Crafts Board, see Jennifer McLerran, *A New Deal for Native Art: Indian Arts and Federal Policy, 1933–1943* (Tucson: University of Arizona Press, 2009); Robert Fay Schrader, *The Indian Arts and Crafts Board: An Aspect of Indian New Deal Policy* (Albuquerque: University of New Mexico Press, 1983); and Susan Labry Meyn, *More Than Curiosities: A Grassroots History of the Indian Arts and Crafts Board and its Precursors, 1920–1942* (Lanham, MD: Lexington Books, 2001). For an insight into the intersections of federal government policy and the marketing of traditional Diné arts and crafts, see Erika Bsumek, *Indian-Made: Navajo Culture in the Marketplace, 1868–1940* (Lawrence: University Press of Kansas, 2008).

61. Collier, "The Indians' Master Problem," *NSN*, 15.

62. For detailed analysis of government-sponsored New Deal land management and conservation policies, see Sarah Phillips, *This Land, This Nation: Conservation, Rural America, and the New Deal* (Cambridge: Cambridge University Press, 2007). See also Paul Landis, "The New Deal and Rural Life," *American Sociological Review* 1, no. 4 (August 1936): 592–603; Jess Gilbert, "Rural Sociology

and Democratic Planning in the Third New Deal," *Agricultural History* 82, no. 4 (Fall 2008): 421–438.

63. Narration from *The River*, a 1937 film produced by the Resettlement Administration. See Phillips, *This Land, This Nation*, 75.

64. Concern at rural depopulation was rife amongst government agencies in the 1930s. See Cherisse Jones-Branch, "'An Uneasy Alliance': Farm Women and the United States Department of Agriculture, 1913–1965," *Federal History* (2018): 107.

65. For a detailed examination of New Deal rural extension programs and the agendas behind them, see Amanda Coleman, "Rehabilitating the Region: The New Deal, Gender, and the Remaking of the Rural South," *Southeastern Geographer* 50, no. 2 (Summer 2010): 200–217, and Diana Moyer, "The Gendered Boundaries of Child-Centred Education: Elsie Ripley Clapp and the History of US Progressive Education," *Gender and Education* 21, no. 5 (September 2009): 531–547. For a contemporary presentation, and some critical appraisal, of New Deal rural policy, see Landis, "New Deal," 592–603.

66. See Moyer, "Gendered Boundaries," 536–538, 542–543.

67. See Coleman, "Rehabilitating the Region," 200–217.

68. Mabel Carney, "Desirable Rural Adaptations in the Education of Negroes," *Journal of Negro Education* 5, no. 3 (July 1936): 449. Carney taught rural education courses at Teachers College (Columbia University) and was a staunch advocate of progressive education and greater educational opportunities for African Americans, despite extolling the benefits of Arthurdale—a whites-only government community project.

69. Carney, "Desirable Rural Adaptations," 449.

70. John Collier, "A New Deal for the American Indian," *Literary Digest* (April 7, 1934): 21.

71. John Collier to All Superintendents, "Circular 2970: Indian Religious Freedom and Indian Culture," Office of Indian Affairs Circulars, January 3, 1934, cited in Collier to Dwight, February 19, 1936, Office Files of John Collier, 1933–1945, microfilm, Roosevelt Institute of American Studies, Middelburg, NL [hereafter cited as Collier Files, RIAS], reel 14. See also *Annual Report of the Department of the Interior* (Washington, DC: US Government Printing Office, 1934), 90.

72. Collier, "Circular 2970."

73. Leslie Denman, "Indian Ritual and Drama," *Women's City Club Magazine* 10, no. 4 (May 1936): 19.

74. Alexander Leighton and Dorothea Leighton, *The Navaho Door* (Cambridge, MA: Harvard University Press, 1944), 30–31.

75. For example, Commissioner of Indian Affairs Thomas Morgan dismissed

Indigenous religions as a "vile mixture of superstition, legends, and meaningless ceremonies." Thomas Morgan, "A Plea for the Papoose: An Address at Albany, New York" (1889), in *Americanizing the American Indians*, 244.

76. Meriam, *Problem of Indian Administration*, 108.

77. Deloria and Lytle, *Nations Within*, 79.

78. In practice, the short-lived Applied Anthropology Unit had limited influence on government policy. Anthropologists had little input on the Navajo stock reduction policy, which was a cultural and economic disaster. On Pine Ridge and Rosebud, anthropologists created confusion by attempting to revive some *tiyospayes* (historic Lakota sociopolitical groups) which hadn't operated for decades and which didn't match the reality and wishes of twentieth-century Lakota society. See Biolsi, *Organizing the Lakota*, 105–108, and Marsha Weisiger, "Navajos, New Dealers, and the Metaphysics of Nature," in *Indigenous Knowledge and the Environment in Africa and North America*, ed. David Gordon and Shepard Krech III (Athens: Ohio University Press, 2012), 137.

79. See Horace Kallen, "Democracy Versus the Melting Pot," *The Nation* 100 (February 18 and February 25, 1915): 190–194, 217–220.

80. See George Boyce, *When Navajos Had Too Many Sheep: The 1940s* (San Francisco: Indian Historian, 1974), 91.

81. Elmer Thomas, Dennis Chavez, Burton Wheeler, "Survey of Conditions of Indians of the United States" (Analysis of the Statement of the Commissioner of Indian Affairs in Justification of Appropriations for 1944, and the Liquidation of the Indian Bureau), June 11, 1943, 17, Collier Papers (Yale), reel 31.

82. Thomas, Chavez, and Wheeler, "Survey of Conditions of Indians of the United States," 20.

83. Elaine Eastman to H. M. Hitchcock, June 29, 1935, H. M. Hitchcock Papers Relating to Elaine Eastman, 1935 (Western Americana Collection, Beinecke Rare Book and Manuscripts Library, Yale University, New Haven, CT).

84. Delos K. Lonewolf, quoted in Philp, *John Collier's Crusade*, 179.

85. Alice Lee Jemison, quoted in *Survey of Conditions of the Indians in the United States: Hearings before a Subcommittee of the Committee on Indian Affairs, United States Senate, 76th Congress: Part 37*, vol. 17 (Washington, DC: US Government Printing Office, 1940), 20700. Emphasis added.

86. Dennis Chavez, quoted in *Survey of Conditions*, 20700.

87. Philp, *Indian Self-Rule*, 59; Schrader, *Indian Arts and Crafts Board*, xi–xii.

88. Brian Dippie, *The Vanishing American: White Attitudes and US Indian Policy* (Middletown, CT: Wesleyan University Press, 1982), 312.

89. See Lomawaima and McCarty, *To Remain an Indian*, and Biolsi, *Organizing the Lakota*.

90. John Collier, "Preservation of Heritage" (1936), 115 (published essay—journal unknown), Collier Papers (Yale), reel 32.

91. Collier, "Preservation of Heritage," 116.

92. John Collier, untitled press release manuscript (May 1935), 2–3, Collier Papers (Yale), reel 31.

93. Collier, "Red Atlantis," 16; Collier, "Preservation of Heritage," 116.

94. Charles Loram, "Comment on Ethnological Training for Indian Service People," *IAW* 2, no. 5 (October 15, 1934): 30.

95. Section 11, Indian Reorganization (Wheeler-Howard) Act (June 18, 1934), accessed 20 February 2025, https://law.marquette.edu.

96. See Szasz, *Education and the American Indian*, 66.

97. John Collier, "Indian Leadership," *IAW* (November 1, 1933): 11.

98. For a useful overview of the New Deal education policy's aims and limitations see Szasz, *Education and the American Indian*, 16–50.

99. "Readjustment of Indian Affairs," discussion at House of Representatives, Committee on Indian Affairs, 73rd Congress, 2nd Session, Washington, DC, February 22, 1934, 7 (Title II: Special Education for Indians, Section 2), Collier Papers (Yale), reel 30.

100. Evelyn Crady Adams, *American Indian Education* (New York: Kings Crown, 1946), 80–81.

101. Evelyn Crady Adams, 80–81; Szasz, *Education and the American Indian*, 60–61.

102. Particularly egregious was Collier's decision to remove high school accreditation from several reservation schools.

103. Jensen, "Teachers and Progressives," 59.

Chapter 2: Presenting Native "Pasts" in the Classroom

A portion of this chapter appeared originally in *Journal of the Southwest* 61, no. 4 (Winter 2019): 821–862.

1. Carson Ryan, "Social and Educational Implications of the Navajo Program," paper presented at National Conference of Social Workers, Kansas City, May 25, 1934, Office Files of John Collier, 1933–1945, microfilm, Roosevelt Institute for American Studies, Middelburg, reel 10. Hereafter cited as Collier Files (RIAS).

2. Leupp was commissioner of Indian Affairs, 1904–9. In one annual report he professed to "have noted also with great pleasure the appearance in some of the school publications of short stories written by the pupils, descriptive of their family life, or putting into their own homely phraseology the folklore

of their people." See Louise Lockard, "Navajo Literacy: Stories of Learning to Write" (PhD diss., University of Arizona, 1993), 86.

3. Lomawaima and McCarty, *To Remain an Indian*, 92, 75–76.

4. Lomawaima and McCarty, *To Remain an Indian*, 72–75.

5. Horne and McBeth, *Essie's Story*, 75, 69–70, 85–86.

6. Stoltz, *Dove Always Cried*, 47.

7. Stoltz, *Dove Always Cried*, 74.

8. *Annual Report of the Commissioner of Indian Affairs* (Washington, DC: US Government Printing Office, 1931), 7.

9. Stoltz, *Dove Always Cried*, 75.

10. See Stoltz, *Dove Always Cried*, 111–148. Stoltz includes twenty-one stories from the Seneca Indian School's 7th, 8th, and 9th grade pupils (1933) and forty-seven stories from the Carson Indian School pupils (1935), no grade cited. The stories have titles but no information concerning individual authors.

11. King, *Earth Memory Compass*, 89.

12. "Long Ago" (Seneca School), and "How Pinenuts Came to Nevada" (Carson School), in Stoltz, *Dove Always Cried*, 119, 147.

13. See "Long Ago" and "Grandmother's Story" (Seneca School), and "A Discovery of Gold" (Carson School), in Stoltz, *Dove Always Cried*, 115, 111–112, 128.

14. "Long Ago" (Seneca School), in Stoltz, *Dove Always Cried*, 114. The author notes of their grandmother, "She told me this about five months before she died," thereby explicitly attributing the narrative content to an elder relative.

15. "The Coyote" (Carson School), in Stoltz, *Dove Always Cried*, 130.

16. "The Bear, the Deer and the Stork" (Carson School), in Stoltz, *Dove Always Cried*, 131.

17. "About Owls" (Carson School), in Stoltz, *Dove Always Cried*, 145.

18. "Yellow Old Lady Who Made Good Teeth" (Carson School), in Stoltz, *Dove Always Cried*, 125–126.

19. "Story of Long Ago" (Seneca School), in Stoltz, *Dove Always Cried*, 117.

20. "How the Indians Get Power" (Carson School), in Stoltz, *Dove Always Cried*, 130–131. Emphasis added.

21. "Indian War Dances" (Seneca School), in Stoltz, *Dove Always Cried*, 112.

22. "The Making of Baskets" (Carson School), in Stoltz, *Dove Always Cried*, 132–133.

23. Stoltz, *Dove Always Cried*, 75.

24. Crawford Goldsby (1876–96), alias "Cherokee Bill," was a Cherokee outlaw in Indian Territory.

25. "Cherokee Bill," "Grandmother's Story," and "Long Ago" (Seneca School), in Stoltz, *Dove Always Cried*, 116, 111–112, 114.

26. Katanski, *Learning to Write "Indian,"* 21.

27. Vine Deloria Jr., "The Perpetual Education Report" in *Power and Place: Indian Education in America*, ed. Vine Deloria Jr. and Daniel Wildcat (Golden, CO: Fulcrum, 2001), 154.

28. Horne and McBeth, *Essie's Story*, 86.

29. Stoltz, *Dove Always Cried*, 74 (emphasis added), 78, 81.

30. Willard Rhodes, quoted in Rae Korson and Joseph Hickerson, "The Willard Rhodes Collection of American Indian Music in the Archive of Folk Song," *Ethnomusicology* 13, no. 2 (May 1969): 298.

31. Fred Richards to George Boyce, June 14, 1941, Record Group 75, BIA Central Classified Files (decimal files), Navajo General Area, Folder 807: "Fort Defiance," box 177, National Archives Federal Record Center: Pacific Region (Laguna Niguel). Hereafter cited as RG75-Navajo-Fldr-box-NARA-LN.

32. For a detailed presentation of Diné Origin narratives, see Lloyd L. Lee, *Diné Identity in a Twenty-First-Century World* (Tucson: University of Arizona Press, 2020), 19–25.

33. Jennifer Nez Denetdale, *Reclaiming Diné History: The Legacies of Navajo Chief Manuelito and Juanita* (Tucson: University of Arizona Press, 2015), 7.

34. Fred Richards to George Boyce, June 14, 1941, RG75-Navajo-Fldr 807: "Fort Defiance," box 177-NARA-LN. Archaeologist and ethnologist Richard Van Valkenburgh published *A Short History of the Navajo People* in 1938. He was then employed by the BIA to research land problems on the Navajo Reservation, and he resigned in 1942 in protest at the coercive stock reduction policy.

35. The fortnightly, in-service BIA publication *Navajo Service News* reported in May 1936 that Fred Richards and his pupils were using the BIA publication *Indians at Work* as "the basis" of much of their study of "current Indian history." This reflects the paucity of available literature on Native histories at the Indian Service schools, as well as the dependence on written history sources. See *NSN* 1, no. 2 (May 15, 1936): 14.

36. Collier, *From Every Zenith*, 202.

37. Meriam, *Problem of Indian Administration*, 372.

38. Lucy Adams, "Program for Navajo Schools," December 6, 1937, 7–8, RG75-Navajo-Fldr 800: "Education 1936–1938," box 165-NARA-LN.

39. Lucy Adams to E. Fryer, memorandum: "Navajo School Program 1938–1939: An Outline of School Plans for the Coming Year," September 3, 1938, 2, RG75-Navajo-Fldr 800: "Education 1936–1938," box 165-NARA-LN. Bureau officials demonstrated no interest in inviting Diné elders to contribute to history lessons.

40. Eight "Life and Customs" texts were published, including seven by Ruth Underhill.

41. Willard Beatty, quoted in Ruth Underhill, *The Papago Indians of Arizona and Their Relatives the Pima* (Lawrence, KS: Haskell Institute Press, 1941), 71.

42. "Sherman Pamphlets," *Indian Education* 38 (March 1, 1940): 5–6. *Indian Education* described itself as "a fortnightly field letter of the Education Division, US Office of Indian Affairs."

43. Underhill, *Papago Indians*, 71.

44. Underhill, *Papago Indians*, 7, 49, 60.

45. Underhill, *Papago Indians*, 34.

46. A 1949 anthropological study of the Tohono O'odham nation noted that many people refrained from discussing traditional religion with outsiders, partly due to past experience of government-mandated suppression. The researchers concluded that medicine rituals and smaller group ceremonies were widely practiced. See Alice Joseph, Rosamond Spicer, and Jane Chesky, *The Desert People: A Study of the Papago Indians* (Chicago: University of Chicago Press, 1949), 72–73.

47. Underhill, *Papago Indians*, 13.

48. Underhill, *Papago Indians*, 34 (on warfare), 42 (on medicine and astronomy), 44 (on parenting).

49. Underhill, *Papago Indians*, 34.

50. Underhill, *Papago Indians*, 41–42.

51. Underhill, *Papago Indians*, 47 (on Creation beliefs), 49–56 (on ceremonies).

52. Underhill, *Papago Indians*, 65.

53. Underhill, *Papago Indians*, 65. This forms part of the book's brief concluding section, "Papago and Pima Today."

54. Joseph, Spicer, and Chesky, *Desert People*, 27.

55. Underhill, *Papago Indians*, 49. See also 56–57.

56. Underhill, *Papago Indians*, 33–34 (on governance), 34–35 (on warfare), 57 (on visions), 62 (on medicine).

57. Ruth Underhill, *Workaday Life of the Pueblos* (Phoenix: Phoenix Indian School Printing Department, 1946), 4.

58. Underhill refers to the "legend" of Salt Woman and "the War Twins, famous in pueblo mythology." She opined, "Some [pueblo communities] met the god of seeds, or perhaps only another tribe with greater knowledge." Underhill, *Workaday Life*, 75–76, 18.

59. Underhill, *Workaday Life*, 18–20, 141, 127.

60. Ruth Underhill, *Here Come the Navaho!* (Lawrence, KS: Haskell Institute Press, 1953), 15. For contributors, see page 6.

61. Underhill, *Here Come the Navaho!*, 17–24.

62. Gram, *Education at the Edge of Empire*, 88.

63. Scudder Mekeel, "An Anthropologist's Observations on Indian Education," *Progressive Education* 14 (March 1936): 157. Underhill referred to the Pueblos' seventeenth-century "wild enemies, the Apache" and claimed that "the Navajo and Apache ran wild" in New Mexico in the 1820s–30s—"wildness" here seems equated with warfare/raiding. See Underhill, *Workaday Life*, 24, 28.

64. Underhill, *Workaday Life*, 162.

65. Underhill, *Papago Indians*, 6–7.

66. See Carrie A. Lyford, *The Crafts of the Ojibwa* (Phoenix: Phoenix Indian School Printing Department, 1943), 4. See also Carrie A. Lyford, *Quill and Beadwork of the Western Sioux* (Lawrence, KS: Haskell Institute Press, 1940), 9.

67. Willard Beatty, cited in Lyford, *Crafts of the Ojibwa*, 4.

68. Lyford, *Crafts of the Ojibwa*, 28, 30.

69. Lyford, *Crafts of the Ojibwa*, 154.

70. Lyford, *Quill and Beadwork*, 58, 60.

71. Lyford, *Quill and Beadwork*, 82. Emphasis added.

72. Lyford, *Crafts of the Ojibwa*, 28.

73. Lyford, *Crafts of the Ojibwa*, 121.

74. Lyford, *Quill and Beadwork*, 71.

75. See Lyford, *Quill and Beadwork*, 55 (on quillwork). See Lyford, *Crafts of the Ojibwa*, 29 (on cedar bark and rush mats), 61 (on wicker baskets), 93 (on cedar-bark mats), 149 (on birch-bark bitten patterns).

76. Lyford, *Crafts of the Ojibwa*, 154.

77. Ruth Underhill, *Pueblo Crafts* (Phoenix: Phoenix Indian School Printing Department, 1944), 137.

78. Underhill, *Pueblo Crafts*, 137, 9, 135, 89, 91.

79. Underhill, *Pueblo Crafts*, 105.

80. Underhill, *Pueblo Crafts*, 105.

81. McLerran, *New Deal for Native Art*, 227.

82. Underhill, *Pueblo Crafts*, 136–137.

83. For detailed analyses of the Indian Arts and Crafts Board, see McLerran, *New Deal for Native Art*; Meyn, *More Than Curiosities*; Schrader, *Indian Arts and Crafts Board*. See also Molly Mullin, *Culture in the Marketplace: Gender, Art, and Value in the American Southwest* (Durham, NC: Duke University Press, 2001).

84. Willard Beatty, "Greatest of Indian Resources," *IAW* 3, no. 18 (May 1, 1936): 27; Harold Ickes, quoted in "Advancement in the Cause of Indian Arts and Crafts," *IAW* 1, no. 11 (January 15, 1934): 19.

85. Rose Brandt, quoted in "Pueblo Children Represent the United States in an International Art Exhibit," *IAW* 2, no. 13 (February 15, 1935): 27–28.

86. Fern Harris, "Navajo Weaving," *IAW* 4, no. 3 (September 15, 1936): 29–31.

87. Nonabah Gorman Bryan and Stella Young, *Navajo Native Dyes: Their Preparation and Use* (Chilocco, OK: Chilocco Agricultural School Printing Department, 1940), 5–6.

88. For discussion of the San Ildefonso craft revival, see McLerran, *New Deal for Native Art*, 109–112; and Henrietta Burton, *The Re-establishment of the Indians in their Pueblo Life through the Revival of Their Traditional Crafts: A Study in Home Extension Education* (New York: Columbia University Press, 1936). For the Seneca Arts Project, see Hauptman, *Iroquois and the New Deal*, 136–164.

89. Arthur C. Parker, "Museum Motives behind the NY Arts Project," *IAW* 2, no. 21 (June 15, 1935): 11–12.

90. Cephas Hill, "Reviving Indian Arts among the Senecas," *IAW* 2, no. 21 (June 15, 1935): 15.

91. Meyn, *More Than Curiosities*, 68–69.

92. John Adair, *The Navajo and Pueblo Silversmiths* (Norman: University of Oklahoma Press, 1944), 40, 201, 100.

93. Ann Clark, "Twenty Months in an Indian Day School" (n.d.), 11, Collier Papers (Yale), reel 29.

94. See Underhill, *Pueblo Crafts*, 105.

95. Flora Goforth, "Weaving Comes to Pine Ridge—and Stays," in *Education for Action: Selected Articles from Indian Education, 1936–43*, ed. Willard Beatty (Chilocco, OK: Chilocco Agricultural School Printing Department, 1944), 316–317.

96. Clark, "Twenty Months in an Indian Day School," 19–20; Burton, *Re-Establishment of the Indians*, 68.

97. Burton, *Re-Establishment of the Indians*, 68.

98. Evelyn Crady Adams, *American Indian Education*, 87. Collier wrote the introduction to her 1946 evaluation of US Indian education policy.

99. Willard Beatty, "Planning Indian Education in Terms of Pupil and Community Needs," *IAW* 4, no. 2 (September 1, 1936): 6.

100. For insight into the cultural processes involved in traditional Diné weaving and dye making, including protocol on plant collection, see Jennifer McLerran, *A New Deal for Navajo Weaving: Reform and Revival of Diné Textiles* (Tucson: University of Arizona Press, 2022), 204–207.

101. The annual Navajo Tribal Fair began in September 1938. It featured livestock competitions, horse races, rodeo, dances, and arts and crafts exhibitions. See "Navajo Tribal Fair" in Flagstaff Chamber of Commerce, "1941 Flagstaff All-Indian Powwow Program," 18, Arizona Memory Project, accessed 2 February 2025, https://azmemory.azlibrary.gov/nodes/view/39309.

102. E. Fryer to All Personnel, memorandum, April 22, 1940, RG75-Navajo-Fldr 894: "Pageants Indian Education [2/2]," box 197-NARA-LN. Pageant

organizer Earl Raines also promoted the educational aspect of the pageant, informing Navajo Service headteachers it "has a great deal of educational value." See Earl Raines to School Area Heads, August 26, 1940, RG75-Navajo-Fldr 894: "Pageants Indian Education [1/2]," box 197-NARA-LN.

103. "Pageant of Navajo History," final script, August 1940, RG75-Navajo-Fldr 894: "Pageants Indian Education [1/2]," box 197-NARA-LN. Hereafter cited as "Pageant of Navajo History," final script.

104. Earl Raines to School Area Heads, August 26, 1940, RG75-Navajo-Fldr 894: "Pageants Indian Education [1/2]," box 197-NARA-LN.

105. Fryer to All Personnel, memorandum, April 22, 1940, RG75-Navajo-Fldr 894: "Pageants Indian Education [2/2]," box 197-NARA-LN.

106. Earl Raines to Lucy Adams, July 20, 1940, RG75-Navajo-Fldr 894: "Pageants Indian Education [1/2]," box 197-NARA-LN.

107. Raines to School Area Heads, August 26, 1940.

108. Ralph Davol, "Pageantry as a Fine Art," *Art and Progress* 5, no. 8 (June 1914): 299.

109. Earl Raines to Pageant Committee, memorandum, May 18, 1940, RG75-Navajo-Fldr 894: "Pageants Indian Education [1/2]," box 197-NARA-LN.

110. Lomayumtewa C. Ishii, "Western Science Comes to the Hopis: Critically Deconstructing the Origins of an Imperialist Canon," *Wicazo Sa Review* 25, no. 2 (2010): 65–88.

111. Virginia Tanner, quoted in David Glassberg, *American Historical Pageantry: The Uses of Tradition in the Early Twentieth Century* (Chapel Hill: University of North Carolina Press, 1990), 117.

112. Standing Bear, *Land of the Spotted Eagle*, chapter 9.

113. Earl Raines to Lucy Adams, May 4, 1940, RG75-Navajo-Fldr 894: "Pageants Indian Education [1/2]," box 197-NARA-LN.

114. Howard Gorman to Lucy Adams, May 13, 1940, RG75-Navajo-Fldr 894: "Pageants Indian Education [1/2]," box 197-NARA-LN.

115. Raines to Adams, July 20, 1940.

116. Lee, *Diné Identity*, 19.

117. "Pageant of Navajo History," final script. Emphasis added.

118. Raines to Adams, July 20, 1940.

119. "Pageant of Navajo History," final script.

120. For an analysis of Juanita's important role, see Denetdale, *Reclaiming Diné History*.

121. "Pageant of Navajo History," final script.

122. Lucy Adams to Earl Raines, June 20, 1940, RG75-Navajo-894: "Pageants Indian Education [1/2]," box 197-NARA-LN.

123. Glassberg, *American Historical Pageantry*, 139.

124. "Pageant of Navajo History," final script.

125. Flagstaff Chamber of Commerce, "1941 Flagstaff All-Indian Powwow Program," Arizona Memory Project, accessed January 29, 2025, https://azmemory.azlibrary.gov/nodes/view/39309.

126. Lucy Adams to Earl Raines, May 9, 1940, RG75-Navajo-894: "Pageants Indian Education," box 197-NARA-LN.

127. See David Wallace Adams, *Education for Extinction*, 191–206. See also Benjamin Rader, "'The Greatest Drama in Indian Life': Experiments in Native American Identity and Resistance at the Haskell Institute Homecoming of 1926," *Western Historical Quarterly* 35, no. 4 (2004): 429–453. Rader describes how Blackfeet visitors delayed a scheduled homecoming performance of *Hiawatha* with an impromptu dance to celebrate Haskell's football victory. See also John Gram, "Acting Out Assimilation: Playing Indian and Becoming American in the Federal Indian Boarding Schools," *American Indian Quarterly* 40, no. 3 (2016): 251–273.

128. Iverson, *Diné*, 174.

129. L. G. Moses, *Wild West Shows and the Images of American Indians, 1883–1933* (Albuquerque: University of New Mexico Press, 1996), 222 (quotation).

130. The Arthurdale project (West Virginia) was run by the US Division of Subsistence Homesteads and has been described as "an experiment in large-scale community-based progressive education." While the settlement was meant to promote community cooperation and local democracy, the restriction of membership to whites only, and refusal to acknowledge historic (and ongoing) racial and labor tensions, suggests the government's reluctance to engage with uncomfortable realities that challenged the notion of a united nation. See Moyer, "Gendered Boundaries," 531–547, quotation on 539.

131. See Susan Miller, "Native America Writes Back: The Origins of the Indigenous Paradigm in Historiography," *Wicazo Sa Review* 23, no. 2 (2008): 9–28; and Susan Miller, "Native Historians Write Back: The Indigenous Paradigm in American Indian Historiography," *Wicazo Sa Review* 24, no. 1 (2009): 25–45.

132. Denetdale, *Reclaiming Diné History*, 177.

133. Glenn Adams and Phia Salter, "They (Color) Blinded Me with Science: Counteracting Coloniality of Knowledge in Hegemonic Psychology," in *Seeing Race Again: Countering Colorblindness across the Disciplines*, ed. Kimberlé Crenshaw (Berkeley: University of California Press, 2019), 280.

134. Nellie Star Boy Menard, NEA National Heritage fellow, was a renowned maker of Lakota star quilts.

135. Nellie Star Boy Menard, quoted in Susan Labry Meyn, "Fighting for Indian Artisans: John Collier, Rene d'Harnoncourt and the Indian Arts and Crafts

Board," in *Politics and Progress: American Society and the State since 1865*, ed. Andrew Edmund Kersten and Kriste Lindenmeyer (Westport, CT: Praeger, 2001), 64.

136. Lyford, *Quill and Beadwork*, 60.

137. Lyford, *Quill and Beadwork*, 9.

138. For more detail on the Navajo dye and weaving projects, see McLerran, *New Deal for Navajo Weaving*, 129–131, 161–162.

139. Horne and McBeth, *Essie's Story*, 85.

140. Horne and McBeth, *Essie's Story*, 83.

141. Horne and McBeth, *Essie's Story*, 84.

142. Horne and McBeth, *Essie's Story*, 85–86. Horne found that reservation communities and Native school staff were often happy to advise on dances and costumes: "The reason that people were willing to help me learn these skills is that I was helping to keep our Indian culture alive in this off-reservation boarding school."

143. Marion Billbrough Dreamer, quoted in Laura Woodworth-Ney, "The Diaries of a Day-School Teacher: Daily Realities on the Pine Ridge Indian Reservation, 1932–1942," *South Dakota History* 24, no. 3 (Fall/Winter 1994): 208. Dreamer taught at Day School Number 5, near Oglala, 1932–39.

144. Horne and McBeth, *Essie's Story*, 84. Horne also attended an in-service summer school at the University of New Mexico, including Diné weaving and Acoma pottery courses, taught by Native teachers. See Horne and McBeth, *Essie's Story*, 80.

145. Hill, "Reviving Indian Arts," 15.

146. Patrick Wolfe, quoted in Veracini, *Settler Colonialism*, 40.

Chapter 3: Soil Conservation, Science, and Health on the Curriculum

A small portion of this chapter appeared originally in *Journal of the Southwest* 61, no. 4 (Winter 2019): 821–862.

1. For analysis of the impact of stock reduction, see Marsha Weisiger, *Dreaming of Sheep in Navajo Country* (Seattle: University of Washington Press, 2009); Peter Iverson, *The Navajo Nation* (Westport, CT: Bloomsbury Academic, 1981), 27–65; Richard White, *The Roots of Dependency* (Lincoln: University of Nebraska Press, 1983), 260–323; and Rose Mitchell and Charlotte Frisbie, *Tall Woman: The Life Story of Rose Mitchell* (Albuquerque: University of New Mexico Press, 2001).

2. Manley Begay Jr. defines *Hózhójii* as "the state of harmony, peace, beauty, wellness, and balance with all." In contrast, *Hochxójii* is "the state of

disharmony." See Manley Begay Jr., "The Path of Navajo Sovereignty in Traditional Education," in *Navajo Sovereignty: Understandings and Visions of the Diné People*, ed. Lloyd L. Lee (Tucson: University of Arizona Press, 2017), 61.

3. Iverson, *Navajo Nation*, 54.

4. Weisiger, "Navajos, New Dealers, and Metaphysics," 140.

5. For analysis of the economic misery caused by stock reduction, see Weisiger, *Dreaming of Sheep*, 213–214, 222–223.

6. Weisiger, "Navajos, New Dealers, and Metaphysics," 133.

7. Weisiger, "Navajos, New Dealers, and Metaphysics," 133–135.

8. Weisiger, "Navajos, New Dealers, and Metaphysics," 138.

9. Weisiger, "Navajos, New Dealers, and Metaphysics," 135.

10. Weisiger, "Navajos, New Dealers, and Metaphysics," 135–136.

11. See Underhill, *Workaday Life*, 21. For a fuller description of dendrochronology, see Underhill, *Here Come the Navaho!*, 26–27. According to Underhill, "The ring is wide if there has been plenty of rain, narrow if there was little."

12. John Collier, "A Birdseye View of Indian Policy Historic and Contemporary," submitted to Sub-Committee of the Appropriation Committee of the House of Representatives, December 30, 1935, upon request of Rep. Marion Zioncheck, 12, William Zimmerman, Jr. Papers, 1933–1965, box 5: folder 3, Center for Southwest Research, University of New Mexico Libraries (Albuquerque). Hereafter cited as Zimmerman, Jr. Papers.

13. John Collier to Harold Ickes, memorandum: "The Set-Up for the Navajo Community Day Schools, Community Centers and Sub-Agencies," August 9, 1934, 2, Zimmerman, Jr. Papers, box 10: folder 4: "Navajo, 1933–1938." The underlining is Collier's.

14. "Primary Objectives of Indian Schools," enclosed with Shiprock Agricultural High School catalog, RG75-Navajo-Fldr 806: "1941–1942," box 176-NARA-LN. These points formed objectives 3, 4, and 7 out of a list of 9. Vocational education and health education were points 5 and 6.

15. "Primary Objectives," objective 1.

16. Begay Jr., "Path of Navajo Sovereignty," 61.

17. Clif Stratton, in his history of citizenship education in American schools, notes, "For school geographers, the history of imperial conquest had proven whites adaptable to climate variation, primarily through technological ingenuity, while weaker races remained subject to geographic determinism." See Stratton, *Education for Empire*, 27. A 1933 history textbook proudly asserted that "civilization has been developed and history has been made chiefly by the white race." See Zoe Burkholder, *Color in the Classroom: How American Schools Taught Race, 1900–1954* (New York: Oxford University Press, 2011), 58.

18. John Collier, "Memorandum Concerning Points Raised in Mr. Blair's Letter of August 12, 1935," August 15, 1935, RG75-Navajo-Fldr 806: "1935–1939 [2/2]," box 176-NARA-LN.

19. John Collier to Clyde Blair, August 15, 1935, RG75-Navajo-Fldr 806: "1935–1939 [2/2]," box 176-NARA-LN.

20. Clyde Blair, "The Day School System of the Navajo Reservation" (Summer 1936), 13, RG75-Navajo-Fldr 800: "Education, 1943–1946 [1/2]," box 166-NARA-LN.

21. "Special Summer Courses on Soil Conservation at Arizona State Teachers' College," *IAW* 4, no. 20 (June 1, 1937): 15.

22. Fryer was Navajo general superintendent, 1936–42. He was a staunch defender of stock reduction.

23. E. Fryer to Willard Beatty, December 10, 1936, RG75-Navajo-Fldr 800: "Education 1936–1938," box 165-NARA-LN.

24. E. Fryer to H. G. Calkins, August 11, 1937, RG75-Navajo-Fldr 800: "Education 1936–1938," box 165-NARA-LN.

25. Lucy Adams, "Program for Navajo Schools" (December 6, 1937), 1, RG75-Navajo-Fldr 800: "Education 1936–1938," box 165-NARA-LN.

26. Willard Beatty to E. Fryer, August 17, 1936, RG75-Navajo-Fldr 800: "Education 1936–1938," box 165-NARA-LN.

27. John Collier to Willard Beatty, "Memorandum: Subject: Beatty letter to Fryer, August 17, 1936," August 25, 1936; and John Collier to William Zimmerman, "Memorandum," March 12, 1937, both in RG75-Navajo-Fldr 800: "Education 1936–1938," box 165-NARA-LN.

28. John Collier, "Office of Indian Affairs Report," in *Annual Report to the Secretary of the Interior* (Washington, DC: US Government Printing Office, 1940), 387. Hereafter cited as ARSI (1940).

29. Jensen, "Teachers and Progressives," 58. Jensen notes teachers "regularly avoided the subject" of land management.

30. Material for Tuba City Vocational High School Catalogue, January 13, 1942, 2, RG75-Navajo-Fldr 806: "1941–1942," box 176-NARA-LN.

31. Shiprock Agricultural High School Catalogue, February 1942, 1–2, RG75-Navajo-Fldr 806: "1941–1942," box 176-NARA-LN.

32. See McLerran, *New Deal for Navajo Weaving*, 130–131.

33. For a fuller discussion of the sheep laboratory see Weisiger, *Dreaming of Sheep*, 192–195. Red Shirt's Wife, a leading weaver, requested that "our Old Navajo sheep" be saved from increasing domination by rambouillet hybrids. See also McLerran, *New Deal for Navajo Weaving*, 158–166.

34. British colonial and BIA officials were keen to draw links between land and soil conservation issues in the 1930s. South African and Rhodesian soil

conservation officers toured the American Southwest and discussed range management with Collier, who eagerly emphasized the issue's universality. For an insight into this colonial-BIA interaction, see Jacob Tropp, "US Indian Affairs, British Imperial Africa, and Transcolonial Dialogues over Conservation and 'Native Development' in the 1930s," *Journal of World History* 33, no. 3 (September 2022): 459–489.

35. Lucy Adams, "Program for Navajo Schools," 10.

36. Walter Stepp to George Boyce, "Memorandum: Visit to Hunter's Point Day School, April 23, 1943," April 28, 1943, RG75-Navajo-Fldr 806: "Schools, 1943–1944," box 177-NARA-LN. Stepp was acting principal of Fort Defiance Boarding School. He visited Hunter's Point Day School for half a day and was favorably impressed with the school activities and the school-community relationship.

37. For discussion of the Arthurdale project and progressive education, see Moyer, "Gendered Boundaries," 539–541. See also Carney, "Desirable Rural Adaptations in the Education of Negroes," 449.

38. Herbert King Jr., untitled report, December 1939, accompanying letter from H. Bogard to Lucy Adams, December 28, 1939, RG75-Navajo-Fldr 800: "Education 1938–1939," box 166-NARA-LN.

39. George Boyce, paraphrased by E. Fryer, in E. Fryer to Willard Beatty, November 28, 1939, RG75-Navajo-Fldr 800: "Education 1938–1939," box 166-NARA-LN.

40. E. Fryer to John Collier, "Memorandum: Re. Dioramas to be Constructed by Mr Graves," November 16, 1938, RG75-Navajo-Fldr 800: "Education 1936–1938," box 165-NARA-LN.

41. "Problems of Navajo and Pueblo Economy and Their Demands on the Schools," [speech transcript?], Fort Wingate Agricultural and Range Management Training Conference, February 20–26, 1939, 4–5, RG75-Navajo-Fldr 800: "Education 1938–1939," box 166-NARA-LN.

42. Indian Wells Chapter officials (May 1937), cited in *Survey of Conditions of the Indians of the United States: Hearings before a Subcommittee of the Committee on Indian Affairs, United States Senate, 76th Congress Part 37* (Washington, DC: US Government Printing Office, 1940), 21018.

43. Veracini, *Settler Colonialism*, 46. Veracini argues this in relation to settler colonial welfare policies which ostensibly seek to "close the [socioeconomic] gap" between Indigenous and non-Indigenous communities.

44. Clyde Kluckhohn and Dorothea Leighton, *The Navaho*, rev. ed. (1946; Cambridge, MA: Harvard University Press, 1974), 50.

45. Ann Clark, *Little Herder in Spring* (Phoenix: Phoenix School Printing Department, 1940), 70–75.

46. Ann Clark, *Little Herder in Autumn* (Phoenix: Phoenix School Printing Department, 1940), 43.

47. Clark, *Little Herder in Spring*, 91–95.

48. Ann Clark, *Little Herder in Spring; Little Herder in Summer*, combined ed. (Phoenix: Phoenix School Printing Department, 1950), 210–215.

49. Underhill, *Workaday Life*, 160–161.

50. Underhill, *Workaday Life*, 160.

51. Collier's enthusiastic depiction of Pueblo cooperation with stock reduction and soil conservation obscured a varied and complex set of reactions. See Tropp, "US Indian Affairs, British Imperial Africa, and Transcolonial Dialogues," 468–471.

52. NMAIA Report (1940), 25.

53. Phelps-Stokes Report, 4.

54. Valentine Salomore to George Boyce, June 14, 1941, RG75-Navajo-Fldr 807: "Fort Defiance," box 177-NARA-LN.

55. See Hildegard Thompson, *The Navajos' Long Walk for Education* (Tsaile Lake, AZ: Navajo Community College, 1975), 45, 65.

56. Gertrude Giesen, "Work with Beginners, Ages 5–8 Inclusive," [June 1941?], RG75-Navajo-Fldr 807: "Fort Defiance," box 177-NARA-LN.

57. Fred Richards to George Boyce, June 14, 1941, "Statement on 8th Grade Activities, Fort Defiance," RG75-Navajo-Fldr 807: "Fort Defiance," box 177-NARA-LN.

58. Norma Runyan to George Boyce, memorandum, February 8, 1943, RG75-Navajo-Fldr 806: "1943," box 176-NARA-LN.

59. Runyan's stance appears to anticipate the "either/or" attitude of science teachers at public and BIA schools in the later twentieth century. According to Gregory Cajete, science teachers "have determined that if non-western explanations of natural phenomena do not fit the western scientific framework, they are not scientific." See Cajete, "Native American Learner and Bicultural Science Education," 146–147.

60. Basil Johnston, *Indian School Days* (Norman: University of Oklahoma Press, 1988), 186–188. Johnston attended St. Peter Claver's Indian Residential School (Spanish, Northern Ontario), 1939–44.

61. Vine Deloria Jr., "American Indian Metaphysics" in *Power and Place: Indian Education in America*, ed. Vine Deloria Jr. and Daniel Wildcat (Golden, CO: Fulcrum, 2001), 4.

62. George Boyce to Willard Beatty, November 25, 1938, RG75-Navajo-Fldr 800: "Education 1936–1938," box 165-NARA-LN.

63. Willard Beatty to Lucy Adams, September 22, 1938, RG75-Navajo-Fldr 806: "1935–1939," box 176-NARA-LN.

64. George Boyce to Willard Beatty, November 25, 1938, RG75-Navajo-Fldr 800: "Education 1936–1938," box 165-NARA-LN.

65. Phelps-Stokes Report, 1, 24, 3.

66. Phelps-Stokes Report, 86–87.

67. Phelps-Stokes Report, 110.

68. Carney, "Desirable Rural Adaptations," 451. Carney lambasted the inadequate funding of African American schools in the segregated South. Despite her commitment to social justice, Carney's writings suggest a paternalistic attitude to African American rural culture. For more on her career, see Walter Daniel, "Negro Welfare and Mabel Carney at Teachers College, Columbia University," *Journal of Negro Education* 11, no. 4 (October 1942): 560–562; and Mable Carney, "Recently They Said: Rural Negro Youth," *Clearing House* 14, no. 9 (May 1940): 547.

69. Annie Hansen, "The Work of the Domestic Educator," in *Education of the Immigrant: Abstracts of Papers Read at a Public Conference under the Auspices of the New York-New Jersey Committee of the North American Civic League for Immigrants, Held at New York City, May 16 and 17, 1913* (Washington, DC: US Government Printing Office, 1913), 8–9.

70. An exception is provided by Shiprock Boarding School teacher Earl D. Alexander's "Science Report" sent to George Boyce in May 1941. In the first paragraph Alexander states that a school science program "must help students to interpret their environment in terms of scientific habits of thinking instead of superstition." See Earl Alexander, "Science Report, 1940-1941," RG75-Navajo-Fldr 807: "Shiprock," box 177-NARA-LN.

71. Clyde Blair, "The Day School System of the Navajo Reservation, School Year 1936–1937," 3–6, RG75-Navajo-Fldr 800: "Education 1943–1946," box 166-NARA-LN.

72. Lucy Adams, "Program for Navajo Schools," December 6, 1937, 2, RG75-Navajo-Fldr 800: "Education 1936–1938," box 165-NARA-LN.

73. Fred Richards to George Boyce, June 14, 1941, RG75-Navajo-Fldr 807: "Fort Defiance," box 177-NARA-LN.

74. "Allan Hulsizer's notes," in Carson Ryan, "Notes on the Navajo Community Program," [1934?], 5, Zimmerman, Jr. Papers, box 10: folder 4: "Navajo, 1933–1938." According to Ryan (page 1), the schools' main objectives were soil erosion, trachoma and health, milk goats, and fence/hogan improvement.

75. Phelps-Stokes Report, 87.

76. Fred Richards to George Boyce, June 14, 1941, RG75-Navajo-Fldr 807: "Fort Defiance," box 177-NARA-LN. The prioritization of health education echoes the curricular hierarchy for immigrant children promoted by the

superintendent of public schools (New York City) in 1913. See William Maxwell, "Education of the Immigrant Child," in *Education of the Immigrant*, 19.

77. Gertrude Giesen, "Work with Beginners, Ages 5–8 Inclusive," 1, RG75-Navajo-Fldr 807: "Fort Defiance," box 177-NARA-LN.

78. Norma Runyan to George Boyce, memorandum, "Observations of Red Rock Day School," February 8, 1943 [visit: January 11, 1943], RG75-Navajo-Fldr 806: "1943," box 176-NARA-LN.

79. Ora Medley, "Summary of Work for the School Year, 1940–1941 (6th grade)," May 1941, RG75-Navajo-Fldr 807: "Fort Defiance," box 177-NARA-LN.

80. Underhill, *Here Come the Navaho!*, 251.

81. Phelps-Stokes Report, 83–84.

82. W. Peter, "The Land's Health—Basis for a People's Health," *IAW* 4, no. 20 (June 1, 1937): 32.

83. Giesen, "Work with Beginners," 2.

84. Parman, *Navajos and the New Deal*, 218.

85. Joseph, Spicer, and Chesky, *Desert People*, 140; McCarty's Day School Attendance Report, September 30, 1937, Record Group 75, BIA Decimal File, United Pueblos Agency, folder 842: "McCarty's Day School Quarterly Reports, File 1 (October 6, 1936–June 30, 1938)," box 258, NARA Federal Record Center: Rocky Mountain Region (Denver). Hereafter cited as RG75-UPA-Fldr, Box-NARA-Denver.

86. McCarty's Day School Attendance Report, June 30, 1938, RG75-UPA-Fldr 842: "McCarty's Day School Quarterly Reports, File 1 (October 6, 1936–June 30, 1938)," box 258-NARA-Denver.

87. Joseph, Spicer, and Chesky, *Desert People*, 233.

88. Hansen, "Work of the Domestic Educator," 7.

89. Hansen, "Work of the Domestic Educator," 8, 9. Emphasis added.

90. Philander Claxton to Secretary of the Interior, November 1, 1913, "Letter of Transmittal," in *Education of the Immigrant*, 6.

91. See Coleman, "Rehabilitating the Region," 200–217; Jones-Branch, "'An Uneasy Alliance,'" 98–114; Mary Summers, "The New Deal Farm Programs: Looking for Reconstruction in American Agriculture," *Agricultural History* 74, no. 2 (Spring 2000): 241–257.

92. For greater insight into the "family wage ideal" and government attitudes towards women and welfare, see Ruth Feldstein, *Motherhood in Black and White: Race and Sex in American Liberalism, 1930–1965* (Ithaca, NY: Cornell University Press, 2000), 13–37. See also Mimi Abramovitz, *Regulating the Lives of Women: Social Welfare Policy from Colonial Times to the Present*, 3rd ed. (New York: Routledge, 2017), chapters 7 and 8. For an examination of New

Dealers' disregard of Diné women's status regarding stock reduction, see Marsha Weisiger, "Gendered Injustice: Navajo Livestock Reduction in the New Deal Era," *Western Historical Quarterly* 38, no. 4 (December 2007): 437–455.

93. Iverson, *Diné*, 177. See also Lomawaima and McCarty, *To Remain an Indian*, 76–77.

94. Howard Roberts to L. T. Hoffman, "Agriculture Report," October 11, 1938, RG75-Navajo-Fldr 806: "1935–1939," box 176-NARA-LN.

95. Joseph, Spicer, and Chesky, *Desert People*, 182–183. Joseph, Spicer, and Chesky describe the Tohono O'odham diet as "largely dependent upon the limited agricultural resources of the desert and upon cultural traditions" which rendered it "extremely monotonous and limited in its main components." They therefore ascribed the perceived dietary inadequacies to Tohono O'odham culture in addition to the desert environment.

96. Collier, ARSI (1940), 384. The "Indian Affairs" section comprised pages 354–401 of the report. The dietary segment featured under the subheadings "Indian Health" and "Health through Education."

97. Giesen, "Work with Beginners," 2.

98. Collier, ARSI (1940), 384.

99. Former students of Old Leupp Boarding School (Navajo Reservation) in the 1930s remembered grandparents bringing much-appreciated food for the pupils. See Davina Ruth Two Bears, "Decolonizing Research for My Diné (Navajo) Community: The Old Leupp Boarding School Historic Site," *Archaeological Papers of the American Anthropological Association* 33, no. 1 (July 2022): 65.

100. Taos Day School Quarterly Report, June 1937, RG75-UPA-Folder 842: "Taos Day School Quarterly Reports, File 1," General Correspondence File, 1935–43, box 258-NARA-Denver; Taos Day School Quarterly Report, March 31, 1938, RG75-UPA-Folder 842: "Taos Day School Quarterly Reports, File 1," General Correspondence File, 1935–43, box 258-NARA-Denver.

101. Nutria Day School Attendance Report, March 31, 1937, RG75-UPA-Folder 842: "Nutria Day School Quarterly Reports, File 1," General Correspondence File, 1935–43, box 258-NARA-Denver; Cochiti Day School Quarterly Report, March 31, 1939, RG75-UPA-Folder 842: "Cochiti Day School Quarterly Reports, File 1," box 395-NARA-Denver.

102. San Juan Day School Quarterly Report, May 31, 1943, RG75-UPA-Folder 842: "San Juan Day School Quarterly Reports, File 1," box 396-NARA-Denver; Picuris Day School Quarterly Report, December 31, 1937, RG75-UPA-Folder 842: "Picuris Day School Quarterly Reports, File 1," box 258-NARA-Denver.

103. Cochiti Day School Quarterly Report, September 30, 1936; Cochiti Day School Quarterly Report, March 31, 1937; Cochiti Day School Quarterly Report, June 30, 1938, all in RG75-UPA-Folder 842: "Cochiti Day School Quarterly

Reports, File 1," box 258-NARA-Denver. See also Cochiti Day School Quarterly Report, March 31, 1939, and March 31, 1940, both in RG75-UPA-Folder 842: "Cochiti Day School Quarterly Reports, File 1: from 7-1-1938," box 395-NARA-Denver.

104. R. H. McCurtain (principal, Shiprock Boarding School) to Lucy Adams, January 23, 1939, RG75-Navajo-Fldr 806: "1935–1939," box 176-NARA-LN.

105. Laguna Day School Quarterly Report, November 30, 1941, RG75-UPA-Folder 842: "Laguna Day School Quarterly Reports, File 1," box 395-NARA-Denver.

106. Miguel Trujillo to Almira Franchville, September 16, 1937, RG75-UPA-Folder 801.13: "Paraje Day School," box 251 (FRC 163345–50)-NARA-Denver.

107. William Shoop to Sophie Aberle, September 9, 1937, RG75-UPA-Folder 801.4: "Isleta Day School, 1/36–6/38," box 256 (FRC 163351–56)-NARA-Denver.

108. Sophie Aberle to William Shoop, September 14, 1937, RG75-UPA-Folder 801.4: "Isleta Day School, 1/36–6/38," Box 256-NARA-Denver.

109. Louise Wiberg to Leonard Otipoby, October 24, 1938, RG75-UPA-Folder 801.4–801.9: "Education, Schools, Miscellaneous, etc, 1938–44," box 392-NARA-Denver.

110. Leroy Jackson to Sophie Aberle, March 16, 1936, RG75-UPA-Folder 801.24: "Taos Day School," box 251 (FRC 163345–50)-NARA-Denver.

111. Max Kramer to A. G. Sianz, September 23, 1937, RG75-UPA-Folder 801.24: "Taos Day School," box 251 (FRC 163345–50)-NARA-Denver.

112. Underhill, *Here Come the Navaho!*, 251. Underhill, while extolling the beauty and sincerity of Diné religion, claimed it didn't have answers to "new diseases" and to practical problems including flies: "It was time that the Navaho, again, should adopt new ways."

113. Collier, ARSI (1940), 380.

114. Norma Runyan to George Boyce, "Memo: Observations of Red Rock Day School, January 11, 1943," February 8, 1943, RG75-Navajo-Folder 806: "1943," box 176-NARA-LN.

115. James Cohoe to Chester Faris, January 20, 1936, RG75-Navajo-Folder 806: "1935–1939 [2/2]," box 176-NARA-LN.

116. Chester Faris to James Cohoe, February 12, 1936, RG75-Navajo-Folder 806: "1935–1939 [2/2]," box 176-NARA-LN.

117. Robert Martin (NTC delegate), quoted in Robert Trennert, *White Man's Medicine: Government Doctors and the Navajo, 1863–1935* (Albuquerque: University of New Mexico Press, 1998), 177.

118. Davies, *Healing Ways*, 31.

119. Meriam, *Problem of Indian Administration*, 13.

120. See testimony of Miguel Trujillo, W. P. Martin, and Roland Durand, and

comments by Senator Lynn Frazier and Superintendent Chester Faris, in *Survey of Conditions of the Indians in the United States: Hearings before a Subcommittee of the Committee on Indian Affairs, United States Senate, 70th Congress, 2nd Session* (Washington, DC: US Government Printing Office, 1932), 10183–10184, 10190–10193.

121. See McLerran, *New Deal for Navajo Weaving*, 165–166.

122. S. J. Kunitz, *Disease Change and the Role of Medicine: The Navajo Experience* (Berkeley: University of California Press, 1983), 129.

123. In 1946, medical anthropologists Clyde Kluckhohn and Dorothea Leighton argued that "physicians have been often too openly contemptuous of all Navaho [sic] 'medical' practices, too fierce in their condemnations of Navaho [sic] lack of cleanliness and sanitation, generally too little able or willing to see things from the Indians' point of view." See Kluckhohn and Leighton, *The Navaho*, 154.

124. Trennert, *White Man's Medicine*, 179–180. See also Davies, *Healing Ways*, 27, 37.

125. Collier, ARSI (1940), 379.

126. Collier, ARSI (1940), 379.

127. John Collier, letter to the editor, *Christian Century*, November 2, 1934, Collier Files (RIAS), reel 1.

128. Jacob Morgan, "Navajo Chautauqua," newspaper article, unnamed publication (clipping), September 14, 1934, Collier Files (RIAS), reel 1. Morgan was a Christian missionary and boarding school graduate who rejected aspects of traditional Diné culture, while defending Diné sovereignty and identity. He strongly opposed the Indian New Deal.

129. Collier, ARSI (1940), 380.

130. John Collier, preface to *Navaho Door*, Leighton and Leighton, xii, xv.

131. Leighton and Leighton, *Navaho Door*, 24, 40.

132. Leighton and Leighton, *Navaho Door*, 28. See also Collier, ARSI (1940), 379. Collier stated that "through generations of testing, these 'Medicine Men' had acquired an extensive knowledge of medicinal herbs and the use of practical therapeutics in the form of massage, sweat baths, cathartics, and cauterizations."

133. Leighton and Leighton, *Navaho Door*, 28.

134. Leighton and Leighton, *Navaho Door*, 30.

135. Louis Goll, quoted in William Powers, *Oglala Religion* (Lincoln: University of Nebraska Press, 1975), 114. Goll was the Holy Rosary Mission superior on Pine Ridge Reservation, 1920–26.

136. Sallie Wagner, *Wide Ruins: Memories from a Navajo Trading Post* (Albuquerque: University of New Mexico Press, 1997), 77–78. Wagner moved to the

Navajo Reservation in 1938. The memoir is largely sympathetic to Diné culture and community but also paternalistic and supportive of stock reduction.

137. Alexander Leighton and Dorothea Leighton, "Therapeutic Values in Navaho Religion," essay sent by John Collier to Dr. Winfred Overheimer, June 11, 1942, 12, Collier Files (RIAS), reel 7.

138. Leighton and Leighton, "Therapeutic Values," 12.

139. Davies, *Healing Ways*, 59.

140. Leighton and Leighton, *Navaho Door*, 64. Emphasis added.

141. Leighton and Leighton, "Therapeutic Values," 12.

142. Joseph, Spicer, and Chesky, *Desert People*, 80.

143. John Collier, letter to the editor, *Christian Century*, November 2, 1934, Collier Files (RIAS), reel 1.

144. John Cooper, "Anthropology and the Indian Problems of the Americas," in *Indians of the United States*, ed. Clark Wissler (New York: Doubleday, 1940), 19.

145. Joseph, Spicer, and Chesky, *Desert People*, 102. The study was commissioned as part of the Indian Education Research Project sponsored by the BIA and the University of Chicago. The research was conducted 1942–43.

146. Leighton and Leighton, "Therapeutic Values," 13.

147. Leighton and Leighton, *Navaho Door*, 37, 84, 37, 92.

148. Collier, ARSI (1940), 379–380. Emphasis added.

149. For the list of course titles (excluding "Navajo Medicine Men and Their Cures"), see Homer Howard to Lucy Adams, February 7, 1939, RG75-Navajo-Fldr 800: "Education 1938–1939," box 166-NARA-LN. For the reference to "Navajo Medicine Men and Their Cures," see John Provinse to Homer Howard, memorandum, "Proposed Course for Summer School at Fort Wingate," RG75-Navajo-Fldr 800: "Education 1938–1939," box 166-NARA-LN.

150. John Provinse to Homer Howard, memorandum, "Proposed Course for Summer School at Fort Wingate," RG75-Navajo-Fldr 800: "Education 1938–1939," box 166-NARA-LN. An advocate of applied anthropology, John Provinse conducted surveys for the SCS on the Navajo Reservation (1936–38) and joined the Navajo Service in 1939. He was assistant commissioner of Indian Affairs, 1946–52.

151. Provinse, "Proposed Course for Summer School."

152. Provinse, "Proposed Course for Summer School."

153. Provinse, "Proposed Course for Summer School."

154. Homer Howard to Lucy Adams, February 7, 1939, RG75-Navajo-Fldr 800: "Education 1938–1939," box 166-NARA-LN.

155. Clayton W. Dumont Jr., "The Politics of Scientific Objections to Repatriation," *Wicazo Sa Review* 18, no. 1 (Spring 2003): 109.

156. Laura Thompson, *Culture in Crisis: A Study of the Hopi Indians* (New York: Harper, 1950), 54–55. Thompson's fieldwork was conducted July 1942–September 1943.

157. Kluckhohn and Leighton, *The Navaho*, 26.

158. Indian Wells chapter officials (May 1937), in *Survey of Conditions of the Indians in the United States* (1940), 21018.

159. Earl Alexander, "Science Report, 1940–1941," RG75-Navajo-Fldr 807: "Shiprock," box 177-NARA-LN.

160. Leighton and Leighton, *Navaho Door*, 30. Emphasis added.

161. John Collier, "Red Atlantis," 16.

Chapter 4: Indigenous Religions and the Indian Service School Program

A small portion of this chapter appeared originally in *Journal of the Southwest* 61, no. 4 (Winter 2019): 821–862.

1. In 1907, the Hopi leader and elder-in-residence Tawaquaptewa led Hopi pupils in an Eagle Dance at Sherman Institute. Superintendent Harwood Hall briefly sought to use Hopi dances to promote the Sherman Institute to the public and so increase donations. See Matthew Sakiestewa Gilbert, "'The Hopi Followers'": Chief Tawaquaptewa and Hopi Student Advancement at Sherman Institute, 1906–1909," *Journal of American Indian Education* 44, no. 2 (Fall 2005): 1–23.

2. For a discussion of the dance bans, see Treglia, "Consistency and Inconsistency of Cultural Oppression."

3. The Meriam Report predicted that Hopi traditional religion, which it dismissed as "superstition," would "depart to return no more" once a regular water supply was introduced. See Meriam, *Problem of Indian Administration*, 846.

4. John Collier, "Statement on Missionaries" (1934), Collier Files (RIAS), reel 14.

5. Chee Dodge, cited in "Proceedings of the Navajo Tribal Council" (Fort Defiance, July 7–8, 1926), Major Council Meetings of the American Indian Tribes, 1907–1956, microfilm, reel 1 (Hayden Library, Arizona State University). Hereafter cited as MCMAIT.

6. Tom Dodge, address to the Navajo Tribal Council (1933), excerpt in *"For Our Navajo People": Diné Letters, Speeches, and Petitions, 1900–1960*, ed. Peter Iverson (Albuquerque: University of New Mexico Press, 2002), 168–169.

7. Phelps-Stokes Report, 94, 99, 105.

8. Meriam, *Problem of Indian Administration*, 16.

9. Editorial, *Christian Advocate* 84, no. 4 (January 24, 1935): 4, Collier Files (RIAS), reel 14.

10. Philip Gordon, "Annual Report on 'Our Negro and Indian Missions' (Survey of Indian Missions)," sent to all Catholic clergy in US, [March 1935?], Collier Files (RIAS), reel 14.

11. M. A. Dawber, report on the Madison Conference, "For the Committee," [July 1935?], 4, Collier Files (RIAS), reel 14. This was the Indian Missionary Conference held at Madison, Wisconsin, July 11, 1935.

12. Elaine Eastman was a day-school teacher on the Great Sioux Reservation in the 1890s. A staunch assimilationist, she was highly critical of the Indian New Deal, especially cultural tolerance. See Elaine Eastman, "Does Uncle Sam Foster Paganism?," *Christian Century* 51 (August 8, 1934), 1016–1018. See also Elaine Eastman, "The American Indian and His Religion," *Missionary Review of the World* (March 1937), 30; and Elaine Eastman, "Invitation to a Pageant," *Christian Advocate* (October 31, 1935), 986. Reverend G. Lee Phelps, a Baptist missionary from Oklahoma, criticized "practically every religious ceremony practiced among the Indians" which he viewed as "exceedingly degrading"—he opposed Circular 2970 ("the circular is calculated to do immense harm") and the IRA. See G. Lee Phelps to John Collier, October 24, 1934, Collier Files (RIAS), reel 14. See also J. Golden to John Collier, May 1, 1936, Collier Files (RIAS), reel 14.

13. W. O. Roberts (superintendent, Pine Ridge) to John Collier, July 6, 1937, BIA-CCF: Series B, reel 8.

14. J. Golden to John Collier, May 1, 1936, Collier Files (RIAS), reel 14.

15. Boyce, *When Navajos Had Too Many Sheep*, 163–164.

16. Jacob Morgan, "Navajo Chatauqua," newspaper article (no visible title), September 14, 1934, Collier Files (RIAS), reel 1.

17. Nevill Joyner to Asbury, October 3, 1933, Collier Files (RIAS), reel 14.

18. J. H. Boscher and F. Vander Stoep, interviewed by Donald Parman, October 29, 1971, transcript, tape 880, microfilm, reel 6, American Indian Oral History Collection, Center for Southwest Research, University Libraries, University of New Mexico (Albuquerque). Hereafter cited as AIOHC (CSWR).

19. David Daily, *Battle for the BIA: G. E. E. Lindquist and the Missionary Crusade against John Collier* (Tucson: University of Arizona Press, 2004), 103–105.

20. Daily, *Battle for the BIA*, 103.

21. John Collier, "Statement on Government-Missionary Relations," [1934?], 3, Collier Files (RIAS), reel 14. Emphasis added.

22. Unnamed matron, quoted in Thompson, *Culture in Crisis*, 138. The reference to a "breach of federal regulation" is Thompson's assessment, not the matron's.

23. Daily, *Battle for the BIA*, 70.

24. John Collier to William Zeh, March 11, 1935, Zimmerman, Jr. Papers, box 4: folder 7.

25. Almira Franchville to Loretta Leroux, September 28, 1936, RG75-UPA:Fldr 801.22: "San Juan Pueblo," box 251 (FRC 163345–50)-NARA-Denver.

26. General Superintendent (UPA) to Governor (Isleta), February 14, 1938; Pablo Abeita to Sophie Aberle, February 16, 1938, both in RG75-UPA-Fldr 801.4: "Isleta Day School 1/36–6/38," box 256 (FRC 163351–56)-NARA-Denver.

27. Almira Franchville and Louise Wiberg: Circular 3 to Day School Teachers, August 31, 1940, RG75-UPA-Fldr 102c: "Day Schools: Circulars," box 255-NARA-Denver.

28. E. Fryer to G. Bloomfield, January 29, 1942, RG75-Navajo-Fldr 800: "Education, 1943–46 [1/2]," box 166-NARA-LN.

29. Norma Runyan to George Boyce, memorandum, February 8, 1943, "Observations of Burnhams Day School" (January 15, 1943), RG75-Navajo-Fldr 806: "1943," box 176-NARA-LN.

30. Jacob Morgan to Leola Kessler, December 9, 1941, RG75-Navajo-Fldr 806: "1940–41 [1/2]," box 176-NARA-LN.

31. Leola Kessler to Jacob Morgan, December 11, 1941, RG75-Navajo-Fldr 806: "1940–41 [1/2]," box 176-NARA-LN.

32. Phelps-Stokes Report, 110.

33. Jacob Morgan to Arthur Snyder, December 9, 1941, RG75-Navajo-Fldr 806: "1940–41 [1/2]," box 176-NARA-LN.

34. Arthur Snyder to Jacob Morgan, December 11, 1941, RG75-Navajo-Fldr 806: "1940–41 [1/2]," box 176-NARA-LN.

35. Morris Burge, interviewed by Donald Parman, July 21, 1970, transcript, 22–23, tape 890, reel 6, AIOHC (CSWR).

36. Phelps-Stokes Report, 110, 116.

37. See Lomawaima and McCarty, *To Remain an Indian*, 96–98. See also Ann Clark, *Sun Journey: A Story of Zuni Pueblo* (Chilocco, OK: Chilocco Printing Department, 1945).

38. Taos Day School Quarterly Report, April 1, 1937, March 31, 1938, RG75-UPA-Fldr 842: "Taos Day School Quarterly Reports: File 1," box 258-NARA-Denver.

39. Seth Wilson to Sophie Aberle, March 1, 1940, RG75-UPA-Fldr 810: "Students, 1938–43," box 77-NARA-Denver.

40. Gram, *Education at the Edge of Empire*, 105.

41. According to John Gram, "Superintendents focused on traditional dances and traditional authority figures as the greatest challenges that students would face upon returning home." See Gram, 145–146.

42. Sophie Aberle to J. B. Vernon, December 6, 1935, RG75-UPA-Fldr 802.1: "Santa Fe Boarding School," box 252-NARA-Denver.

43. Almira Franchville to Margaret Deal, January 17, 1938, RG75-UPA-Fldr

801.8: "McCarty's Day School, January 1935-June 1938," box 256 (FRC 163351–56)-NARA-Denver.

44. Ann Clark, *Little Boy with Three Names: A Story of Taos Pueblo* (Chilocco, OK: Chilocco Printing Department, 1940), 56.

45. Lucy Adams, "Program for Navajo Schools," December 6, 1937, 5, RG75-Navajo-Fldr 800: "Education 1936–1938," box 165-NARA-LN.

46. See Gram, *Education at the Edge of Empire*, 33–34, for insight into SFIS Superintendent John DeHuff's sporadic permittance of term-time, feast-day attendance in the early 1920s.

47. Nutria Day School Quarterly Report, December 31, 1936, RG75-UPA-Fldr 842.1: "General Correspondence File, 1935–43," box 258-NARA-Denver.

48. Louise Wiberg to Margaret Deal, February 7, 1939, RG75-UPA-Fldr 801.4–801.9: "Education, Schools, Miscellaneous, etc, 1938–44," box 392-NARA-Denver.

49. Cochiti Day School Quarterly Report, November 30, 1942, RG75-UPA-Fldr 842: "File 1," box 395-NARA-Denver.

50. Lucy Adams, "Program for Navajo Schools," December 6, 1937, 5; George Boyce to G. S. Browne, March 9, 1945, RG75-Navajo-Fldr 800: "Education 1945–1946," box 167-NARA-LN. Adams noted that "the scattered population, bad roads and weather, dances and ceremonials, and the economic activities of the children make attendance fluctuating." Boyce accepted the impact of bad roads but also ascribed poor attendance to "the mobility of the people in their sheepherding and ceremonial life."

51. D. P. Trent (for J. M. Stewart) to Office of Indian Affairs (Attn: Beatty), October 5, 1943, RG75-Navajo-Fldr 806: "Schools 1943–1944," box 177-NARA-LN.

52. D. Ellis to George Boyce, memorandum, September 28, 1943, "Report on Visit to Seba Dalkai Day School, September 16, 1943," RG75-Navajo-Fldr 806: "1943," box 176-NARA-LN.

53. Taos Day School Quarterly Report, March 31, 1938, RG75-UPA-Fldr 842: "File 1," box 258-NARA-Denver.

54. Walter Stepp to George Boyce, memorandum, November 5, 1943, "Visit to Crystal Day School, November 3, 1943," RG75-Navajo-Fldr 806: "Schools 1943–1944," box 177-NARA-LN.

55. Virgil Whitaker to Warren Ondelacy, December 3, 1943, RG75-UPA-Fldr 802.1: "Santa Fe Boarding School," box 76 (FRC 163285–90)-NARA-Denver. See also Warren Ondelacy to Mrs. [Brannon? handwriting unclear], November 30, 1943, same file.

56. Education superintendent Virgil Whitaker appears to have tried to curtail UPA pupil absences at Thanksgiving. See Virgil Whitaker to Mrs. Samuel Thompson, November 13, 1944, RG75-UPA-Fldr 802.1: "Santa Fe Boarding

School," box 76 (FRC 193285–90)-NARA-Denver. See also Virgil Whitaker to Jesus Beca, October 11, 1944, same file.

57. Lucia Page to Vernon Beggs, November 1, 1945, RG75-UPA-Fldr 802.1: "Santa Fe Boarding School," box 76 (FRC 193285–90)-NARA-Denver.

58. Julian Martinez to Sophie Aberle, February 1941, RG75-UPA-Fldr 061: "Dances, 1939–41," box 112 (FRC 163293–97)-NARA-Denver.

59. Lomawaima and McCarty, "Examining and Applying Safety Zone Theory," 8.

60. Report from Rhoda Hughes to George Boyce, June 7, 1941, Hunter's Point Day School, RG75-Navajo-Fldr 807: "Fort Defiance," box 177-NARA-LN.

61. Hughes to Boyce, June 7, 1941.

62. Norma Runyan began teaching at Tuba City Boarding School in 1937 and brought an owl into the classroom. See Thompson, *Navajos' Long Walk*, 45, 65.

63. Horne and McBeth, *Essie's Story*, 86.

64. This was printed on the back inside covers of the Indian Life and Customs books. They were additionally billed as "suitable for use in any school."

65. See Underhill, *Papago Indians*; Underhill, *Workaday Life*; Underhill, *Here Come the Navaho!*

66. Underhill, *Workaday Life*, 129; Underhill, *Here Come the Navaho!*, 251.

67. Underhill, *Workaday Life*, 96–97. Underhill equated the kiva's sacred significance to a "special chapel in a Christian cathedral."

68. Underhill, *Workaday Life*, 141. This ambitious overview text on the history and cultures of all Pueblo communities was the fourth installment in the Indian Life and Customs series.

69. Underhill, *Here Come the Navaho!*, 251.

70. Underhill, *Workaday Life*, 96.

71. Underhill, *Workaday Life*, 141.

72. Gertrude Giesen, "Work with beginners, ages 5–8 inclusive," RG75-Navajo-Fldr 807: "Fort Defiance," box 177-NARA-LN.

73. Flora Gregg Iliff, *People of the Blue Water: A Record of Life Among the Walapai and Havasupai Indians* (Tucson: University of Arizona Press, 1985; first published 1954), 252–253.

74. Adam Fortunate Eagle, *Pipestone: My Life in an Indian Boarding School* (Norman: University of Oklahoma Press, 2012), 123.

75. Fortunate Eagle, *Pipestone*, 143–144. Bea Burns was the boys' matron at Pipestone from 1929, following posts at other BIA boarding schools.

76. Fortunate Eagle, afterword to *Pipestone*.

77. Mrs. William McGranahan to John Collier, August 14, 1937, BIA-CCF: Series B, reel 9.

78. Paul Fickinger to Miss Hall, August 25, 1937, BIA-CCF: Series B, reel 9.

79. Scudder Mekeel to Miss Hall, BIA-CCF: Series B, reel 9. Mekeel also

expressed concern that McGranahan referred to "the" Hé Dog community, despite the school serving six communities. In Mekeel's view, "This looks bad from the wife of the Principal of the school."

80. Scudder Mekeel to John Collier, BIA-CCF: Series B, reel 9.

81. John Collier to Mrs. McGranahan, November 17, 1937, BIA-CCF: Series B, reel 9.

82. Memorandum referenced in Harold Ickes to John Collier, October 12, 1933, BIA-CCF: Series B, reel 6.

83. John Collier to Samuel Stacher, October 12, 1933, BIA-CCF: Series B, reel 6.

84. Samuel Stacher to John Collier, October 16, 1933, BIA-CCF: Series B, reel 6.

85. Harold Ickes to John Collier, October 23, 1933, BIA-CCF: Series B, reel 6.

86. Stoltz, *Dove Always Cried*, 68.

87. E. R. Fryer, interviewed by Donald Parman, July 21, 1970, transcript, 3, tape 890, reel 6, AIOHC (CSWR).

88. Kluckhohn and Leighton, *The Navaho*, 176–77.

89. Landis, "New Deal and Rural Life," 596–597. A professor of rural sociology at the State College of Washington, Landis welcomed increased research into rural needs but lamented rural case workers' lack of training.

90. Collier, "Office of Indian Affairs Report," in ARSI (1940), 393. Collier noted the experimental program "has demonstrated the feasibility of job-training for administrators."

91. Collier, "Office of Indian Affairs Report," 393.

92. Walter Olson, "Report" (August 1940), RG75-Navajo-Folder 890: "Southwest Field Training Program," box 197-NARA-LN.

93. Olson, "Report" (August 1940). In his report Olson referred to Diné men as "bucks" and Diné women as "squaws."

94. Phelps-Stokes Report, 42.

95. Evelyn Crady Adams, *American Indian Education*, 103.

96. Phelps-Stokes Report, 45–46.

97. Collier, ARSI (1940), 385.

98. Thompson, *Culture in Crisis*, 145.

99. King, *Earth Memory Compass*, 94–95.

100. Lucy Adams, "Program for Navajo Schools," December 6, 1937, 2, RG75-Navajo-Fldr 800: "Education, 1936–1938," box 165-NARA-LN.

101. Sophie Aberle to Sarah Gertrude Knott, September 23, 1940, RG75-UPA-Fldr 060: "Customs, 1940," box 112 (FRC 163293–97)-NARA-Denver. Aberle was responding to an information request from National Folk Festival director Gertrude Knott.

102. Anthropologists Clyde Kluckhohn and Dorothea Leighton advised

the BIA in 1946 to involve Diné elders so as to improve cooperation with the schools. This suggests the day schools were not seen to be teaching Diné culture and values. See Kluckhohn and Leighton, *The Navaho*, 151.

103. Unnamed "older boy" and unnamed Diné adult, quoted in Dorothea Leighton and Clyde Kluckhohn, *Children of the People: The Navaho Individual and His Development* (Cambridge, MA.: Harvard University Press, 1947), 68–70.

104. Kluckhohn and Leighton, *The Navaho*, 151–152.

105. See Collier's comments on religious liberty, medicine men, and health policy in ARSI (1940), 379–380.

106. T. B. Hall, "Editorials to the Papagos," *IAW* 3, no. 18 (May 1, 1936): 20–21.

107. Miguel Trujillo, "Indian Education throughout the Years," *IAW* 4, no. 18–19 (May 1937): 29.

Chapter 5: Bilingual Education and Dual-Language Primers

A small portion of this chapter appeared originally in *Journal of the Southwest* 61, no. 4 (Winter 2019): 821–862.

1. Willard Beatty, quoted in Louise Lockard, "New Paper Words: Historical Images of Navajo Language Literacy," *American Indian Quarterly* 19, no. 1 (Winter 1995): 25. The quotation is from an essay by Beatty published March 1935.

2. Willard Beatty, afterword to Ann Clark, *About the Slim Butte Raccoon* (Lawrence, KS: Haskell Institute Press, 1942), 75. Emphasis added. This section is replicated in Ann Clark, *Bringer of the Mystery Dog* (Lawrence, KS: Haskell Institute Press, 1943), 77.

3. Willard Beatty, afterword to Ann Clark, *Little Herder in Spring* (Phoenix, Phoenix School Printing Department, 1940), 107.

4. Diné bizaad plays a crucial connective role between the Holy People (*Diyin Dine'é*) and the people (Diné) through ceremonies that maintain and restore harmony and balance. According to Lloyd Lee,

> Diné bizaad is an essential tool for this connection, and it is also a means of transforming chaos into cosmos and the reversal of cosmos to chaos. The language is part of the good and order as well as the bad and disorder. Both are intertwined, and language acknowledges this, yet good and order have the advantage. Language cannot be without knowledge, thought, and speech. Diné bizaad was used to create the world. It is sacred and has power.

See Lee, *Diné Identity in a Twenty-First-Century World*, 51.

5. Willard Beatty, "The Direction of Education," in *Education for Action*, 13.

6. Boyce, *When Navajos Had Too Many Sheep*, 91.

7. Phelps-Stokes Report, 57–58. Evelyn Crady Adams also confirmed the emphasis on English: "A healthy literate self maintaining [sic] Indian is the school goal trilogy." See Evelyn Crady Adams, *American Indian Education*, 106.

8. Lucy Adams, "Program for Navajo Schools" (December 6, 1937), 1, RG75-Navajo-Fldr 800: "Education 1936–1938," box 165-NARA-LN.

9. Florence Little, "Some Schoolroom Activities," 2, RG75-Navajo-Fldr 807: "Fort Defiance," box 177-NARA-LN.

10. Gertrude Giesen, "Work with beginners, ages 5–8 inclusive," [Summer 1941?], RG75-Navajo-Fldr 807: "Fort Defiance," box 177-NARA-LN. According to Giesen, a key objective of her teaching was "to have children learn English and develop initiative in using it."

11. Ora Medley, "Summary of Work for the School Year, 1940–1941" (May 1941), RG75-Navajo-Fldr 807: "Fort Defiance," box 177-NARA-LN. Fifth-grade teacher Valentine Salomore also emphasized English language instruction in his curriculum summary; see Valentine Salomore, untitled curriculum summary (Fort Defiance) sent to George Boyce, June 14, 1941, RG75-Navajo-Fldr 807: "Fort Defiance," box 177-NARA-LN.

12. "Tuba City: Material for School Catalogue" (January 13, 1942), 1–2, RG75-Navajo-Fldr 806: "1941–1942," box 176-NARA-LN.

13. "Fort Defiance Boarding School Outline on work done in classroom for 1940–41," June 6, 1941, RG75-Navajo-Folder 807: "Fort Defiance," box 177-NARA-LN.

14. According to Kluckhohn and Leighton, "The principal conscious educational goal expressed by Navahos [sic] today seems to be the ability to use English." See Kluckhohn and Leighton, *The Navaho*, 145. Alice Joseph noted a similar viewpoint amongst Tohono O'odham parents: "Most of the Papago want some sort of schooling for their children, as they realize the value and the practical necessity of speaking English. Thus it is the rare family that does not make some effort to send its children to school." See Joseph, Spicer, and Chesky, *Desert People*, 100.

15. Unnamed father of 11th grade Shiprock pupil, quoted in Leighton and Kluckhohn, *Children of the People*, 65.

16. Howard Gorman paraphrased in [Homer Howard?], "Discussion of Written Navajo Language," a report on BIA conference held at Fort Wingate, July 24-August 1, 1939, 8 (July 26, 1939), RG75-Navajo-Fldr 800: "Education, 1938–1939," box 166-NARA-LN. The event was held to establish a standard written Diné orthography.

17. Unnamed 5th grade Diné schoolgirl, quoted in Leighton and Kluckhohn, *Children of the People*, 66.

18. NMAIA Report, 27.

19. "Meeting held in the boys' sitting room (chair: John Gorman)," Fort Wingate, December 17, 1939, RG75-Navajo-Fldr 800: "Education 1938–1939," box 166-NARA-LN.

20. "General Meeting for Boys," December 11, 1939, RG75-Navajo-Fldr 800: "Education 1938–1939," box 166-NARA-LN. The meeting featured, as guest speakers, eight of the adult male participants addressing the male school pupils.

21. Florence Little, "Some Schoolroom Activities," [Summer 1941?], 2, RG75-Navajo-Fldr 807: "Fort Defiance," box 177-NARA-LN.

22. Norma Runyan to George Boyce, memorandum, "Observations on Huerfano Day School," November 27, 1941, RG75-Navajo-Fldr 806: "1940–1941 [1/2]," box 176-NARA-LN.

23. Davina Ruth Two Bears, "My Grandmother's and Grandfather's School: The Old Leupp Boarding School, A Historic Archaeological Site on the Navajo Reservation," (PhD. diss., Indiana University, 2019), 187, 190, 205, 215. A former student also recalled that Crownpoint Boarding School tried to enforce an English-only policy on campus in the late 1930s; see King, *Earth Memory Compass*, 104.

24. Harold Ickes to Superintendents, Principals and Teachers in the Indian Service (August 16, 1934), Collier Papers (Yale), reel 32. The banning of harsh, physical punishments at the boarding schools was also noted by Dorothea Leighton and Clyde Kluckhohn—"former militaristic, coercive methods have been abandoned"—and by Alice Joseph. See Leighton and Kluckhohn, *Children of the People*, 64; and Joseph, Spicer, and Chesky, *Desert People*, 99.

25. Two Bears, "My Grandmother's and Grandfather's School," 170, 191, 195, 197.

26. Almira Franchville to Sophie Aberle, July 15, 1937, RG75-UPA-Fldr 801.11: "Nambe Day School," box 251 (FRC 163345–50)-NARA-Denver.

27. W. Peter to E. Fryer, memorandum, "A Land Management Visual Education Device," June 9, 1939, RG75-Navajo-Fldr 800: "Education, 1938–1939," box 166-NARA-LN. Peter had publicly expressed his support for the land management program, linking improved soil to improved health: "We must achieve better Navajo health by better land management." See W. Peter, "The Land's Health—Basis for a People's Health," *IAW* 4, no. 20 (June 1, 1937): 32.

28. In early 1939, Superintendent Fryer discussed leadership values with people he referred to as "the old Navajos." He reported three key leadership qualities: the ability to lead sacred dances ("This ability was regarded as an absolute essential to leadership"); "economic independence" (secondary to the first quality); and "the ability to interpret correctly." According to Fryer, "A good interpreter is regarded as a leader," and Howard Gorman was cited "as a man who is a leader because of this quality." See E. Fryer to "The Files,"

memorandum, "Navajo Leadership," February 8, 1939, RG75-Navajo-Fldr 800: "Education, 1938–1939," box 166-NARA-LN.

29. Clyde Blair, "The Day School System of the Navajo Reservation," [report on 1936–37 school year?], 4, RG75-Navajo-Fldr 800: "Education 1943–1946 [1/2]," box 166-NARA-LN.

30. John Provinse to W. G. McGinnies (Director, SCS), memorandum, "Navajo Translations," July 13, 1937, RG75-Navajo-Fldr 800: "Education 1936–1938," box 165-NARA-LN. Provinse is paraphrasing Howard Gorman.

31. J. Nixon Hadley to John Provinse, memorandum, "Navajo Interpretations," October 26, 1938, RG75-Navajo-Fldr 800: "Education 1936–1938," box 165-NARA-LN.

32. Howard Gorman to E. Fryer, memorandum, "Navajo Translation," August 2, 1939, 1, RG75-Navajo-Fldr 800: "Education, 1938–1939," box 166-NARA-LN.

33. NMAIA Report, 24; Phelps-Stokes Report, 85.

34. Phelps-Stokes Report, 46; NMAIA Report, 24.

35. "The Navajo Language," *NSN* (May 1, 1936), 12. One class was held at the Navajo Agency and one at Fort Defiance Boarding School.

36. NMAIA Report, 24.

37. For example, see Beatty, afterword to Clark, *Little Herder in Spring*, 107.

38. Evelyn Crady Adams, *American Indian Education*, 86.

39. Willard Beatty, quoted in Boyce, *When Navajos Had Too Many Sheep*, 233.

40. For example, Rep. William Lemke (Republican, North Dakota), argued, "Indian languages ought to be considered like the Greek and Latin ... as a matter of history rather than general use." See Boyce, *When Navajos Had Too Many Sheep*, 234–235.

41. Boyce, *When Navajos Had Too Many Sheep*, 233. This is particularly galling considering the crucial role played by Diné bizaad in US military intelligence in World War II.

42. Watkins, quoted in Boyce, *When Navajos Had Too Many Sheep*, 235. The first Diné-English bilingual primer was *Little Herder in Autumn* (1940). The 1943 dictionary, utilized by military personnel supervising Diné recruits, was compiled by linguists Robert Young and William Morgan.

43. Boyce, *When Navajos Had Too Many Sheep*, 124.

44. Clyde Beyale (Torreon district), paraphrased in "General Meeting for Boys" (December 11, 1939), Adult Navajo Short-course (Wingate), RG75-Navajo-Fldr 800: "Education, 1938–1939," box 166-NARA-LN.

45. Willard Beatty, quoted in Peter Iverson, "Speaking Their Language: Robert W. Young and the Navajos," in *Between Indian and White Worlds: The Cultural Broker*, ed. Margaret Connell Szasz (Norman: University of Oklahoma Press, 1994), 264. See also Teresa McCarty, *Language Planning and Policy in*

Native America: History, Theory, Praxis (Bristol, UK: Multilingual Matters, 2013), 75–76.

46. Albert "Chic" Sandoval Sr. devoted his life to preserving Diné bizaad and to developing Diné studies as part of the school curriculum. Elected to the Navajo Tribal Council in 1928, he also worked with Berard Haile on a Navajo orthography. See Miranda Jensen Haskie, "Preserving a Culture: Practicing the Navajo Principles of Hozho doo K'é" (PhD diss., Fielding Graduate Institute, 2002), 1–8.

47. Willard Beatty to E. R. Fryer, July 28, 1939, RG75-Navajo-Fldr 800: "Education, 1938–1939," box 166-NARA-LN.

48. Howard Gorman to E. R. Fryer, memorandum, "Navajo Translation," August 2, 1939, 1, RG75-Navajo-Fldr 800: "Education, 1938–1939," box 166-NARA-LN.

49. Beatty to Fryer, July 28, 1939.

50. Gorman to Fryer, "Navajo Translation," August 2, 1939, 2.

51. John Harrington, words reported in "Discussion of Written Navajo Language," day-by-day report on language workshop held at Fort Wingate, July 24–August 1, 1939, 3, 10, RG75-Navajo-Fldr 800: "Education, 1938–1939," box 166-NARA-LN. Hereafter cited as Wingate Language Report. Much of the report contains paraphrasing of attendees' words, possibly by Homer Howard, with an excerpt from Gerhardt Laves's notes.

52. Richard Van Valkenburgh, paraphrased in Wingate Language Report, 3.

53. John Harrington, paraphrased in Wingate Language Report, 19.

54. Gerhardt Laves, "Copy of Notes made by Mr Laves—Friday, July 28," in Wingate Language Report, 14.

55. John Charles, paraphrased in Wingate Language Report, 3–4.

56. John Charles to E. Fryer, April 18, 1939, RG75-Navajo-Fldr 800: "Education, 1938–1939," box 166-NARA-LN.

57. Howard Gorman, paraphrased in Wingate Language Report, 2.

58. Gorman to Fryer, "Navajo Translation," August 2, 1939, 2.

59. Albert Sandoval, paraphrased in Wingate Language Report, 16.

60. Willetto Antonio, paraphrased in Wingate Language Report, 15.

61. Gorman to Fryer, "Navajo Translation," August 2, 1939, 1.

62. Gorman to Fryer, "Navajo Translation," August 2, 1939, 2.

63. Howard Gorman, paraphrased in Wingate Language Report, 17.

64. Gorman to Fryer, "Navajo Translation," August 2, 1939, 2.

65. Beatty to Fryer, July 28, 1939.

66. John Charles, paraphrased in Wingate Language Report, 3, 4, 16.

67. Howard Gorman, paraphrased in Wingate Language Report, 10.

68. John Harrington, paraphrased in Wingate Language Report, 7.

69. Richard Van Valkenburgh, paraphrased in Wingate Language Report, 7.

70. Homer Howard, paraphrased in Wingate Language Report, 10–11.

71. Howard Gorman, paraphrased in Wingate Language Report, 11.

72. Wingate Language Report, 5.

73. Howard Gorman, paraphrased in Wingate Language Report, 10; Gorman to Fryer, "Navajo Translation," August 2, 1939, 2.

74. Gorman to Fryer, "Navajo Translation," August 2, 1939, 2.

75. Lee, *Diné Identity*, 51.

76. Homer Howard and Howard Gorman, paraphrased in Wingate Language Report, 11. Homer Howard also raised this concern on page 4.

77. Willard Beatty, afterword to Clark, *Little Herder in Spring*, 108.

78. Beatty, afterword to Clark, *Little Herder in Spring*, 108.

79. Beatty, afterword to Clark, *Little Herder in Autumn*, 90.

80. Iverson, "Speaking Their Language," 264.

81. Marguerite Stoltz recalled an unsuccessful reading lesson at Southern Ute Boarding School in 1927. A story about a golden chair elicited little engagement from the Diné teens, and Stoltz lamented the alien and "childish" reading material. Stoltz, *Dove Always Cried*, 11.

82. Mekeel, "An Anthropologist's Observations on Indian Education," 156.

83. Qoyawayma translated the Burrowing Owl song, the Prairie Dog song, Coyote song, and the story of Squirrel picking pinons. See Qoyawayma, *No Turning Back*, 125–126.

84. Qoyawayma, *No Turning Back*, 151. Qoyawayma gave a demonstration at the 1941 institute at Chemawa.

85. Beatty, afterword to Clark, *Little Herder in Spring*, 108.

86. Ann Clark, *Young Hunter of Picuris* (Chilocco, OK: Chilocco Printing Department, 1943), afterword, 55.

87. Clark, *Young Hunter of Picuris*, 55.

88. Anthropologist Harvey Markowitz has commented on the translation challenge posed by the non-Lakota language structure in Clark's prose. See Lomawaima and McCarty, *To Remain an Indian*, 104.

89. Lomawaima and McCarty, *To Remain an Indian*, 91, 98.

90. Ann Clark, *About the Pine Ridge Porcupine* (Lawrence, KS: Haskell Institute Press, 1940), digitized version (no page numbers).

91. Underhill, *Here Come the Navaho!*, 93.

92. Clark, *About the Slim Butte Raccoon*.

93. Lomawaima and McCarty argue that the giveaway is the focus of attack—that Clark sought to promote thrift, frugality, and hard work *over* Lakota

customs. See Lomawaima and McCarty, *To Remain an Indian*, 102. However, the Lakota giveaway in the tale is not criticized—just the raccoon's bastardized version.

94. Ann Clark, *About the Grass Mountain Mouse* (Lawrence, KS: Haskell Institute Press, 1943).

95. Bryan and Young, *Navajo Native Dyes*, 7. Home economics teacher Stella Young wrote the short introduction chapter.

96. Clark, *About the Grass Mountain Mouse*.

97. Vine Deloria Jr. argued that anthropologists visiting Lakota and Dakota communities after World War II harbored erroneous beliefs that dances occurred constantly, and they were disappointed by the reality. They misguidedly urged communities to sponsor multiple dances through the summer, which exacerbated poverty: "Gone are the little gardens which used to provide fresh vegetables in the summer and canned goods in the winter. Gone are the chickens which provided eggs and Sunday dinner. In the winter the situation becomes critical for families who spent the summer dancing." See Vine Deloria Jr., *Custer Died for Your Sins: An Indian Manifesto* (Toronto: MacMillan, 1969), 86–87.

98. Ann Clark, *The Hen of Wahpeton* (Lawrence, KS: Haskell Institute Press, 1943), 2, 26, 38, 86.

99. Lomawaima and McCarty argue that the Just for Fun stories were intended "to inculcate values, especially the value of adhering to federal directives." See Lomawaima and McCarty, *To Remain an Indian*, 98, 100.

100. Clark, *Hen of Wahpeton*, 67.

101. Clark, *Hen of Wahpeton*, 80.

102. The reference to high-maintenance "government chickens" is from the recollections of U. T. Miller, a research assistant to rural sociologist Arthur Raper on his 1941–42 study of the USDA's United Farm Program projects in Georgia. See Summers, "New Deal Farm Programs," 241–257.

103. Clark, *Hen of Wahpeton*, 75.

104. Beatty, afterword to Clark, *Little Herder in Autumn*, 89.

105. Clark, *Little Herder in Autumn*, 69, 75–77. The Little Herder series begins with autumn and ends with summer, though spring was the first instalment published. See "Meet Little Herder," *Indian Education* 38 (March 1, 1940), 4.

106. Ann Clark, *Little Herder in Winter* (Phoenix: Phoenix School Printing Department, 1940), no page numbers.

107. Clark, *Sun Journey*.

108. Clark, *Little Boy with Three Names*.

109. Lomawaima and McCarty, *To Remain an Indian*, 98.

110. Clark, *Little Boy with Three Names*, 45.

111. Clark, *Little Boy with Three Names*, 56.

112. Clark, *Little Boy with Three Names*, 56.

113. S. Prock, "Report of Academic Department on Adult School Dec. 11–22 inclusive," RG75-Navajo-Fldr 800: "Education 1938–39," box 166-NARA-LN. For Raines's dismissive attitude, see Raines to Pageant Committee, memorandum, May 18, 1940, RG75-Navajo-Fldr 894: "Pageants Indian Education [1/2]," box 197-NARA-LN.

114. "Report of meeting held in the boys' sitting room, Fort Wingate" (December 17, 1939), 2, RG75-Navajo-Fldr 800: "Education, 1938–39," box 166-NARA-LN.

115. "Report of participants' meeting held in the boys' sitting room" (December 17, 1939), Chair: John Gorman, Wingate adult short-course, RG75-Navajo-Fldr 800: "Education 1938–1939," box 166-NARA-LN.

116. Yellowman, cited in Navajo Tribal Council Meeting, 22–24 June 1942, 18, MCMAIT, reel 3.

117. Hoskie Cronemeyer (1952), quoted in Iverson, *"For Our Navajo People,"* 107–108.

118. Lily Neil (1947), quoted in Iverson, *"For Our Navajo People,"* 105.

119. "General Meeting for Boys," December 11, 1939, RG75-Navajo-Fldr 800: "Education, 1938–39," box 166-NARA-LN.

120. Ella Deloria, *Speaking of Indians* (Lincoln: University of Nebraska Press, 1998; first published 1944), 144. She argued, "As it looks now, that idea of a special course of study set up for Indians alone [for life on the reservation] shows up a bit negatively as a kind of race discrimination. What is right and necessary for the majority of American school children and is made available to them ought not to be denied to other American children."

121. Qoyawayma, *No Turning Back*, 125–126.

122. Joe Sando, quoted in Howard C. Ellis, "From the Battle in the Classroom to the Battle for the Classroom," *American Indian Quarterly* 11, no. 3 (Summer 1987): 258. The interviews were conducted 1967–72 for the American Indian Research Project.

123. Cronemeyer, quoted in Iverson, *"For Our Navajo People,"* 107–108.

124. Underhill, *Here Come the Navaho!*, 6. Underhill listed a number of Diné contributors who were "deeply interested in their own history and in the teaching of it to their descendants."

125. Lomawaima and McCarty, *To Remain an Indian*, 94.

126. Beatrice Medicine, *Learning to Be an Anthropologist and Remaining "Native,"* 50, 42.

Chapter 6: Evaluating the New Deal Education Reforms

1. Elmer Thomas, Denis Chavez, Burton Wheeler, and Henrik Shipstead, *Survey of Conditions of Indians of the United States*, Analysis of the Statement of the Commission on Indian Affairs in Justification of Appropriations for 1944, and the Liquidation of the Indian Bureau (June 11, 1943), 17, Collier Papers (Yale), reel 31.

2. The total BIA budget granted for 1944 was $28,843,902—in 1932, before the addition of New Deal day schools and revolving credit fund, it was $30,445,092. See Szasz, *Education and the American Indian*, 111. For Beatty's discussions with congresspersons, see Boyce, *When Navajos Had Too Many Sheep*, 233–235.

3. For fuller discussions of World War II's impact on the BIA education program see Szasz, *Education and the American Indian*, 106–22, and Boyce, *When Navajos Had Too Many Sheep*, 116–53. See also Jensen, "Teachers and Progressives," 59–60.

4. House Select Committee to Investigate Indian Affairs and Conditions (1944), quoted in Szasz, *Education and the American Indian*, 109.

5. Alice Lee Jemison, quoted in *Survey of Conditions of the Indians in the United States*, vol. 17, part 37 (Washington, DC: US Government Printing Office, 1940), 20698.

6. Thomas, Chavez, Burton, and Shipstead, *Survey of Conditions of Indians of the United States* (1943), 17.

7. Thomas, Chavez, Burton, and Shipstead, *Survey of Conditions of Indians of the United States* (1943), 20.

8. According to the director of education, George Boyce, active service in World War II inspired servicepersons to seek formal schooling for their relatives. See Boyce, *When Navajos Had Too Many Sheep*, 133, 130.

9. *Treaty between the United States of America and the Navajo Tribe of Indians* (1868), in *Indian Affairs: Laws and Treaties, Volume II (Treaties)*, ed. Charles J. Kappler (Washington, DC: US Government Printing Office, 1904), 1017.

10. Boyce, *When Navajos Had Too Many Sheep*, 195–197.

11. Boyce, *When Navajos Had Too Many Sheep*, 145, 195. Tohatchi Boarding School closed in 1946 due to "continuous pollution of the water system from broken down sewer lines and water mains"—see *Gallup Independent*, March 2, 1946. By spring 1946 four on-reservation boarding schools had closed (including Chinle and Shiprock), leaving fifteen thousand Diné children without school provision. The remaining boarding schools had capacity for 1,582 children; the 1946 enrollment neared 2,500.

12. Boyce, *When Navajos Had Too Many Sheep*, 198.

13. Boyce, *When Navajos Had Too Many Sheep*, 198.

14. Boyce, *When Navajos Had Too Many Sheep*, 201, 200. See also Szasz, *Education and the American Indian*, 116–120.

15. Boyce, *When Navajos Had Too Many Sheep*, 201.

16. Boyce, *When Navajos Had Too Many Sheep*, 200–202.

17. Willard Beatty, September 1951 preface to *Education for Cultural Change: Selected Articles from Indian Education, 1944–51*, ed. Willard Beatty (Washington, DC: US Department of the Interior, 1953), 11.

18. Beatty, *Education for Cultural Change*, 11.

19. Beatty, *Education for Cultural Change*, 11.

20. For an analysis of the futility of "progressive" and "traditionalist" labels in the context of Indigenous individuals and communities in the late nineteenth and early twentieth centuries, see David Rich Lewis, "Reservation Leadership and the Progressive-Traditional Dichotomy: William Wash and the Northern Utes, 1865–1928," *Ethnohistory* 38, no. 2 (Spring 1991): 124–148.

21. Keith Sullivan, "Bicultural Education in Aotearoa/New Zealand: Establishing a Tauiwi Side to the Partnership," *New Zealand Annual Review of Education* 3 (December 1993): 208–210.

22. James Banks and Cheryl McGee Banks, eds., *Multicultural Education: Issues and Perspectives*, 4th ed. (Wiley, 2003), 249.

23. Lomawaima and McCarty, *To Remain an Indian*.

24. Clark, *Little Herder in Winter*.

25. Clark, *Little Boy with Three Names*, 45.

26. For quotation see Lomawaima and McCarty, *To Remain an Indian*, 98.

27. See Sullivan, "Bicultural Education in Aoteroa/New Zealand," 212. Keith Sullivan places Banks's cultural difference paradigm within his "multicultural stage" of education—just falling short of cultural pluralism. To Sullivan, cultural difference *acknowledges* ethnic identification as a positive, whereas cultural pluralism in education actively *promotes* ethnic identification and the maintenance of ethnic cultures, resting upon active involvement of the community in curriculum design.

28. Freire, *Pedagogy of the Oppressed*, 133–134.

29. Nyamnjoh, "'Potted Plants in Greenhouses,'" 129–154.

30. Nyamnjoh, "'Potted Plants in Greenhouses,'" 129.

31. Nyamnjoh, "'Potted Plants in Greenhouses,'" 135.

32. Nyamnjoh, "'Potted Plants in Greenhouses,'" 129.

33. In 1891, Lake Mohonk conference president Merill Gates proclaimed: "We are going to conquer the Indians by a standing army of school-teachers, armed with ideas, winning victories by industrial training, and by the gospel of love and the gospel of hard work." Army captain-turned-educator Richard

Henry Pratt, founder of Carlisle School, has been credited with the slogan "Kill the Indian to save the Man." See quotations in James Wilson, *The Earth Shall Weep: A History of Native America* (London: Picador, 1998), 311–312.

34. Nyamnjoh, "'Potted Plants in Greenhouses,'" 131.

35. Clayton W. Dumont Jr., "Politics of Scientific Objections to Repatriation," 125.

36. Nyamnjoh, "'Potted Plants in Greenhouses,'" 129; Dumont Jr., "Politics of Scientific Objections to Repatriation," 110.

37. Dumont Jr., "Politics of Scientific Objections to Repatriation," 109.

38. Michel Foucault, "Truth and Power" in *Power/Knowledge: Selected Interviews and Other Writings, 1972–1977*, ed. Colin Gordon (New York: Pantheon Books, 1980), 131–133.

39. *The Farmer's Irrigation Guide, Conservation Bulletin* no. 2 (Washington, DC: Department of the Interior, Bureau of Reclamation, US Government Printing Office, 1939). The guide was cited approvingly in the BIA publication *Indian Education*, published fortnightly by the Education Division and circulated to BIA schools—see "Plan before You Irrigate," *Indian Education* 38 (March 1, 1940), 3–4.

40. *Public Health in Arizona* (Phoenix: Arizona State Board of Health, 1938), 18–19.

41. Morris Cooke, quoted in Phillips, *This Land, This Nation*, 136.

42. Mississippi Valley Committee Report (1934), quoted in Phillips, *This Land, This Nation*, 133. Emphasis added.

43. Landis, "New Deal and Rural Life," 599.

44. Landis, "New Deal and Rural Life," 597.

45. Landis, "New Deal and Rural Life," 601–602; Jones-Branch, "'An Uneasy Alliance,'" 106–108; Coleman, "Rehabilitating the Region," 200–217; Summers, "New Deal Farm Programs," 241–257.

46. Landis, "New Deal and Rural Life," 598.

47. Nyamnjoh, "'Potted Plants in Greenhouses,'" 129.

48. Forbes, "New Assimilation Movement," 27–28.

49. Veracini, *Settler Colonialism*, 98. Emphasis added.

50. Freire, *Pedagogy of the Oppressed*, 137.

51. For a useful summary of the federal government's use of social scientists in the 1930s, see Thomas James, "Rhetoric and Resistance," 600.

52. Tsosie, "Reclaiming Native Stories," 336.

53. Donald Fixico, *The American Indian Mind in a Linear World* (New York: Routledge, 2003), 127.

54. Paulo Freire, *Education for Critical Consciousness* (London: Sheed and Ward, 1974), 106–108.

55. Mekeel, "An Anthropologist's Observations on Indian Education," 155.

56. This echoes what James Banks has dubbed the "Ethnic Additive paradigm." See Sullivan, "Bicultural Education in Aotearoa/New Zealand," 209–10. See also James Banks, "Approaches to Multicultural Curriculum Reform" in *Beyond Heroes and Holidays: A Practical Guide to K-12 Anti-Racist, Multicultural Education and Staff Development*, ed. Enid Lee, Deborah Menkart, and Margo Okazawa-Rey (Washington, DC: Teaching for Change, 2006), 37–38.

57. Colleen O'Neill, *Working the Navajo Way: Labor and Culture in the Twentieth Century* (Lawrence: University Press of Kansas, 2005), 157–159.

58. Jensen, "Teachers and Progressives," 51.

Epilogue: Monocultural Resurgence and Bicultural Education in Practice

Epigraph: John Tippeconnic III, "Tribal Control of American Indian Education: Observations Since the 1960s with Implications for the Future," in *Next Steps: Research and Practice to Advance Indian Education*, ed. Karen Gayton Swisher and John Tippeconnic III (Charleston, WV: ERIC Clearinghouse, 1999), 34.

1. Forbes, "New Assimilation Movement," 7–28.

2. Carol Robinson-Zanartu and Juanita Majel-Dixon, "Parent Voices: American Indian Relationships with Schools," *Journal of American Indian Education* 36, no. 1 (Fall 1996): 45, 39, 46.

3. Robinson-Zanartu and Majel-Dixon, "Parent Voices," 50.

4. Indian Nations at Risk Task Force Report (1992), quoted in Jon Reyhner, "American Indian Cultures and School Success," 36.

5. Timothy Begaye, "Native Teacher Understanding of Culture as a Concept for Curricular Inclusion," *Wicazo Sa Review* 22, no. 1 (Spring 2007): 35–52.

6. Begaye, "Native Teacher Understanding," 47.

7. Begaye, "Native Teacher Understanding," 44, 47.

8. Murray L. Wax and Robert G. Breunig, *Study of the Community Impact of the Hopi Follow Through Program* (Washington DC: US Department of Health, Education and Welfare, 1973). The Follow Through Program, established in 1968, aimed to provide for parental involvement in Hopi schools. Between 1970–72 (Project No. 2–0647), Wax and Breunig interviewed 178 parents and observed PTA meetings and classroom instruction. They concluded that Follow Through had made little difference in how Hopi parents viewed the schools, largely because "the program, designed and implemented from without the community, tended to reinforce and perpetuate the basic patterns of interactions between Anglos and Hopis within the school context as they existed over the past 100

years." See Wax and Bruenig, *Study of the Community Impact of the Hopi Follow Through Program*, 1.

9. Unnamed Hotevilla parent interviewed April 14, 1972, in Wax and Bruenig, *Study of the Community Impact of the Hopi Follow Through Program*, 16.

10. Iseke and Desmoulins, "Two-Way Street," 48. For the need to protect sacred knowledge in education, see Cajete, "Native American Learner," 142–143; and Ananda Marin and Megan Bang, "Designing Pedagogies for Indigenous Science Education: Finding Our Way to Storywork," *Journal of American Indian Education* 54, no. 2 (Summer 2015): 40–41.

11. See Iseke and Desmoulins, "Two-Way Street," 31–53; Cajete, "Native American Learner," 136–137.

12. Paul Boyer, Testimony for the Carnegie Foundation Special Report on Tribal Colleges, before the Oversight Hearing on Tribally Controlled Community Assistance Act, Committee on Education and Labor, April 21, 1990, quoted in Delores J. Huff, *To Live Heroically: Institutional Racism and American Indian Education* (Albany: State University of New York Press, 1997), 176–177.

13. Boyer, *Tribal Colleges*, 25.

14. Gloria Emerson (Ramah Navajo High School) testifying before 1972 congressional hearing, quoted in Boyce, *When Navajos Had Too Many Sheep*, 248.

15. Ned Hatathli, testifying before 1972 congressional hearing, quoted in Boyce, *When Navajos Had Too Many Sheep*, 248.

16. Raymond Nakai, quoted in T. Gregory Barrett and Lourene Thaxton, "Robert A. Roessel Jr. and Navajo Community College: Cross-Cultural Roles of Key Individuals in Its Creation, 1951–1989," *American Indian Culture and Research Journal* 31, no. 4 (2007): 29–30. Nakai was chairman of the Navajo Tribal Council, 1964–71.

17. Howard Gorman, quoted in Barrett and Thaxton, "Robert A. Roessel Jr.," 33.

18. *Materials Prepared All or in Part as Result of Office of Education Small Research Grant OEG-9-9-120076-0050 (057) to Navajo Community College*, Project No. 9-1-076, Navajo Studies Program, NCC (Many Farms, Arizona: Navajo Community College, 1971). Hereafter cited as NCC (1971). The publication is a collation of curriculum materials (project overview, course overviews, curriculum outline and objectives, textbook material) produced for the NCC 1970 fall semester.

19. NCC (1971), introduction section, 5.

20. NCC (1971), course description for Navajo Studies 131: "Navajo History and Culture 1," 196, and "Navajo History and Culture 1: The Origin of the Navajo," 120.

21. NCC (1971), introduction section, 6.

22. NCC (1971), course description of Navajo Studies 132: "Navajo History and Culture II," 206.

23. NCC (1971), "An Expanded Course Outline: Navajo History and Culture II (1860–1960)," 8–9, 90–91.

24. NCC (1971), "An Expanded Course Outline: Navajo History and Culture II (1860–1960)," 15–16, 97–98. The sources cited include the *New Mexican*, October 27, 1866, and William Keleher's 1952 monograph *Turmoil in New Mexico, 1846–1868*.

25. NCC (1971), "An Expanded Course Outline: Navajo History and Culture II (1860–1960)," 1–2, 83–84.

26. NCC (1971),"An Expanded Course Outline: Navajo History and Culture II (1860–1960)," 6, 88.

27. NCC (1971), "An Expanded Course Outline: Navajo History and Culture II (1860–1960)," 1, 83.

28. NCC (1971), introduction section, 5, 9.

29. Field trips "to actually see some of the places where these early events took place." NCC (1971), "Navajo History and Culture 1: The Origin of the Navajo," 120, 205. See also NCC (1971), 206: field trips conducted "to historical places of importance to the Navajos." The seventh objective of the Navajo Studies program was "to visit sacred and historical places important to Navajo culture"—see NCC (1971), 195.

30. NCC (1971), "Navajo History and Culture II (NCC Fall Semester, 1970)," 131.

31. NCC (1971), "Navajo History and Culture 1: The Origin of the Navajo," 120.

32. "Transcript of Council Proceedings between W. T. Sherman and Samuel F. Tappan and Chiefs and Headmen of the Navajo Tribe (28–30 May 1868)," in NCC (1971), "An Expanded Course Outline: Navajo History and Culture II," 17–20, 100–103.

33. NCC (1971), introduction section, 4.

34. NCC (1971), "Other Navajo Crafts (NS 102B): Basketmaking," 204.

35. NCC (1971), "Objectives of the Navajo Studies Program," 195.

36. Scholar and educator Ruth Roessel has been described as a "champion of Navajo teachings." She was a founder of Rough Rock Demonstration School and of Navajo Community College, and she served as director of Navajo studies at both. See *Navajo-Hopi Observer*, April 16, 2012.

37. Ruth Roessel, in NCC (1971), "Navajo Studies at NCC," 194.

38. Roessel, in NCC (1971), "Navajo Studies at NCC," 193.

39. NCC (1971), introduction section, 5.

40. NCC (1971), "Course Description for Navajo Studies," 197–198.

41. B.A. Diné Studies, "About Diné Studies track" (course information, job prospects), Diné College, accessed 8 September 2024, https://www.dinecollege.edu/academics/b-a-dine-studies-dine-studies-track/.

42. Sinte Gleska University serves the Sicangu Lakota Nation. See Lakota Studies Department, Sinte Gleska University, accessed 28 March 2025, sintegleska.edu/Lakota-studies.html.

43. See Marin and Bang, "Designing Pedagogies," 29–51; Iseke and Desmoulins, "Two-Way Street," 31–53.

44. Standing Bear, *Land of the Spotted Eagle*, chapter 9.

SELECTED BIBLIOGRAPHY

Primary Sources

MANUSCRIPT/ARCHIVAL SOURCES

American Indian Oral History Collection, microfilm, Center for Southwest Research, University Libraries, University of New Mexico, Albuquerque.

H. M. Hitchcock Papers Relating to Elaine Eastman, 1935, Western Americana Collection, Beinecke Rare Book and Manuscripts Library, Yale University, New Haven, CT.

IRA Papers, Pennsylvania Historical Society, Philadelphia.

John Collier Papers, microfilm, Manuscripts and Archives, Yale University Library, New Haven, CT.

Major Council Meetings of the American Indian Tribes, 1907–1956, microfilm, Hayden Library, Arizona State University, Tempe.

Office Files of John Collier, 1933–1945, microfilm, Roosevelt Institute for American Studies, Middelburg, NL.

Records of the Bureau of Indian Affairs, Record Group 75: Navajo Area Office, Central Classified Files, 1924–1954 (800: Education), National Archives, Pacific Region, Laguna Niguel, CA.

Records of the Bureau of Indian Affairs, Record Group 75: United Pueblos Agency, Central Classified Files, 1933–1950 (060: Indian Customs; 102: Administration and Control; 800: Education), National Archives, Rocky Mountain Region, Denver.

Records of the Bureau of Indian Affairs Central Classified Files, 1907–1939, Series B: Customs and Social Relations, microfilm, Cambridge University Library, Cambridge.

William Zimmerman, Jr. Papers, 1933–1965, Center for Southwest Research, University of New Mexico Libraries, Albuquerque.

NEWSPAPERS, PERIODICALS

American Magazine of Art 1934
Christian Advocate 1935
Christian Century 1925–34
Gallup Independent 1946
Good Housekeeping Magazine 1934
Indian Education 1940
Indians at Work 1933–45
Literary Digest 1934
Missionary Review of the World 1937

Nation 1915
Navajo-Hopi Observer 2012
Navajo Service News 1936–38
New York Times 1923
Progressive Education 1936
Searchlight 1923
Sunset 1923–24
Survey 1922
Women's City Club Magazine 1936

Books, Reports, Memoirs, Essays

Adair, John. *The Navajo and Pueblo Silversmiths*. Norman: University of Oklahoma Press, 1944.
Adams, Evelyn Crady. *American Indian Education: Government Schools and Economic Progress*. New York: Kings Crown, 1946.
Annual Report of the Commissioner of Indian Affairs. Washington, DC: US Government Printing Office, 1931.
Annual Report of the Department of the Interior. Washington, DC: US Government Printing Office, 1934.
Annual Report to the Secretary of the Interior. Washington, DC: US Government Printing Office, 1940.
Beatty, Willard, ed. *Education for Action: Selected Articles from Indian Education, 1936–43*. Chilocco, OK: Chilocco Agricultural School Printing Department, 1944.
Beatty, Willard, ed. *Education for Cultural Change: Selected Articles from Indian Education, 1944–51*. Washington, DC: US Department of the Interior, 1953.
Boyce, George. *When Navajos Had Too Many Sheep: The 1940s*. San Francisco: Indian Historian, 1974.
Bryan, Nonabah Gorman, and Stella Young. *Navajo Native Dyes: Their Preparation and Use*. Chilocco, OK: Chilocco Agricultural School Printing Department, 1940.
Burton, Henrietta. *The Re-establishment of the Indians in Their Pueblo Life through the Revival of Their Traditional Crafts: A Study in Home Extension Education*. New York: Columbia University Press, 1936.
Carney, Mable. "Desirable Rural Adaptations in the Education of Negroes." *Journal of Negro Education* 5, no. 3 (July 1936): 448–454.
Clark, Ann. *About the Grass Mountain Mouse*. Lawrence, KS: Haskell Institute Press, 1943.
Clark, Ann. *About the Pine Ridge Porcupine*. Lawrence, KS: Haskell Institute Press, 1940.

Clark, Ann. *About the Slim Butte Racoon*. Lawrence, KS: Haskell Institute Press, 1942.

Clark, Ann. *Bringer of the Mystery Dog*. Lawrence, KS: Haskell Institute Press, 1943.

Clark, Ann. *The Hen of Wahpeton*. Lawrence, KS: Haskell Institute Press, 1943.

Clark, Ann. *Little Boy with Three Names*. Chilocco, OK: Chilocco Printing Department, 1940.

Clark, Ann. *Little Herder in Autumn*. Phoenix: Phoenix School Printing Department, 1940.

Clark, Ann. *Little Herder in Spring*. Phoenix: Phoenix School Printing Department, 1940.

Clark, Ann. *Little Herder in Spring; Little Herder in Summer*. Combined ed. Phoenix: Phoenix School Printing Department, 1950.

Clark, Ann. *Little Herder in Winter*. Phoenix: Phoenix School Printing Department, 1940.

Clark, Ann. *Sun Journey: A Story of Zuni Pueblo*. Chilocco, OK: Chilocco Printing Department, 1945.

Clark, Ann. *Young Hunter of Picuris*. Chilocco, OK: Chilocco Printing Department, 1943.

Collier, John. "Collier's Reply to Eastman." *Christian Century* 51 (October 8, 1934): 1018–1020.

Collier, John. "Does the Government Welcome the Indian Arts?" in Mrs Franklin D. Roosevelt, "Proceedings of the Twenty-Fifth Annual Convention of the American Federation of Arts: Washington DC, May 14–16, 1934," *American Magazine of Art* 27, no. 12 (December 1934): 11.

Collier, John. "Do Indians Have Rights of Conscience?" *Christian Century* (March 12, 1925): 346–349.

Collier, John. *From Every Zenith: A Memoir*. Denver: Sage Books, 1963.

Collier, John. *The Indians of the Americas*. New York: New American Library, 1947.

Collier, John. "A New Deal for the American Indian." *Literary Digest* (April 7, 1934): 21.

Collier, John. "Persecuting the Pueblos: The Indian Bureau Denies Its Wards Religious Liberty." *Sunset* 53, no. 7 (July 1924): 50, 92–93.

Collier, John. "Politicians Pillage the Pueblos." *Searchlight* 7, no. 8 (January 31, 1923): 15–19.

Collier, John. "The Pueblos' Last Stand." *Sunset* 50 (February 1923): 19–22, 65–66.

Collier, John. "The Red Atlantis." *Survey* 49 (October 1, 1922): 16–19, 63–66.

Collier, John. "US Indian Administration." *Social Research* 12 (September 1945): 274–303.

Cooper, John. "Anthropology and the Indian Problems of the Americas." In *Indians of the States*, ed. Clark Wissler, 19. New York: Doubleday, 1940.

Daniel, Walter. "Negro Welfare and Mabel Carney at Teachers College, Columbia University." *Journal of Negro Education* 11, no. 4 (October 1942): 560–562.

Davol, Ralph. "Pageantry as a Fine Art." *Art and Progress* 5, no. 8 (June 1914): 299.

Deloria, Ella. *Speaking of Indians*. Lincoln: University of Nebraska Press, 1998. First published 1944.

Denman, Leslie. "Indian Ritual and Drama." *Women's City Club Magazine* 10, no. 4 (May 1936): 19.

Eastman, Elaine. "Does Uncle Sam Foster Paganism?" *Christian Century* 51 (October 8, 1934): 1016–1018.

Education of the Immigrant: Abstracts of Papers Read at a Public Conference under the Auspices of the New York-New Jersey Committee of the North American Civic League for Immigrants, Held at New York City, May 16 and 17, 1913. Washington, DC: US Government Printing Office, 1913.

The Farmer's Irrigation Guide, Conservation Bulletin no. 2. Washington, DC: Department of the Interior, Bureau of Reclamation, US Government Printing Office, 1939.

Fortunate Eagle, Adam. *Pipestone: My Life in an Indian Boarding School*. Norman, University of Oklahoma Press, 2012.

Horne, Esther Burnett, and Sally McBeth, *Essie's Story: The Life and Legacy of a Shoshone Teacher*. Lincoln: University of Nebraska Press, 1998.

Iliff, Flora Gregg. *People of the Blue Water: A Record of Life Among the Walapai and Havasupai Indians*. Tucson: University of Arizona Press, 1985. First published 1954.

Johnston, Basil. *Indian School Days*. Norman: University of Oklahoma Press, 1988.

Joseph, Alice, Rosamond Spicer, and Jane Chesky. *The Desert People: A Study of the Papago Indians*. Chicago: University of Chicago Press, 1949.

Kallen, Horace. "Democracy Versus the Melting Pot." *Nation* 100 (February 18 and 25, 1915): 190–194, 217–220.

Kluckhohn, Clyde, and Dorothea Leighton. *The Navaho*. Revised ed. Cambridge, MA: Harvard University Press, 1974. First published 1946.

Landis, Paul. "The New Deal and Rural Life." *American Sociological Review* 1, no. 4 (August 1936): 592–603.

Leighton, Alexander, and Dorothea Leighton. *The Navaho Door*. Cambridge, MA: Harvard University Press, 1944.

Leighton, Dorothea, and Clyde Kluckhohn. *Children of the People: The Navaho Individual and His Development*. Cambridge, MA: Harvard University Press, 1947.

Lyford, Carrie A. *The Crafts of the Ojibwa.* Phoenix: Phoenix School Printing Department, 1943.

Lyford, Carrie A. *Quill and Beadwork of the Western Sioux.* Lawrence, KS: Haskell Institute Press, 1940.

Materials Prepared All or in Part as Result of Office of Education Small Research Grant OEG- 9-9-120076-0050 (057) to Navajo Community College, Project No. 9-1-076, Navajo Studies Program, Navajo Community College. Many Farms, AZ: Navajo Community College, 1971.

Mekeel, Scudder. "An Anthropologist's Observations on Indian Education." *Progressive Education* 14 (March 1936): 151–159.

Meriam, Lewis, et al. *The Problem of Indian Administration.* Baltimore, MD: Johns Hopkins Press, 1928.

The Navajo Indian Problem: An Inquiry Sponsored by the Phelps-Stokes Fund. New York: Phelps-Stokes Fund, 1939.

Public Health in Arizona. Phoenix: Arizona State Board of Health, 1938.

Qoyawayma, Polingaysi. *No Turning Back: A True Account of a Hopi Indian Girl's Struggle to Bridge the Gap Between the World of Her People and the World of the White Man.* Albuquerque: University of New Mexico Press, 1964.

Standing Bear, Luther. *Land of the Spotted Eagle.* Boston: Houghton Mifflin, 1933.

Stoltz, Marguerite Bigler. *The Dove Always Cried: Narratives of Indian School Life.* Blacksburg, VA: Pocahontas, 1994.

Survey of Conditions of the Indians in the United States: Hearings before a Subcommittee of the Committee on Indian Affairs, United States Senate, 70th Congress, 2nd Session. Washington, DC: US Government Printing Office, 1932.

Survey of Conditions of the Indians in the United States: Hearings before a Subcommittee of the Committee on Indian Affairs, United States Senate, 76th Congress: Part 37. Washington, DC: US Government Printing Office, 1940.

Thompson, Hildegard. *The Navajos' Long Walk for Education.* Tsaile Lake, AZ: Navajo Community College, 1975.

Thompson, Laura. *Culture in Crisis: A Study of the Hopi Indians.* New York: Harper, 1950.

Underhill, Ruth. *Here Come the Navaho!* Lawrence, KS: Haskell Institute Press, 1953.

Underhill, Ruth. *The Papago Indians of Arizona and Their Relatives the Pima.* Lawrence, KS: Haskell Institute Press, 1941.

Underhill, Ruth. *Pueblo Crafts.* Phoenix: Phoenix Indian School Printing Department, 1944.

Underhill, Ruth. *Workaday Life of the Pueblos.* Phoenix: Phoenix Indian School Printing Department, 1946.

Urgent Navajo Problems: Observations and Recommendations Based on a Recent Study by the New Mexico Association on Indian Affairs. Santa Fe: New Mexico Association on Indian Affairs, 1940.

Wagner, Sallie. *Wide Ruins: Memories from a Navajo Trading Post*. Albuquerque: University of New Mexico Press, 1997.

Secondary Sources

Abramovitz, Mimi. *Regulating the Lives of Women: Social Welfare Policy from Colonial Times to the Present*. 3rd ed. New York: Routledge, 2017.

Adams, David Wallace. *Education for Extinction: American Indians and the Boarding School Experience, 1875–1928*. Lawrence: University Press of Kansas, 1995.

Adams, David Wallace. "Education in Hues: Red and Black at Hampton Institute, 1878–1893." *South Atlantic Quarterly* 76, no. 2 (Spring 1977): 159–176.

Adams, Glenn, and Phia Salter. "They (Color) Blinded Me with Science: Counteracting Coloniality of Knowledge in Hegemonic Psychology." In *Seeing Race Again: Countering Colorblindness across the Disciplines*, ed. Kimberlé Crenshaw, 271–292. Berkeley: University of California Press, 2019.

Adams, Jane. "Resistance to 'Modernity': Southern Illinois Farm Women and the Cult of Domesticity." *American Ethnologist* 20, no. 1 (February 1993): 89–113.

Andrews, Thomas G. "Turning the Tables on Assimilation: Oglala Lakotas and the Pine Ridge Day Schools, 1889–1920s." *Western Historical Quarterly* 33, no. 4 (Winter 2002): 407–430.

Au, Wayne, Anthony L. Brown, and Dolores Calderon. *Reclaiming the Multicultural Roots of the US Curriculum: Communities of Color and Official Knowledge in Education*. New York: Teachers College Press, 2016.

Banks, James. "Approaches to Multicultural Curriculum Reform." In *Beyond Heroes and Holidays: A Practical Guide to K-12 Anti-Racist, Multicultural Education and Staff Development*, ed. Enid Lee, Deborah Menkart, and Margo Okazawa-Rey, 37–38. Washington, DC: Teaching for Change, 2006.

Banks, James, and Cheryl McGee Banks. *Multicultural Education: Issues and Perspectives*. 4th ed. Wiley, 2003.

Barrett, T. Gregory, and Lourene Thaxton. "Robert A. Roessel Jr. and Navajo Community College: Cross-Cultural Roles of Key Individuals in Its Creation, 1951–1989." *American Indian Culture and Research Journal* 31, no. 4 (2007): 25–50.

Begay, Manley, Jr. "The Path of Navajo Sovereignty in Traditional Education."

In *Navajo Sovereignty: Understanding and Visions of the Diné People*, ed. Lloyd L. Lee, 57–90. Tucson: University of Arizona Press, 2017.

Begaye, Timothy. "Native Teacher Understanding of Culture as a Concept for Curricular Inclusion." *Wicazo Sa Review* 22, no. 1 (Spring 2007): 35–52.

Berthrong, Donald J. "Legacies of the Dawes Act: Bureaucrats and Land Thieves at the Cheyenne-Arapaho Agencies of Oklahoma." *Arizona and the West* 21, no. 4 (Winter 1979): 335–354.

Biolsi, Thomas. *Organizing the Lakota: The Political Economy of the New Deal on the Pine Ridge and Rosebud Reservations*. Tucson: University of Arizona Press, 1992.

Boyer, Paul. *Tribal Colleges: Shaping the Future of Native America*. Princeton, NJ: Princeton University Press, 1989.

Bsumek, Erica. *Indian-Made: Navajo Culture in the Marketplace, 1868–1940*. Lawrence: University Press of Kansas, 2008.

Burkholder, Zoe. *Color in the Classroom: How American Schools Taught Race, 1900–1954*. New York: Oxford University Press, 2011.

Cajete, Gregory. "The Native American Learner and Bicultural Science Education." In *Next Steps: Research and Practice to Advance Indian Education*, ed. Karen Gayton Swisher and John W. Tippeconnic III, 135–160. Charleston, WV: ERIC Clearinghouse, 1999.

Child, Brenda. *Boarding School Seasons: American Indian Families 1900–1940*. Lincoln: University of Nebraska Press, 1998.

Coleman, Amanda. "Rehabilitating the Region: The New Deal, Gender, and the Remaking of the Rural South." *Southeastern Geographer* 50, no. 2 (Summer 2010): 200–217.

Daily, David. *Battle for the BIA: G. E. E. Lindquist and the Missionary Crusade against John Collier*. Tucson: University of Arizona Press, 2004.

Davies, Wade. *Healing Ways: Navajo Healthcare in the Twentieth Century*. Albuquerque: University of New Mexico Press, 2001.

Deloria, Vine, Jr. "American Indian Metaphysics." In *Power and Place: Indian Education in America*, ed. Vine Deloria Jr. and Daniel Wildcat, 1–6. Golden, CO: Fulcrum, 2001.

Deloria, Vine, Jr. *Custer Died for Your Sins: An Indian Manifesto*. Toronto: MacMillan, 1969.

Deloria, Vine, Jr. "The Perpetual Education Report." In *Power and Place: Indian Education in America*, ed. Vine Deloria Jr. and Daniel Wildcat, 151–162. Golden, CO: Fulcrum, 2001.

Deloria, Vine, Jr., and Clifford Lytle. *The Nations Within: The Past and Future of Native American Sovereignty*. New York: Pantheon, 1984.

Deloria, Vine, Jr., and Daniel Wildcat, eds. *Power and Place: Indian Education in America*. Golden, CO: Fulcrum, 2001.

Denetdale, Jennifer Nez. *Reclaiming Diné History: The Legacies of Navajo Chief Manuelito and Juanita*. Tucson: University of Arizona Press, 2015.

Dippie, Brian. *The Vanishing American: White Attitudes and US Indian Policy*. Middletown, CT: Wesleyan University Press, 1982.

Dumont, Clayton W., Jr. "The Politics of Scientific Objections to Repatriation." *Wicazo Sa Review* 18, no. 1 (Spring 2003): 109–128.

Eittreim, Elisabeth. *Teaching Empire: Native Americans, Filipinos, and US Imperial Education, 1879–1918*. Lawrence: University Press of Kansas, 2019.

Ellis, Clyde. *A Dancing People: Powwow Culture on the Southern Plains*. Lawrence: University Press of Kansas, 2003.

Ellis, Clyde. "'There Is No Doubt . . . The Dances Should Be Curtailed': Indian Dances and Federal Policy on the Southern Plains, 1880–1930." *Pacific Historical Review* 70, no. 4 (November 2001): 543–569.

Ellis, Clyde. "'We Don't Want Your Rations, We Want This Dance': The Changing Use of Song and Dance on the Southern Plains." *Western Historical Quarterly* 30, no. 2 (Summer 1999): 133–154.

Ellis, Howard C. "From the Battle in the Classroom to the Battle for the Classroom." *American Indian Quarterly* 11, no. 3 (Summer 1987): 255–264.

Fear-Segal, Jacqueline. *White Man's Club: Schools, Race, and the Struggle of Indian Acculturation*. Lincoln: University of Nebraska Press, 2007.

Feldstein, Ruth. *Motherhood in Black and White: Race and Sex in American Liberalism, 1930–1965*. Ithaca, NY: Cornell University Press, 2000.

Fixico, Donald. *The American Indian Mind in a Linear World*. New York: Routledge, 2003.

Forbes, Jack D. "The New Assimilation Movement: Standards, Tests, and Anglo-American Supremacy." *Journal of American Indian Education* 39, no. 2 (Winter 2000): 7–28.

Foucault, Michel. "Truth and Power." In *Power/Knowledge: Selected Interviews and Other Writings, 1972–1977*, ed. Colin Gordon, 131–133. New York: Pantheon Books, 1980.

Freire, Paulo. *Education for Critical Consciousness*. London: Sheed and Ward, 1974.

Freire, Paulo. *Pedagogy of the Oppressed*. London: Penguin, 1996. First published 1968.

Gerstle, Gary. "Liberty, Coercion, and the Making of Americans." *Journal of American History* 84, no. 2 (September 1997): 524–558.

Gilbert, Jess. "Rural Sociology and Democratic Planning in the Third New Deal," *Agricultural History* 82, no. 4 (Fall 2008): 421–438.

Glassberg, David. *American Historical Pageantry: The Uses of Tradition in the Early Twentieth Century*. Chapel Hill: University of North Carolina Press, 1990.

Gram, John R. "Acting Out Assimilation: Playing Indian and Becoming American in the Federal Indian Boarding Schools." *American Indian Quarterly* 40, no. 3 (2016): 251–273.

Gram, John R. *Education at the Edge of Empire: Negotiating Pueblo Identity in New Mexico's Indian Boarding Schools*. Seattle: University of Washington Press, 2015.

Haskie, Miranda Jensen. "Preserving a Culture: Practicing the Navajo Principles of Hozho doo K'é." PhD. diss., Fielding Graduate Institute, 2002.

Hauptman, Laurence. "Africa View: John Collier, the British Colonial Service and American Indian Policy, 1933–1945." *Historian* 48, no. 3 (1986): 359–374.

Hauptman, Laurence. *The Iroquois and the New Deal*. Syracuse, NY: Syracuse University Press, 1981.

Hinsley, Curtis, Jr. *The Smithsonian and the American Indian: Making a Moral Anthropology in Victorian America*. Washington, DC: Smithsonian Institution, 1981.

Holm, Tom. *The Great Confusion in Indian Affairs: Native Americans and Whites in the Progressive Era*. Austin: University of Texas Press, 2005.

Hoxie, Frederick. *A Final Promise: The Campaign to Assimilate the Indians, 1880–1920*. Lincoln: University of Nebraska Press, 1984.

Huff, Delores J. *To Live Heroically: Institutional Racism and American Indian Education*. Albany: State University of New York Press, 1997.

Hyer, Sally. *One House, One Voice, One Heart: Native American Education at the Santa Fe Indian School*. Santa Fe: Museum of New Mexico Press, 1990.

Iseke, Judy, and Leisa Desmoulins. "A Two-Way Street: Indigenous Knowledge and Science Take a Ride." *Journal of American Indian Education* 54, no. 3 (Fall 2015): 31–53.

Ishii, Lomayumtewa C. "Western Science Comes to the Hopis: Critically Deconstructing the Origins of an Imperialist Canon." *Wicazo Sa Review* 25, no. 2 (2010): 65–88.

Iverson, Peter. *Diné: A History of the Navajos*. Albuquerque: University of New Mexico Press, 2002.

Iverson, Peter. *The Navajo Nation*. Westport, CT: Bloomsbury Academic, 1981.

Iverson, Peter. "Speaking Their Language: Robert W. Young and the Navajos." In *Between Indian and White Worlds: The Cultural Broker*, ed. Margaret Connell Szasz, 255–272. Norman: University of Oklahoma Press, 1994.

Iverson, Peter, ed. *"For Our Navajo People": Letters, Speeches, and Petitions, 1900–1960*. Albuquerque: University of New Mexico Press, 2002.

Jacobs, Margaret D. "Making Savages of Us All: White Women, Pueblo Indians, and the Controversy over Indian Dances in the 1920s." *Frontiers* 17, no. 3 (1996): 178–209.

James, Keith. "Identity, Cultural Values, and American Indians' Perceptions of Science and Technology." *American Indian Culture and Research Journal* 30, no. 3 (2006): 45–58.

James, Thomas. "Rhetoric and Resistance: Social Science and Community Schools for Navajos in the 1930s." *History of Education Quarterly* 28, no. 4 (1988): 599–626.

Jensen, Katherine. "Teachers and Progressives: The Navajo Day School Experiment." *Arizona and the West* 25, no. 1 (Spring 1983): 49–62.

Jones-Branch, Cherisse. "'An Uneasy Alliance': Farm Women and the United States Department of Agriculture, 1913–1965." *Federal History* (2018): 98–114.

Katanski, Amelia. *Learning to Write "Indian": The Boarding-School Experience and American Indian Literature*. Norman: University of Oklahoma Press, 2005.

Kelly, Lawrence. *The Assault on Assimilation: John Collier and the Origins of Indian Policy Reform*. Albuquerque: University of New Mexico Press, 1983.

King, Farina. *The Earth Memory Compass: Diné Landscapes and Education in the Twentieth Century*. Lawrence: University Press of Kansas, 2018.

Korson, Rae, and Joseph Hickerson. "The Willard Rhodes Collection of American Indian Music in the Archive of Folk Song." *Ethnomusicology* 13, no. 2 (May 1969): 296–304.

Kunitz, S. J. *Disease Change and the Role of Medicine: The Navajo Experience*. Berkeley: University of California Press, 1983.

Kunitz, S. J. "The Social Philosophy of John Collier." *Ethnohistory* 18, no. 3 (Summer 1971): 213–229.

Lawrence, Adrea. *Lessons from an Indian Day School: Negotiating Colonization in Northern New Mexico, 1902–1907*. Lawrence: University Press of Kansas, 2011.

Lee, Lloyd L. *Diné Identity in a Twenty-First-Century World*. Tucson: University of Arizona Press, 2020.

Lee, Lloyd L., ed. *Navajo Sovereignty: Understandings and Visions of the Diné People*. Tucson: University of Arizona Press, 2017.

Lewis, David Rich. "Reservation Leadership and the Progressive-Traditional Dichotomy: William Wash and the Northern Utes, 1865–1928." *Ethnohistory* 38, no. 2 (Spring 1991): 124–148.

Lockard, Louise. "Navajo Literacy: Stories of Learning to Write." PhD diss., University of Arizona, 1993.

Lockard, Louise. "New Paper Words: Historical Images of Navajo Language Literacy." *American Indian Quarterly* 19, no. 1 (Winter 1995): 17–30.

Lomawaima, K. Tsianina. "Estelle Reel, Superintendent of Indian Schools, 1898–1910: Politics, Curriculum and Land." *Journal of American Indian Education* 35, no. 3 (May 1996): 5–31.

Lomawaima, K. Tsianina. *They Called It Prairie Light: The Story of Chilocco Indian School*. Lincoln: University of Nebraska Press, 1994.

Lomawaima, K. Tsianina, and Teresa McCarty. "Concluding Commentary: Revisiting and Clarifying the Safety Zone." *Journal of American Indian Education* 53, no. 3 (2014): 63–67.

Lomawaima, K. Tsianina, and Teresa McCarty. "Introduction to the Special Issue: Examining and Applying Safety Zone Theory: Current Policies, Practices, and Experiences." *Journal of American Indian Education* 53, no. 3 (2014): 1–10.

Lomawaima, K. Tsianina, and Teresa McCarty. *To Remain an Indian: Lessons in Democracy from a Century of American Indian Education*. New York: Teachers College Press, 2006.

Marin, Ananda, and Megan Bang. "Designing Pedagogies for Indigenous Science Education: Finding Our Way to Storywork." *Journal of American Indian Education* 54, no. 2 (Summer 2015): 29–51.

McCarty, Teresa. *Language Planning and Policy in Native America: History, Theory, Praxis*. Bristol, UK: Multilingual Matters, 2013.

McCarty, Teresa. "Revitalizing Indigenous Language in Homogenizing Times." *Comparative Education* 39, no. 2 (2003): 147–163.

McDonnell, Janet. *The Dispossession of the American Indian, 1887–1934*. Bloomington: Indiana University Press, 1991.

McLerran, Jennifer. *A New Deal for Native Art: Indian Arts and Federal Policy, 1933–1943*. Tucson: University of Arizona Press, 2009.

McLerran, Jennifer. *A New Deal for Navajo Weaving: Reform and Revival of Diné Textiles*. Tucson: University of Arizona Press, 2022.

Medicine, Beatrice. *Learning to Be an Anthropologist and Remaining "Native": Selected Writings*. Urbana: University of Illinois Press, 2001.

Meyn, Susan Labry. "Fighting for Indian Artisans: John Collier, Rene d'Harnoncourt and the Indian Arts and Crafts Board." In *Politics and Progress: American Society and the State since 1865*, ed. Andrew Edmund Kersten and Kriste Lindenmeyer, 55–70. Westport, CT: Praeger, 2001.

Meyn, Susan Labry. *More Than Curiosities: A Grassroots History of the Indian Arts and Crafts Board and its Precursors, 1920–1942*. Lanham, MD: Lexington Books, 2001.

Miller, Susan. "Native America Writes Back: The Origins of the Indigenous Paradigm in Historiography." *Wicazo Sa Review* 23, no. 2 (2008): 9–28.

Miller, Susan. "Native Historians Write Back: The Indigenous Paradigm in American Indian Historiography." *Wicazo Sa Review* 24, no. 1 (2009): 25–45.

Mitchell, Rose, and Charlotte Frisbie. *Tall Woman: The Life Story of Rose Mitchell*. Albuquerque: University of New Mexico Press, 2001.

Moses, L. G. *Wild West Shows and the Images of American Indians, 1883–1933*. Albuquerque: University of New Mexico Press, 1996.

Moyer, Diana. "The Gendered Boundaries of Child-Centred Education: Elsie Ripley Clapp and the History of US Progressive Education." *Gender and Education* 21, no. 5 (September 2009): 531–547.

Nyamnjoh, Francis. "'Potted Plants in Greenhouses': A Critical Reflection on the Resilience of Colonial Education in Africa." *Journal of Asian and African Studies* 47, no. 2 (2012): 129–154.

O'Neill, Colleen. *Working the Navajo Way: Labor and Culture in the Twentieth Century*. Lawrence: University Press of Kansas, 2005.

Parman, Donald. *The Navajos and the New Deal*. New Haven, CT: Yale University Press, 1976.

Phillips, Sarah. *This Land, This Nation: Conservation, Rural America, and the New Deal*. Cambridge: Cambridge University Press, 2007.

Philp, Kenneth R. *John Collier's Crusade for Indian Reform, 1920–1954*. Tucson: University of Arizona Press, 1977.

Philp, Kenneth R. *Termination Revisited: American Indians on the Trail to Self-Determination, 1933–1953*. Lincoln: University of Nebraska Press, 1999.

Philp, Kenneth R., ed. *Indian Self-Rule: First-Hand Accounts of Indian-White Relations from Roosevelt to Reagan*. Logan: Utah State University Press, 1986.

Powers, William. *Oglala Religion*. Lincoln: University of Nebraska Press, 1975.

Prucha, Francis Paul, ed. *Americanizing the American Indians: Writings by the "Friends of the Indian," 1880–1900*. Cambridge, MA: Harvard University Press, 1973.

Prucha, Francis Paul, ed. *Documents of United States Indian Policy*. Lincoln: University of Nebraska Press, 1975.

Rader, Benjamin. "'The Greatest Drama in Indian Life': Experiments in Native American Identity and Resistance at the Haskell Institute Homecoming of 1926." *Western Historical Quarterly* 35, no. 4 (2004): 429–453.

Reinhardt, Akim. "A Crude Replacement: The Indian New Deal, Indirect Colonialism, and Pine Ridge Reservation." *Journal of Colonialism and Colonial History* 6, no. 1 (2005).

Reinhardt, Akim. *Ruling Pine Ridge: Oglala Lakota Politics from the IRA to Wounded Knee*. Lubbock: Texas Tech University Press, 2007.

Reyhner, Jon. "American Indian Cultures and School Success." *Journal of American Indian Education* 32, no. 1 (October 1992): 30–39.

Reyhner, Jon, and Jeanne Eder, eds. *American Indian Education: A History*. Norman: University of Oklahoma Press, 2015.

Robinson-Zanartu, Carol, and Juanita Majel-Dixon. "Parent Voices: American Indian Relationships with Schools." *Journal of American Indian Education* 36, no. 1 (Fall 1996): 33–54.

Rusco, Elmer. *A Fateful Time: The Background and Legislative History of the Indian Reorganization Act*. Reno: University of Nevada Press, 2000.

Sakiestewa Gilbert, Matthew. *Education beyond the Mesas: Hopi Students at Sherman Institute, 1902–1929*. Lincoln: University of Nebraska Press, 2010.

Sakiestewa Gilbert, Matthew. "'The Hopi Followers': Chief Tawaquaptewa and Hopi Student Advancement at Sherman Institute, 1906–1909." *Journal of American Indian Education* 44, no. 2 (Fall 2005): 1–23.

Sando, Joe S. *Pueblo Profiles: Cultural Identity through Centuries of Change*. Santa Fe, NM: Clear Light, 1998.

Schrader, Robert Fay. *The Indian Arts and Crafts Board: An Aspect of Indian New Deal Policy*. Albuquerque: University of New Mexico Press, 1983.

Schwartz, E. A. "Red Atlantis Revisited: Community and Culture in the Writings of John Collier." *American Indian Quarterly* 18, no. 4 (September 1994): 507–531.

Smith, Sherry. *Reimagining Indians: Native Americans through Anglo Eyes, 1880–1940*. New York: Oxford University Press, 2000.

Smoak, Gregory. *Ghost Dances and Identity: Prophetic Religion and American Indian Ethnogenesis in the Nineteenth Century*. Berkeley: University of California Press, 2008.

Stratton, Clif. *Education for Empire: American Schools, Race, and the Paths of Good Citizenship*. Berkeley: University of California Press, 2016.

Sullivan, Keith. "Bicultural Education in Aotearoa/New Zealand: Establishing a Tauiwi Side to the Partnership." *New Zealand Annual Review of Education* 3 (December 1993): 208–210.

Summers, Mary. "The New Deal Farm Programs: Looking for Reconstruction in American Agriculture." *Agricultural History* 74, no. 2 (Spring 2000): 241–257.

Swisher, Karen Gayton, and John Tippeconnic III, eds. *Next Steps: Research and Practice to Advance Indian Education*. Charleston, WV: ERIC Clearinghouse, 1999.

Szasz, Margaret Connell. *Education and the American Indian: The Road to Self-Determination since 1928*. 3rd ed. Albuquerque: University of New Mexico Press, 1999.

Szasz, Margaret Connell, ed. *Between Indian and White Worlds: The Cultural Broker*. Norman: University of Oklahoma Press, 1994.

Talbot, Steve. "Spiritual Genocide: The Denial of American Indian Religious Freedom, from Conquest to 1934." *Wicazo Sa Review* 21, no. 2 (2006): 7–39.

Taylor, Graham. *The New Deal and American Indian Tribalism: The Administration of the Indian Reorganization Act, 1934–45*. Lincoln: University of Nebraska Press, 1980.

Tlanusta Garrett, Michael. "'Two People': An American Indian Narrative of Bicultural Identity." *Journal of American Indian Education* 36, no. 1 (Fall 1996): 1–21.

Treglia, Gabriella. "The Consistency and Inconsistency of Cultural Oppression: American Indian Dance Bans, 1900–1933." *Western Historical Quarterly* 44, no. 2 (Summer 2013): 145–166.

Treglia, Gabriella. "Cultural Pluralism or Cultural Imposition? Examining the Bureau of Indian Affairs' Education Reforms during the Indian New Deal (1933–1945)." *Journal of the Southwest* 61, no. 4 (Winter 2019): 821–862.

Treglia, Gabriella. "Using Citizenship to Retain Identity: The Native American Dance Bans of the Later Assimilation Era, 1900–1933." *Journal of American Studies* 47, no. 3 (August 2013): 777–800.

Trennert, Robert. *White Man's Medicine: Government Doctors and the Navajo, 1863–1955*. Albuquerque: University of New Mexico Press, 1998.

Tropp, Jacob. "US Indian Affairs, British Imperial Africa, and Transcolonial Dialogues over Conservation and 'Native Development' in the 1930s." *Journal of World History* 33, no. 3 (September 2022): 459–489.

Tsosie, Rebecca. "Introduction: Symposium on Cultural Sovereignty." *Arizona State Law Journal* 34 (2002): 1–14.

Tsosie, Rebecca. "Reclaiming Native Stories: An Essay on Cultural Appropriation and Cultural Rights." *Arizona State Law Journal* 34 (2002): 299–358.

Two Bears, Davina Ruth. "Decolonizing Research for My Diné (Navajo) Community: The Old Leupp Boarding School Historic Site." *Archaeological Papers of the American Anthropological Association* 33, no. 1 (July 2022): 55–72.

Two Bears, Davina Ruth. "My Grandmother's and Grandfather's School: The Old Leupp Boarding School, a Historic Archaeological Site on the Navajo Reservation." PhD diss., Indiana University, 2019.

Veracini, Lorenzo. *Settler Colonialism: A Theoretical Overview*. New York: Palgrave-Macmillan, 2011.

Wax, Murray L., and Robert G. Breunig. *Study of the Community Impact of the Hopi Follow Through Program*. Washington, DC: US Department of Health, Education and Welfare, 1973.

Weisiger, Marsha. *Dreaming of Sheep in Navajo Country*. Seattle: University of Washington Press, 2009.

Weisiger, Marsha. "Gendered Injustice: Navajo Livestock Reduction in the New Deal Era." *Western Historical Quarterly* 38, no. 4 (December 2007): 437–455.

Weisiger, Marsha. "Navajos, New Dealers, and the Metaphysics of Nature." In *Indigenous Knowledge and the Environment in Africa and North America*, ed. David Gordon and Shepard Krech III, 129–150. Athens: Ohio University Press, 2012.

Wenger, Tisa. *We Have a Religion: The 1920s Pueblo Indian Dance Controversy and American Religious Freedom*. Chapel Hill: University of North Carolina Press, 2009.

Whalen, Kevin. "Finding the Balance: Student Voices and Cultural Loss at Sherman Institute." *American Behavioral Scientist* 58, no. 1 (2014): 124–144.

Whalen, Kevin. *Native Students at Work: American Indian Labor and Sherman Institute's Outing Program, 1900–1945*. Seattle: University of Washington Press, 2016.

White, Richard. *The Roots of Dependency*. Lincoln: University of Nebraska Press, 1983.

Wilson, James. *The Earth Shall Weep: A History of Native America*. London: Picador, 1996.

Wolfe, Patrick. "Settler Colonialism and the Elimination of the Native." *Journal of Genocide Research* 8, no. 4 (2006): 387–409.

Woodworth-Ney, Laura. "The Diaries of a Day-School Teacher: Daily Realities on the Pine Ridge Indian Reservation, 1932–1942." *South Dakota History* 24, no. 3 (Fall/Winter 1994): 194–211.

ILLUSTRATIONS SOURCES

Photo 1
Photograph No. 48.1 Photos ca. 1940–ca. 1940 (National Archives Identifier: 295151), "Teacher and students in day school classroom," Central Classified Files, 1924–1954, Navajo Area Office (National Archives Identifier: 295145), Records of the Bureau of Indian Affairs, Record Group 75, National Archives and Records Administration—Riverside, CA.

Photo 2
Photograph No. 48.1 Photos ca. 1940–ca. 1940 (National Archives Identifier: 295160), "Teacher with students learning sanitary kitchen practices in day school," Central Classified Files, 1924–1954, Navajo Area Office (National Archives Identifier: 295145), Records of the Bureau of Indian Affairs, Record Group 75, National Archives and Records Administration–Riverside, CA.

Photo 3
Photograph No. 48.1 Photos ca. 1940–ca. 1940 (National Archives Identifier: 295169), "Young female day school student concentrating on spelling work book," Central Classified Files, 1924–1954, Navajo Area Office (National Archives Identifier: 295145), Records of the Bureau of Indian Affairs, Record Group 75, National Archives and Records Administration—Riverside, CA.

Photo 4
Photograph No. 48.1 Photos ca. 1940–ca. 1940 (National Archives Identifier: 295168), "Male student dramatizing story," Central Classified Files, 1924–1954, Navajo Area Office (National Archives Identifier: 295145), Records of the Bureau of Indian Affairs, Record Group 75, National Archives and Records Administration—Riverside, CA.

Photo 5
Photograph No. 48.1 Photos ca. 1940–ca. 1940 (National Archives Identifier: 295150), "Older students learning penmanship in day school," Central Classified Files, 1924–1954, Navajo Area Office (National Archives Identifier: 295145), Records of the Bureau of Indian Affairs, Record Group 75, National Archives and Records Administration—Riverside, CA.

INDEX

Aberle, Sophie, 99, 124, 127, 138
academic involvement in New Deal, 8, 30, 58; New Deal prioritization of academic knowledge, 47–50, 52–53, 62–63, 66–67, 70–71, 108, 129, 149, 150–151, 154–155, 169, 182–183; in New Deal rural policy, 27–28, 184–185, 187
Adams, David Wallace, 3, 207n16
Adams, Lucy Wilcox, 47, 64, 77–78, 80, 90, 92, 125, 138
Akimel O'odham, 48–49
Albuquerque Indian Boarding School (AIS), 16, 78–79, 125, 175
All-Pueblo Council, 24, 209n46
American Indian Defense Association (AIDA), 24
American Pageantry Association (APA), 62
Annual Report of the Commissioner of Indian Affairs, 41–42
Annual Report to the Secretary of the Interior, 79, 97, 106–107, 135, 137
anthropologists, 6, 14, 30, 58, 62, 96, 170, 181, 187, 196; criticism of government policy, 108, 134, 137; influence on New Deal, 4, 52, 84, 212n78; school textbooks and, 47–48, 129–130, 157; on traditional medicine, 103–107. *See also individual anthropologists*
Applied Anthropology Unit, 131, 212n78
Arizona State Board of Health, 184
assimilation, 8, 124, 127, 148; Assimilation Era policy, 2, 13–18, 36–37, 40, 44, 48, 52, 71, 115, 125, 142, 181–182; and immigrants, 21–22; in Meriam Report, 18–19, 21–23; in New Deal, 33, 70–71, 137, 145, 157, 159, 160, 162; post–New Deal, 36, 174–176, 178, 191; scholarship on Assimilation Era, 5–6

Banks, James, 178, 180, 247n27, 249n56
Barboncito, 16, 63, 66, 197
beadwork, 145; Indigenous teachers, 67–68; in textbooks, 53–54, 68
Beatty, Willard W., 4, 41, 56, 60, 70, 90, 127, 138, 173–176, 179, 182, 186–187, 189, 197, 200; on bilingual education, 141–142, 148, 163, 168; on crosscultural primers, 47–48, 52–53, 75, 157, 178; on Diné orthography project, 149–150, 153, 155; on progressive education, 4, 34, 88; on range management, 78–79
Begay, Etsitty, 168–169
Begay, Manley A., Jr., 76, 221–222n2
biculturalism: in education, 2, 4–6, 9, 108–109, 170, 177–178, 189, 193–200; in Meriam Report, 20–21. *See also* double education
bilingualism, 29, 45; primers, 4–6, 84, 141, 149, 151, 155, 170–171, 241n42; teaching, 29, 45, 142, 148, 167, 176, 179–180, 189
Blair, Clyde, 76, 92, 146
boarding schools: in Assimilation Era, 1–2, 19, 23, 115, 132; assimilationist personnel at, 133, 145; closures of, 35, 175; cultural dislocation at, 54, 139; food at, 97–98; medical provision at, 100–101; missionaries at, 116, 120–123; New Deal reforms at, 130–131; scholarship on, 3–4, 203n14, 203n15; and Special Navajo Program, 175; student absences from, 125–126. *See also* students; teachers
Boyce, George, 46, 82, 90, 119, 126, 142, 148, 149, 175–176, 235n50, 246n8
Bryan, Nonabah Gorman, 57–58, 68, 80
Burke, Charles, 15, 132

Cajete, Gregory, 202n5, 225n59, 250n10
Carleton, James, 63, 195
Carlisle Indian Boarding School, 2, 3, 45, 247–248n33
Carney, Mabel, 91, 211n68, 266n68
Carson (Stewart) Indian Boarding School, 41–45, 133, 175
Carson, Christopher "Kit," 63–65, 195
Charles, John, 151, 153
Chemawa Indian Boarding School, 120, 175
Chilocco Indian Boarding School, 39–40, 120
Circular 1665 (and Supplement), 115
Circular 2970, 28–31, 34–35, 117–120, 131–132, 160
civilization hierarchies, 14, 30, 76
Clark, Ann Nolan: pottery revival, 59; primers and textbooks, 86, 157, 160–161, 163–166, 170, 179

Cloud, Henry Roe, 18
Cochiti Day School, 98, 125
Collier, John, 2–3, 6, 27, 33, 47, 58, 87, 96, 110, 132, 135; on academic experts, 187; background in Native rights/New Deal origins, 24–26; on Circular 2970 and religious freedom, 28–31, 127, 179; contemporary criticism of, 32, 119; on education, 34–35; on health education, 100; on Indigenous traditional medicine, 102–103, 106–108; on religious instruction in schools, 116, 120, 123–124; in scholarship, 32–33; on soil conservation education, 75–77; on teaching requirements, 137
colonialism, 18, 20, 27, 33, 65, 67, 71, 80, 84, 88; colonial education paradigms, 180–186; New Deal links to British colonial policy, 37, 80, 223–224n34. *See also* settler colonialism
compartmentalization (cultural), 110, 187–188, 192, 199
Crownpoint Indian Boarding School, 6, 66, 138, 240n23
Crystal Day School, 126
cultural invasion, 8–9, 12, 180–182
cultural pluralism, 3, 6–7, 19, 37, 140, 149, 156, 181, 188, 190, 193, 195, 247n27; Kallen's pluralist model, 30–31
cultural tolerance, 2, 5–6, 14, 21, 29, 31, 33, 36, 76, 96, 106, 108, 115, 119, 127, 130–133, 137–138, 140, 177–178, 183–184, 189

dance bans, 15, 18, 29, 33, 184; scholarship on, 206n7
Dawes Act, 15, 26; scholarship on, 206n1. *See also* land allotment
day schools, 3, 34–36, 165–166; and absences for religious training/ceremonies, 124–126; Diné criticism of, 144, 167–168; health education at, 94–95; illness and risk at, 98–99; medical provision at, 100–101; in Meriam Report, 23–24; and missionaries, 121–122; Pueblo criticism of, 145; in scholarship, 4–5; science education at, 88; and soil conservation, 74, 76–77; in World War II, 173–175. *See also* students; teachers
Deloria, Ella C., 10, 168, 245n120
Deloria, Vine, Jr., 30, 45, 89, 160, 244n97

diet, 69, 96–98, 108–109, 185, 228n95; traditional foods at school, 69, 97, 228n99
Diné Bikéyah, 65, 141–142; sacred significance of, 154, 238n4; at school, 144–145, 147, 152; in translation, 146–147, 148, 152. *See also* Navajo orthography project
Diné College, 199. *See also* Navajo Community College (NCC)
Dodge, Chee, 116–117
Dodge, Tom, 117
double education, 2–3
Dumont, Clayton, Jr., 108, 182–183

Eastman, Elaine, 32, 118, 233n12
elders, 4, 45, 141, 215n39; as cultural educators, 3, 152, 162, 164–166, 170, 179, 192–193, 199; grandparents, 42–44, 128
English language teaching, 1–2, 44, 47, 128, 140, 142–145, 148
English-only policy, 115, 142, 148, 240n23
epistemicide, 8, 12, 18, 180–182
Eurocentrism, 1, 5, 7, 10, 12, 71, 75, 90, 109, 130, 171, 178, 182–183, 187–189, 200

Farm Security Administration (FSA), 28
Federal Emergency Relief Administration (FERA), 134
Forbes, Jack D., 1, 186, 191
Fort Defiance, 64, 128, 196
Fort Defiance Indian Boarding School: Christmas teaching unit, 130; diet, 97; English language teaching, 143; health program, 93; history lessons, 46–47; medical center, 103; science unit, 88
Fortunate Eagle, Adam, 130–131
Foucault, Michel, 183
Franchville, Almira, 121, 145
Freire, Paulo, 8, 180–181, 186–187
Fryer, E. R., 61, 68, 79, 107, 152–154, 223n22; on insensitive personnel, 134; on missionary regulations, 121–122; on soil conservation, 77–78, 146

Ganado, Mucho, 64, 66
Ganado Mission, 102
gender, imposition of attitudes, 96, 227–228n92
Gorman, Howard, 128, 143; on Diné orthography project, 149–155; on Navajo Community College, 195–196;

in Pageant of Navajo History, 63, 65; on translation, 146–147

Hadley, J. Nixon, 147, 150–151, 153
Harrington, Joseph P., 149–155, 170
Haskell Indian Boarding School, 16–17, 39–40
Hatathli, Ned, 194
health, 33, 37, 102–109, 146, 166, 178, 226n76, 240n27; and diet, 96–97; ill-health at schools, 98–101; in Meriam Report, 18, 21–22; on school curricula, 47, 73, 76, 78, 92–95, 97, 109, 143, 199; and traditional Diné healthcare, 101; in wider New Deal rural policy, 27, 96, 184–186. *See also* illness
Hé Dog Day School, 131–132
history, 14, 16, 34–35, 39–40, 67, 79, 167; Navajo Community College course, 194–198; teaching in New Deal, 5, 39–40, 46–47, 63; textbooks, 48–52, 129. *See also* Pageant of Navajo History
hogans, 82–83, 91, 93, 135, 174, 195
home-making, 22, 93–95, 96, 185
Hopi, 5, 108, 120, 124–125, 137, 154; in Meriam Report, 22–23; parents' views on schooling, 168, 192–193; primers, 141, 156–157
Horne, Esther Burnett, 17, 40–41, 45, 68–70, 129, 131, 208n19, 221n142; at BIA summer school, 156
Howard, Homer, 107, 154
Huerfano Day School, 98, 143–144
Hunter's Point Day School, 81, 128, 224n36

Ickes, Harold, 56, 76, 132–133, 145
illness: at boarding schools, 1; at day schools, 98–99; Diné traditional interpretation, 101; education in schools, 94–95, 97; government attitudes towards traditional Diné medicine, 104–107, 109; in Meriam Report, 21; tuberculosis and trachoma, 94, 103. *See also* health
immigrants, attitudes towards, 5, 21–22, 25, 90–91, 95–96
Indian Arts and Crafts Board, 27, 53, 56, 59–60, 68, 80, 173; scholarship on, 210n60, 217n83
Indian Assistants (in schools), 77, 128, 138, 144, 151, 153
Indian Handcrafts series, 52–58, 155

Indian Life and Customs series, 47–52, 129, 156
Indian Life Readers, 141, 156–166, 170
Indian New Deal, 2–3, 8–9; contemporary criticisms of, 31–33, 36, 173–174; education policy, 34–37; ending of, 173–175; evaluation of, 187–190; Indian Reorganization Act, 26–28, 32, 34–35; overview of, 24–28; as part of wider New Deal, 185; scholarship on, 202n11, 203n12
Indians at Work, 16, 33–34, 58, 77, 94, 131, 207n18
Integration stage (education model), 178–179
Isleta Day School, 99, 121
Isleta Pueblo, 16, 129

Jemison, Alice Lee, 32
Joseph, Alice, 95–96, 105, 216n46, 239n14
Just for Fun Stories, 157–163, 165–170, 244n99

King, Farina, 6, 42, 138, 204n31
Kluckhohn, Clyde, 84, 108, 134, 139, 230n123, 237–238n102, 239n14

Laguna Day School, 98–99
Laguna Pueblo, 45, 87, 125
Lakota, 2, 6, 12, 35, 60, 62, 67–68, 104, 132, 199; bilingual primers, 141–142, 148, 156–160, 162, 176; day schools, 4, 69
land allotment, 3, 8, 15, 26, 186, 208n27; Meriam Report's criticism of, 18–20, 23. *See also* Dawes Act
Laves, Gerhardt, 150–151, 153–154
Lee, Lloyd L., 63, 154, 238n4
Leighton, Alexander, 103–106, 110
Leighton, Dorothea, 84, 103–106, 108, 110, 134, 139, 230n123
Leupp, Francis, 16, 36–37, 39, 207n17, 213–214n2
Little, Florence, 142–144
Little Herder primer series: bilingual education, 6, 155, 162; on ecology/soil conservation, 84–86, 163; on sings, 163–164, 179
Lomawaima, K. Tsianina, 5, 9, 39–40, 170, 178; on Meriam Report, 208–209n31; on primers, 124, 157, 165, 243n88, 243–244n93, 244n99. *See also* McCarty, Teresa L.; safety zone

Long Walk, 61, 64, 195
Loram, Charles T., 33
Lyford, Carrie A., 53–56, 58, 67–68, 155

Manuelito, 64, 66
McCarty, Teresa L., 5, 9, 39–40, 170, 178; on Meriam Report, 208–209n31; on primers, 124, 157, 165, 243n88, 243–244n93, 244n99. *See also* Lomawaima, K. Tsianina; safety zone
McCarty's Day School, 94, 125
Medicine, Beatrice, 6, 170
Medley, Ora B., 93, 143
Mekeel, H. Scudder, 30, 52, 131–132, 156, 187, 236–237n79
Menard, Nellie Star Boy, 60, 67–68
Meriam Report, 10, 13, 18, 21, 37; on "artificial" preservation, 20, 31, 45; criticism of Assimilation policy, 18–19; criticism of Indigenous cultures, 22–23, 30, 48; on cultural choice, 19; on education, 23–24, 34, 47; on healthcare, 101; link to Progressive Era attitudes to immigrants, 21–22; on missionaries, 117; scholarship on, 208–209n31
Mesita Day School, 99, 125
missionaries, 24, 102, 116–117, 138, 184; opposition to Circular 2970, 32, 117–120, 233n12; on proselytization in schools, 116–117; relationship with schools in New Deal, 121–124. *See also* National Fellowship of Indian Workers
monocultural education, 1–2, 4, 14, 34–36, 40, 75, 131–132, 177, 193, 202n5
Morgan, Jacob, 65, 102, 119, 122–123, 230n128
Morgan, William, 149, 155, 241n42

Nambe Pueblo, 145
National Fellowship of Indian Workers (NFIW), 118, 120
Native American Church (NAC), 102
Navajo Community College (NCC), 12, 193–198. *See also* Diné College
Navajo language. *See* Diné Bikéyah
Navajo orthography project, 150–156
Navajo Reservation, 33, 36, 100, 102–104, 108, 119, 121, 135, 138–139, 147, 151, 153, 195; and healthcare, 94; soil conservation program on, 74, 76, 82, 87–88; World War II impact on, 173–175
Navajo Service News, 147–148, 215n35

Navajo Tribal Council, 61, 116, 146, 168
New Deal (wider US policy), 27–28, 66, 81, 96, 184–186; scholarship on rural conservation policy, 210–211n62; scholarship on rural extension programs, 211n65
New Mexico Association on Indian Affairs (NMAIA), 9, 205n36
NMAIA 1940 Report, 9–10, 87, 144, 147–148
Nutria Day School, 98, 125
Nyamnjoh, Francis, 8, 18, 181–183, 186

Old Leupp Boarding School, 145, 228n99
Origin narratives (Diné), 46–47, 51, 63, 195–196
Origin narratives (Pueblo), 50

Pageant of Navajo History, 61–67, 128, 167, 195
Papago. *See* Tohono O'odham
Paraje Day School, 56, 99
Parker, Arthur C., 58
paternalism, 3, 10, 13, 56, 62, 70–71, 84, 95, 160, 171, 185
Peter, Dr. W. W., 94, 100, 102–103, 146–147, 240n27
Phelps-Stokes Fund, 9–10, 33, 205n36
Phelps-Stokes Report, 33; on health, 93; on importance of bilingual school staff, 147–148; on intolerant school staff, 136–137; on missionaries, 117, 123–124; on prioritization of English language in school, 142; on prioritization of western science, 90–91; on support for Soil Conservation Service, 87–88
Picuris Day School, 98
Picuris Pueblo, 101, 166
Pima. *See* Akimel O'odham
Pine Ridge Reservation, 60, 68–69, 119, 212n78
Pipestone Indian Boarding School, 130–131
pottery, 54–56, 58–60
Primary Objectives of Indian Schools, 76, 80, 222n14
Problem of Indian Administration. *See* Meriam Report
Program for Navajo Schools, 78, 125, 142, 235n50
progressive education, 4, 10, 23, 36, 91, 127–128, 144, 205n39, 220n130

Provinse, John, 107–108, 231n150
Pueblo Dance Controversy, 24, 209n46
Pueblo Life Readers, 165–166

Q'oyawayma, Polingaysi, 17, 131, 156, 168, 208n21

range management, 7, 75–80, 82–83, 87, 107–108, 134–136, 146, 157–158, 163–164, 184, 198; on links to British colonial land policy, 223–224n34. *See also* Soil Conservation Service
Red Rock Day School, 100
religious freedom, 8, 24, 37, 138, 140, 179–180, 184, 186, 189; and Circular 2970, 28–31; and school absences, 124–127; and traditional medicine, 102–103, 106–107
Richards, Fred, 46–47, 51, 63, 89, 92, 215n35
Roessel, Ruth, 197, 251n36
Rosebud Reservation, 60, 67, 131, 212n78
Runyan, Norma, 63, 88–89, 93, 100, 122, 144–145, 225n59
Ryan, W. Carson, 70, 177, 179, 182, 184, 187, 189, 197; on day schools and homes, 23–24; on history education, 39, 47, 71; on progressive education, 4, 23, 34, 41, 88

safety zone thesis, 5, 7–8, 109–110, 124, 127, 178–179, 189
Sandoval, Albert "Chic," 63, 149–150, 152–154, 195–196, 242n46
San Ildefonso Day School, 56
San Ildefonso Pueblo, 58, 60, 127
San Juan Day School, 56, 98, 121
San Juan potters and pottery, 55
Sanostee Day School, 100
Santa Fe Indian Boarding School (SFIS), 78–79, 125–127, 165
science, 33, 84, 108–110, 161, 177; as colonization, 180–186; and health, 92–96, 100; Indigenous science, 193, 198–199; on school curriculum, 88–91; and stock reduction, 73–74
Seba Dalkai Day School, 126
Seneca Arts and Crafts Project, 58, 70
Seneca Indian Boarding School, 41–44
Settlement House Movement, 5
settler colonialism, 8, 20, 71, 84, 88, 186, 224n43

Shiprock Agricultural High School, 80, 122
singers (Diné traditional medicine practitioners), 101–107, 109
sings, 74, 102, 104, 106, 129–130, 132–133, 135–136, 139, 163–164, 179
Sinte Gleska University, 199
Soil Conservation Service (SCS), 73–74, 94, 184, 186; and criticism of Diné pastoralism, 80, 82–84; insensitive personnel, 134; and schools/curriculum, 76–79; and translation problems, 147
soil erosion: on Navajo Reservation, 73–75, 80–81, 84, 86, 89, 109; wider New Deal rural policy, 27, 184–185
sovereignty, 2–3, 5, 8–10, 13, 16, 32, 36, 70, 88, 154, 183, 186–187, 189
Southwestern Range and Sheep Breeding Laboratory, 80–81
Southwest Field Training Program, 134–135
Special Navajo Program (education), 175–176, 189
Stacher, Samuel, 132–133
Standing Bear, Luther, 2–3, 62, 199–200
stock reduction, 6, 73–75, 86, 96, 145–146, 177, 186, 195, 212n78; scholarship on, 221n1
Stoltz, Marguerite Bigler, 41–42, 44–46, 131, 133, 208n21
storytelling: student compositions, 42–44; traditional learning, 45, 199
students, 46–47, 109, 145; compositions, 41–44; illness, 98–101; resilience at boarding schools, 17, 131, 145; school absences, 124–127
Subsistence Homestead Program, 27
Sullivan, Keith, 178, 247n27
Szasz, Margaret Connell, 4–5

Taos Day School, 56, 98, 99, 124, 126, 166
Taos Pueblo, 25, 33, 101, 110, 166, 179
teachers, 11, 41, 45, 142–145; in Assimilation Era, 17, 23, 45, 130; and Circular 2970, 121, 125–127; criticism of, 145, 147–148, 167–169; on history, 46; Indigenous teachers, 17, 35–36, 40, 45, 67–70, 88, 140, 142–143, 156–157, 177; and language, 136–137; at NCC, 196–197; reporting poor facilities, 99–100; on science, 88–89; and soil conservation, 76–77, 80, 82; training, 48, 152

Teec-Nos-Pos Day School, 98
Tesuque Day School, 56, 169
Tesuque potters and pottery, 55–56, 59–60
Tesuque Pueblo, 25, 33
Tohono O'odham, 48–50, 52, 94–96, 104–105, 140, 143, 182, 216n46, 228n95, 239n14
tribal colleges, 6, 193–200
Trujillo, Miguel, 16–17, 99, 101, 140, 207n18
Tuba City Vocational High School, 80, 88–89, 96, 128, 143

Underhill, Ruth, 30, 47–48, 69–70, 107; Navajo Life and Customs text, 51, 99, 129, 158, 169, 222n11; Pueblo Crafts text, 54–56, 60; Pueblo Life and Customs text, 50, 52, 87, 129–130, 216n58, 217n63; Tohono O'odham Life and Customs text, 48–50, 52
uniform curriculum, 16, 19, 23, 34, 41
United Farm Program, 161–162, 244n102
United Pueblos Agency (UPA), 7, 12, 87, 94, 98–99, 101, 121, 124–127, 135, 138, 145, 166, 177

Van Valkenburgh, Richard, 47, 63, 151, 154, 215n34
vocational education, 2, 10, 16, 28, 34–36, 47, 76, 96, 175, 188, 207n14

Wahpeton Indian Boarding School, 40–41, 68–69
Weaving: at school, 57, 60, 67–68, 80–81, 145, 197; in school texts, 54–55; traditional dyes, 57–58, 68, 218n100
Weisiger, Marsha, 74, 223n33, 228n92
Wingate Adult short course, 81–82, 101, 144, 149, 167–168
Wingate Vocational High School, 57–58, 68, 77, 80, 138, 144, 150, 152

Young, Robert, 149, 150, 155, 241n42

Zuni Pueblo: ceremonies, 29–30, 125–126; orthography project, 154; in Pageant of Navajo History, 63–64; religious training, 124–125; in school primer, 165

www.ingramcontent.com/pod-product-compliance
Lightning Source LLC
Chambersburg PA
CBHW030529230426
43665CB00010B/823